FRAUD
Bringing Light to the Dark Side of Business

FRAUD
Bringing Light to the
Dark Side of Business

W. Steve Albrecht

Gerald W. Wernz

Timothy L. Williams

IRWIN
Professional Publishing®

1333 Burr Ridge Parkway
Burr Ridge, IL 60521
(800) 634-3966

This publication is designed to provide accurate and
authoritative information in regard to the subject matter
covered. It is sold with the understanding that neither the
author or the publisher is engaged in rendering legal, accounting,
or other professional service. If legal advice or other expert
assistance is required, the services of a competent professional
person should be sought.

*From a Declaration of Principles jointly adopted by a Committee
of the American Bar Association and a Committee of Publishers.*

Senior sponsoring editor: Amy Hollands Gaber
Project editor: Karen M. Smith
Copy editor: Georgia Kornbluth
Production manager: Ann Cassady
Designer: Laurie Entringer
Jacket background: M. Angelo/West Light
Art coordinator: Mark Malloy
Compositor: Wm. C. Brown Communications, Inc.
Typeface: 10/12 Times Roman
Printer: Book Press, Inc.

Library of Congress Cataloging-in-Publication Data

Albrecht, W. Steve
    Fraud: bringing light to the dark side of business/W. Steve
Albrecht, Gerald W. Wernz, Timothy L. Williams.
        p. cm.
    Includes index.
    ISBN 1-55623-760-X
    1. Fraud—United States.   2. Fraud.—United States—Prevention.
    3. Fraud investigation—United States.   I. Wernz, Gerald W.
    II. Williams, Timothy L.   III. Title.
    HV6695, A45   1995   94–17523
    364. 1'63'0973—dc20

Printed in the United States of America
 234567890 BP 109876

Preface

Why are we writing this book when so many other books on fraud have been written? Our goal is to provide indepth analysis of fraud, the perpetrators of fraud and their motivations, and the steps that can be taken to detect, investigate, and deter fraud. Collectively, the three authors have investigated and studied hundreds of frauds in numerous organizations. Tim Williams is currently Vice President of Business Ethics at Northern Telecom, a major North American Company, where he is responsible for coordinating response to and prevention of fraud and related ethics issues on a world-wide basis. Prior to his current position, he had over 17 years of corporate security management for three North American corporations. Jerry Wernz is the Director of Internal Audit and Security for Boise Cascade, a Fortune 500 Company. In that position he coordinates fraud prevention, detection, and investigation activities for his organization. Steve Albrecht is a professor and fraud researcher who had conducted numerous fraud-related studies. He has consulted with numerous organizations and is the past president of the Association of Certified Fraud Examiners. Together, the three authors have developed fraud policies for several companies.

These backgrounds allow us to provide you with a fresh look at fraud on a personal level. By reading these pages you will be able to see fraud through the eyes of a perpetrator, the perpetrator's coworkers, and victim organizations. The three elements of fraud and the three factors that motivate someone to commit fraud will be discussed in detail. Using this knowledge of fraud, this book will provide insights into how organizations, individuals, and managers can avoid becoming fraud victims. The book will focus on fraud prevention, where big savings can occur; fraud detection, which is rarely done on a proactive basis; and fraud investigation, which costs millions of dollars in America today and which can be conducted on a more efficient and effective basis.

The book is organized into four parts. Part I, Chapters 1 through 5, focuses on the fraud triangle, which describes why individuals commit fraud. Chapter 1 identifies types of fraud, describes fraud perpetrators, and gives numerous statistics documenting the extent of fraud in the United States. Chapter 2 discusses fraud pressures, Chapters 3 and 4 discuss fraud opportunities, and Chapter 5 discusses fraud rationalizations.

Part II, Chapters 6 through 9, focuses on fraud detection. After an overview of detection considerations in Chapter 6, Chapters 7 through 9 identify those fraud symptoms that can alert you to the fact that fraud is occurring.

Part III, Chapters 10 through 14, focuses on the investigation of fraud. After introducing fraud investigation in Chapter 10, Chapter 11 covers concealment investigative techniques, Chapter 12 covers conversion investigative techniques, Chapter 13 covers inquiry investigative techniques, and Chapter 14 provides an example of a complete investigation report.

Part IV, Chapters 15 and 16 , deal with the prevention of fraud. The book concludes with Chapter 17, which ties the various elements of prevention, detection, and investigation together in an overall fraud plan. We hope you enjoy reading the book.

W. Steve Albrecht
Gerald W. Wernz
Timothy L. Williams

Acknowledgments

This book is possible only through the help of many individuals and organizations. We are grateful to Boise Cascade Corporation and Northern Telecom for providing support to the concepts discussed herein. The internal audit and security departments at Boise Cascade were especially helpful in providing support for the development of many of the concepts.

Thanks is also due to Joseph T. Wells for his personal friendship, to James Ratley, and to the Association of Certified Fraud Examiners for providing a forum where these concepts could be taught, discussed, and further developed. Mr. Wells, Mr. Ratley, and the ACFE have done more than any other people or organization to expand knowledge in this area and to educate and train people in the detection, investigation, and prevention of fraud.

Appreciation is also expressed to several other individuals who have been trusted friends and reviewers including Pete C. Elliott, Gary K. Pruitt, and Richard W. McLaren, Ernst & Young; Carl Warren, University of Georgia; Joanne Niederoest, General Motors Corporation; Philip Trojanowski, Philip Morris Corporation; Jack Bologna, well-known author and fraud consultant; Don Walker, Executive Vice President of Pinkerton Security Services; and Donn Parker, Stanford Research Institute.

This manuscript would have been impossible without the dedicated help of Sheri Winkelkotter, the BYU secretary who typed and corrected its numerous drafts. She is a true professional.

Finally, we are indebted to our wives, LeAnn Albrecht, Fara Wernz, and Teresa Kitson, who provide constant support and who made it possible for the book to be written. They spent many days and nights alone while we were working on this book.

Contents

I

THE NATURE OF FRAUD

This book is divided into five sections, or parts: Part I, The Nature of Fraud (Chapters 1 through 5); Part II, The Detection of Fraud (Chapters 6 through 9); Part III, The Investigation of Fraud (Chapters 10 through 14); Part IV, The Prevention of Fraud (Chapters 15 and 16); and Part V, A Comprehensive Fraud Prevention Program (Chapter 17).

Chapter 1 defines fraud, describes the different types of fraud, identifies elements common to all types of frauds, and provides statistics regarding the amount and kinds of fraud being committed today. Chapter 2 introduces the fraud triangle, which is composed of pressure, opportunity, and rationalization—elements that combine to allow fraud to be committed. Chapter 2 goes on to explain in detail the kinds of pressures that can lead a person to act fraudulently. Chapters 3 and 4 discuss the second element of the fraud triangle—opportunity. In Chapter 3, the focus is on internal control factors that allow fraud to be committed. Chapter 4 discusses factors other than internal control that lead to fraud. The third element of the fraud triangle, rationalization, is explained in Chapter 5.

Chapter One

The Seriousness of the Fraud Problem

There are two principal methods of getting something from others illegally. Either you put a gun next to their heads and force them to give it to you, or you trick or deceive them out of their assets. The first type of theft we call *robbery*, with its many varieties, and the second we call *fraud*. While robbery is certainly more violent than fraud, and attracts much more media attention, losses from fraud far exceed losses from robbery.

Statistics about the extent of fraud are hard to obtain. Fraud statistics are generated by federal agencies, such as the Federal Bureau of Investigation (FBI); by researchers, by companies that are defrauded, and by insurance carriers that insure fraud losses. The reliability of data from all four sources is questionable. Most of the 25 federal agencies that gather statistics on fraud are concerned with only certain aspects of fraud, such as bank embezzlement or Medicare fraud. Research and company statistics suffer because organizations don't want to share "negative" experiences with outsiders and are even often discouraged from doing so by in-house lawyers. Insurance company statistics are incomplete because such companies insure only a small percentage of all fraud perpetrators and victims and don't see the total picture. Worst of all, the actual percentage of frauds that are detected, made public, and/or prosecuted is not known. Indeed, many frauds go undetected and a large number of detected frauds are resolved quietly and internally by victim organizations.

It is not difficult to know, however, that fraud is a growing problem. It is almost impossible to read any newspaper or business magazine without reading about fraud. A recent issue of *USA Today*, for example, contained three fraud-related articles. The first discussed one of the nation's fastest growing grocery store chains, which was alleged to have made sausage with spoiled green pork, to have coated slimy chicken with barbecue sauce before putting it in meat cases, and to have soaked aged stinking fish in bleach before putting it out for sale. In addition, the grocery store chain was being hit with the largest child-labor complaint ever—more than 1,400 violations, including allowing teens to work around meat slicers and other dangerous equipment.

The second article described one state's voter attempt to recall the governor because he was a "crook." Recall backers cited five federal and state probes of the governor, including an Internal Revenue Service (IRS) probe for corruption and tax evasion.

The third example, probably saddest of all, reported an investigation of the Philippine Little League team that won a Little League World Series. Allegedly, all 14 players on the team were ineligible and were allowed to play because of faked names and identification on official documents. The team won the World Series in Pennsylvania by beating Long Beach, California, 15–4, but was stripped of the title in September after officials discovered that the players were ineligible.

FRAUD INVOLVES DECEPTION

All three cases involve the element of deception. In the first case, the grocery store was allegedly deceiving customers by disguising and selling spoiled meat, and was also deceiving federal child-labor law administrators by hiring ineligible teens and exposing them to undue risk. In the second case, a governor was allegedly deceiving his constituency and the IRS by underpaying taxes and by offering bribes to legalize gambling. In the third, a Little League team was using deception to field players who were ineligible.

One of the most famous frauds of all time was the investment scam committed by Charles Biancci (alias Charles Ponzzi), who perpetrated a fraud by promising to pay investors unusually high returns. Two interesting things about Charles Ponzzi were that (1) he never made any of the promised investments, and (2) he actually paid the promised returns—at least initially. To make the investment scam look legitimate and to deceive investors, Charles Ponzzi had to provide returns for a while. If someone invested $1,000 in his scheme, for example, he would pay the promised return of $300 at the end of the year. While the $300 was actually a refund of the original $1,000 and left only $700 in the investment, the investor believed he or she was actually getting a 30 percent "return." Thrilled with the high return, investors quickly poured more money into the investment and told all their friends and neighbors about the great investment. As a result, the fraudulent investment scam grew quickly, and Charles Ponzzi pocketed nearly $20 million.

Ponzzi's scheme is very instructive when one is trying to understand fraud. Certainly, the scheme involved deception. The scheme also involved greed—greed by the perpetrator and even greed by the investors who wanted higher-than-sensible returns. Finally, Ponzzi's scheme involved the element of *confidence*. If he had not paid the original $300 returns, investors wouldn't have contributed additional money. By paying early "returns," Ponzzi earned investors' confidence and convinced customers that he had a legitimate business.

CONFIDENCE IS A NECESSARY INGREDIENT OF FRAUD

Confidence is the single most critical element in fraud. The word "con" comes from the word confidence. No one can con anyone out of anything unless the deceived has confidence in the deceptive person. Husbands cannot con wives unless their wives trust or have confidence in them. Likewise, wives cannot con husbands unless their husbands have confidence in them.

Without confidence, fraud is impossible. One of the authors regularly consults in the area of fraud prevention with banks. After watching banks be defrauded by both employees and customers, he uses the following example to illustrate the element of confidence:

> Assume two individuals enter the bank. Both are males. One is dressed in a business suit and is well groomed. The second has scraggly hair, has tattoos up and down both arms, is wearing tattered jeans, and is carrying a motorcycle helmet under his arm. Which of the two will most likely commit fraud?

The answer, of course, is the first customer, who is dressed in a business suit. He may defraud the bank because bank employees will probably have confidence in him. The second customer cannot commit fraud because bank employees will probably not trust him. He may rob the bank, but he probably could not commit fraud.

All three current authors have investigated frauds and interviewed fraud perpetrators. One of the most common responses of fraud victims is disbelief. Very often we have heard comments like "I can't believe he would do this. That was my most trusted employee." Sure he was, because the ones you don't trust usually cannot commit fraud. Indeed, fraud perpetrators are often the least suspected.

One survey of fraud perpetrators showed that the largest group of perpetrators by age was people 36 to 45 years old. While statistics don't explain why this is the case, one reason is probably that this age group of middle managers have worked themselves into positions of trust.

TYPES OF FRAUD

Fraud involving deception takes many forms. We often categorize frauds according to six types. The first is *employee embezzlement*.[1] In this type of fraud, employees deceive their employers by taking company assets. Embezzlement by employees can be either direct or indirect. Direct fraud occurs when an employee steals company cash, inventory, tools, or other

---

[1] A list of employee frauds is shown in the Appendix to Chapter 1.

assets. It also occurs when an employee sets up a dummy company and has their employer pay for goods that are not delivered. With direct fraud, company assets go directly into the perpetrator's possession without the involvement of third parties.

Indirect employee fraud, on the other hand, occurs when employees take bribes and kickbacks from vendors, customers, or others outside the company to allow for lower sales prices, higher purchase prices, nondelivery of goods, or delivery of inferior goods. In these cases, payment to employees is made by organizations that deal with the perpetrator's employer, not by the employer itself.

A second type of fraud is *management fraud*. Management fraud is distinguished from other types of fraud both by the nature of the perpetrators and by the method of deception. In its most common form, management fraud is deception perpetrated by an organization's top management through the manipulation of financial statements. Well-known examples of alleged management fraud in recent years are Pharmor and Crazy Eddie, Inc., both of which supposedly overstated inventories on financial statements, and ZZZZ Best, ESM Government, Regina Vacuum Company, and Miniscribe Corporation, all of which supposedly overstated revenues and/or receivables. In all these cases, management wanted security holders to believe that the companies' financial positions were better than they really were.

Closely related to management fraud is the *investment scam*. In this type of fraud, fraudulent and usually worthless investments are sold to investors. Telemarketing fraud usually falls into this category, as does the selling of worthless partnership interests and other investment opportunities. Charles Ponzzi is generally regarded as the father of investment scams. Unfortunately, Ponzzi has not lacked imitators; his form of deception is extremely common today.

A fourth type of fraud is *vendor fraud*. Vendor fraud has garnered its share of newspaper headlines in recent years because of significant overcharges by major vendors on defense and other government contracts. Vendor fraud, which is extremely common in the United States, comes in two main varieties: (1) fraud perpetrated by vendors acting alone and (2) fraud perpetrated through collusion between buyers and vendors. Vendor fraud usually results in either an overcharge for purchased goods, the shipment of inferior goods, or the nonshipment of goods even though payment was received.

The fifth type of fraud is *customer fraud*. Customer fraud usually involves customers' not paying for goods purchased, getting something for nothing, or deceiving organizations into giving them something they shouldn't have. For example, a customer walked into a bank one recent Saturday morning and convinced the branch manager to give her a $525,000 cashier's check even though she had only $13,000 in her bank account. The manager thought she was a very wealthy customer who would "make good" on the money, had sales goals to meet, and didn't want to lose her business. Unfortunately, she was a white-collar thief who defrauded the bank of over $500,000. In another customer fraud, six individuals sitting in a Quality Inn Hotel room in downtown Chicago made three calls to a Chicago Bank and had the bank transfer nearly $70 million to their account in another financial institution.

The sixth type of fraud is deception that doesn't fall into one of the other five types and may be for reasons other than financial gain. This kind of deception is simply labeled *miscellaneous fraud.* Altering birth records of Little League players so that a team can compete favorably in the World Series and altering grade reports to get accepted into school are examples of this type of fraud.

WHO COMMITS FRAUD

Anyone can commit fraud. Research into employee embezzlement has found that perpetrators can't be distinguished from other employees on the basis of demographic or psychological characteristics. Most embezzlers have profiles that look exactly like their honest counterparts' profiles.

A study that illustrates the similarities between white-collar criminals and noncriminals was conducted over a period of several years by one of this book's authors and his colleagues.[2] In this empirical study, white-collar criminals were compared with (1) prisoners incarcerated for other property offenses and (2) a noncriminal sample of college students. The personal backgrounds and psychological profiles of the three groups were computed. The results indicated that incarcerated white-collar criminals were generally not similar to other incarcerated prisoners. When compared to other criminals, white-collar criminals were less likely to be caught, turned in, arrested, convicted, and incarcerated; they were also less likely to serve long sentences. In addition, white-collar criminals were considerably older, which might be expected since it usually takes longer to get into managerial positions or other positions of confidence. While only 2 percent of the property offenders were female, 30 percent of the white-collar criminals were women. White-collar criminals tended to have much more stable family situations; they were more likely to be married and less likely to be divorced, they had more children, and they were more likely to be active church members.

Compared to other property offenders, white-collar criminals were better-educated, more religious, less likely to have criminal records or otherwise be criminally inclined, less likely to abuse alcohol, and considerably less likely to use drugs. White-collar criminals were also in

[2]See "Red-Flagging the White-Collar Criminal," *Management Accounting,* by Marshall B Romney, W Steve Albrecht, and David J Cherrington, March 1980, p. 51–57.

better psychological health. They enjoyed more optimism, self-esteem, self-sufficiency, achievement, motivation, and family harmony than did other property offenders, who showed more depression, self-degradation, dependence, lack of motivation, and family discord. White-collar criminals seemed to express more social conformity, self-control, kindness, and empathy, as compared to other property offenders' greater social deviancy, impulsiveness, hostility, and insensitivity to other people.

When they were compared with college students, white-collar criminals differed only slightly. White-collar criminals suffered more psychic pain and were more dishonest, more independent, more sexually mature, more socially deviant, and more empathetic. However, white-collar criminals were much more similar to students than to other property offenders.

It is important to understand the characteristics of white-collar criminals, because they appear to be a close match to people who have the traits that organizations look for in hiring employees, seeking out customers, and selecting vendors. This understanding leads to two quick realizations: (1) that any employee, customer, vendor, or business associate fits the profile of a white-collar criminal and is probably capable of committing fraud, and (2) that it is impossible to predict in advance the employees and others who will cross the line and become dishonest.

THE EXTENT OF FRAUD

While it is difficult to know how extensive fraud is and how much it costs society, several statistics regarding fraud in selected industries for recent years are available. A search for recent articles on fraud revealed the following:

1. The US Chamber of Commerce says that losses from employee embezzlement may be as high as $20 billion to $40 billion annually. These figures place employee theft at a larger amount than burglary, car theft, robbery, and larceny combined.[3] This estimate is slightly higher than the estimate of employee theft by the Bureau of National Affairs, which places the total at between $15 billion and $25 billion annually.

2. The FBI and other federal agencies have estimated that total US fraud losses are between $60 billion and $200 billion annually.[4]

3. Losses related to telephone fraud in 1991 in the US market are estimated to be $10 billion.[5]

---

[3]Robert McGough and Elicia Brown, "Thieves at Work," *Financial World*, December 1990, p. 18.

[4]*The Montreal Gazette*, Apr. 23, 1992.

[5]J Branch Walton, "Phone Fraud: Don't Let Thieves Do a Number on You!" *Security Management*, May 1992, pp. 63–64.

4. A study conducted in 1991 found that 13 percent of all credit card sales resulted in loss due to fraud.[6] In 1991 MasterCard experienced fraud losses of over $300 million, an increase of 42 percent over the previous year.[7]

5. In the aftermath of the savings and loan (S & L) failures, studies found that criminal fraud had been perpetrated in 60 percent of all S & Ls seized by the government.[8]

6. The Federal Trade Commission (FTC) and the Health Insurance Association of America (HIAA) estimate that fraud comprises 10 percent of the nation's health care bill. In 1989, this translated to $60 billion, in 1990 to about $67 billion; by the end of the 1990s, fraudulent charges may cost the nation over $160 billion a year.[9] Another estimate is that fraud may account for up to $75 billion of annual US health care expenditures. The same article states that the Rand Corporation estimates that up to 20 percent of all medical procedures are unnecessary. The total cost of such waste is estimated at $132 billion per year.[10] There is evidence that 3 percent of the nation's doctors routinely commit outright fraud.[11] The US Department of Health and Human Services (DHHS) conducted a study and found that 20 percent of Pennsylvania surgeons inflated their Medicare and Medicaid claims to the federal government.[12]

7. The cost of fraud in the United Kingdom more than doubled between 1987 and 1991—figures that are based only on cases in which charges have been brought.[13]

8. Thirty percent of all business failures are caused by white-collar crime. Crime against small companies accounts for 80 percent of all crimes against business.[14] A spokesman for the US Postal Inspection Service in Washington, DC, says, "fraud investigations in areas that affect small businesses have shot up by over 50 percent in the last four years."[15]

---

[6]Michael Ballard, "On the Safe Side," *Canadian Banker*, January–February 1992, p. 35.

[7]Linda Punch, "A Banner Year for the Crooks," *Credit Card Management*, March 1992, pp. 98–104.

[8]Savings Unit Fraud Cited," *The New York Times*, Feb. 28, 1990, p. C2.

[9]Sarah Kelly, "Impact of Fraudulent Claims on Health Care Costs," *Statistical Bulletin*, October–December 1991, p. 13.

[10]Janice Castro, "Condition: Critical," *Time*, Nov. 25, 1991, pp. 34–41.

[11]Elisabeth Rosenthal, "Insurers Say Growing Fraud In Health Care Costs Billions," *The New York Times*, July 5, 1990, p. A1.

[12]Gilbert M. Gaul, "Study Finds 20% of Pennsylvania Surgeons Inflate Medicare/Medicaid Claims," *Journal of Commerce and Commercial*, Oct. 24, 1991, p. A9.

[13]Robert Chambers, "Give Financial Sleuths the Tools to Catch Big-Time Fraudsters," *The Times*, July 9, 1992.

[14]Richard Andrews, "Protecting Business from Internal Theft," *Vermont Business Magazine*, July 1990.

[15]Brent Browers, "Small Businesses Increasingly Become Targets of Scams," *The Wall Street Journal*, Jan. 14, 1992, p. B2.

9. Studies have shown that 3 out of 10 workers look for ways to steal, another 3 out of 10 will steal if given an opportunity, and 4 out of 10 will usually be honest.[16]

10. Officials claim that all areas of fraud are on the rise. KPMG Peat Marwick found 1991 to be a record year for fraud, and 1992 is expected to be worse.[17] From 1980 to 1989, arrests for fraud in the United States increased 20.8 percent. Males committed 54.3 percent of discovered fraud, while females accounted for 45.7 percent. In 1989, Caucasians accounted for 66.7 percent of fraud arrests, black Americans accounted for 32.6 percent, and all other ethnic groups accounted for the remaining 0.7 percent.[18]

11. In the United States $11.6 billion in merchandise is stolen in 200 million shoplifting incidents each year. This translates into an average cost per American family of $150 per year. In addition to the large dollar value of the problem, the number of people who have engaged in shoplifting is surprisingly high. Approximately 60 percent of Americans have shoplifted at some time in their lives. The vast majority of shoplifters are average people rather than professional criminals, and the average amount per shoplifting incident is $58.[19]

12. In 1990, the IRS claimed that taxpayers paid only $4 of every $5 they owed to the federal government in taxes. This underpayment of taxes created a "tax gap" of approximately $100 billion. The tax gap exceeds $200 billion when unpaid employment taxes and income from illegal activities are included. The worst offenders are individuals and sole proprietors—the two categories that account for 75 percent of the annual tax shortfall.[20] The IRS has uncovered 659 schemes to defraud the government in 1991 by filing phony tax returns in hopes of getting a refund. Fully two-thirds of the 4,775 bogus returns involved tax forms that were filed electronically.[21]

---

[16]John Kula, director of fraud and security consulting for Arthur Andersen & Co., as quoted in Jerry Thomas, "Prosecution of White-Collar Crime Rising," *Chicago Tribune*, June 10, 1991, p. B1.

[17]"Experts Expect '92 to Break Record for Fraud in Britain", *Chicago Tribune*, Business Section, p. 8.

[18]Kathleen Maguire and Timothy J Flanagan (eds.), *Source Book of Criminal Justice Statistics*, 1990, US Department of Justice, Bureau of Justice Statistics, Washington, DC, 1990.

[19]Cox, Dena, "When Consumer Behavior Goes Bad," *Journal of Consumer Research* 17, no. 2 (1990), p. 149.

[20]Albert B Crenshaw, "Billions Cheated from IRS: 'Tax Gap' Created by Errors, Evaders," *The Washington Post*, Apr. 19, 1990, p. B1. Some of the same statistics were included in Marguerite T Smith "Who Cheats on the Income Taxes: Men More than Women," *Money*, Apr. 1991, pp. 100–108.

[21]"IRS Says Tax Fraud Hits High-Tech Level," *The Herald* (Provo, Utah), Apr. 14, 1992, p. 8A.

13. *The Wall Street Journal* reported the findings of a survey of 6,000 students at top colleges across the nation. Researchers reported that two-thirds of students surveyed admitted to cheating on tests and exams. A psychologist quoted in the same article reported that colleges found 40 to 68 percent of students admitted to cheating.[22]

14. Twenty-three percent of all respondents to a study conducted by the Insurance Research Council (IRC) considered padding insurance claims to make up for large deductibles to be acceptable, and similar percentages condoned other sorts of fraudulent insurance-related activities.[23]

15. Telephone marketing swindlers, based largely in southern California, successfully cheat American consumers out of as much as $15 billion a year because federal and state law enforcement agencies are understaffed, poorly coordinated, and often misdirected.[24]

16. The national placement director for Robert Half International, Inc., said that demand for forensic accountants increased by 100 percent in each of the last three years.[25]

17. A recent survey showed that "a surprising one in four scientists suspect their peers of engaging in intellectual fakery." It also revealed that 27 percent of the scientists who encountered fraud did nothing about it and only 2 percent publicly challenged suspected data.[26]

18. Forty-five of the nation's 100 largest defense contractors have been investigated for overbilling the federal government. Companies such as General Electric (GE), Boeing, Rockwell International, Sperry Corporation, and McDonnell Douglas have allegedly submitted false work time cards, altered time cards without employees' knowledge; charged labor costs to wrong contracts; and billed the government for perks for corporate executives, including country club memberships and even tickets to the Metropolitan Opera.[27]

---

[22]William M. Bulkeley, "High Tech Aids Make Cheating in School Easier," *The Wall Street Journal*, Apr. 28, 1992, p. B1.

[23]Kenneth Reich, "Survey Finds Many Condone Lying to Insurers," *The Los Angeles Times*, Nov. 19, 1991, p. A26.

[24]Robert W Stewart, "Phone Swindlers Net $15 Billion a Year," *The Los Angeles Times*, Dec. 29, 1991, p. A5.

[25]Elizabeth M Fowler, "Forensic Accountants in Demand," *The New York Times*, July 16, 1991, p. D17.

[26]William J Broad, "One in Four Scientists in Survey Suspect Fraud by Peers," *The New York Times*, Mar. 27, 1992, p. A16.

[27]Marshall B Clinard, *Corporate Corruption: The Abuse of Power*, Praeger, New York, 1990, pp. 76–77.

19. Since 1965, $17 billion in student loans has been defaulted on by students and paid by the federal government.[28]

20. In 1991, 1,985 defendants were charged in major financial institution fraud cases, with 885 being convicted and 662 sent to jail. These numbers could be much higher if sufficient funding were available to enable the FBI to increase its investigative staff. With present funding, only cases involving amounts greater than $100,000 are being investigated.[29]

21. A study by the Institute of Management Accountants (IMA) indicated that 87 percent of managers were willing to commit fraud in one or more of the cases presented to them, if it would make their organizations look better.[30] Another survey of 400 managers shows that one-third of them distrust their own direct bosses and 55 percent don't believe top management.[31]

CONCLUDING COMMENTS

Any way you look at it, fraud is a major problem in the United States and in other countries. In fact, most studies have suggested that organizations lose between 0.5 and 2 percent of revenues to various types of fraudulent actions. If this is the case, fraud is indeed an expensive proposition for organizations. If, for example, a company with $2 billion in revenues has a profit margin of 10 percent and fraud losses are 1 percent of revenues, the organization must generate an additional $200 million in sales to recover the losses from fraud. This calculation is as follows:

Revenues	$2 billion
Losses from fraud (1 percent of revenues)	20 million
Additional sales needed to recover losses ($20 million × 10)	200 million

Studies have also found that organizations suffer most fraud losses from employees rather than from customers. Several retail studies, for example, have revealed that shoplifting accounts for 30 percent of retail

---

[28]Kerry Hannon, "How You're Getting Stiffed by the Student Loan Mess," *Money*, May 1992, pp. 164–170.

[29]Richard Behar, "Catch Us If You Can: A Dearth of FBI Agents Keep S & L Villains at Large," *Time*, Mar. 26, 1990, p. 60.

[30]*The Wall Street Journal*, Mar. 1, 1990, p. A1.

[31]Selwyn Feinstein, "Labor Letter," *The Wall Street Journal*, Jan. 16, 1990, Section A.1.

fraud losses, while employees take 70 percent. Similar studies conducted in banks have found that employees account for 95 percent of bank losses, while customers and robbers account for only 5 percent. In addition, other studies have found that fraud losses tend to increase when economic times are tough, when organizations become larger, when an organization is having financial difficulties or is merging, and when crash projects are undertaken. Because all these conditions are present today, we can expect the problem only to get worse.

Appendix
THE MOST COMMON EMPLOYEE FRAUDS

- Theft of cash
  Stealing checks
  Diverting cash receipts
  Voiding cash registers
  Altering bank deposits
  Forgery
  Misusing pension fund assets
  Stealing petty cash
  Using company checks to pay personal bills
- Presenting fraudulent invoices
  Fictitious billings
  Overstated billings
- Theft of inventory
- Collusion with customers or suppliers
  Kickbacks
  Bid rigging
  Dummy suppliers
  Overstated prices
- Lapping
- Kiting
- Use of company resources
  Personnel, equipment, or materials
  Purchase orders
- Credit card
- Insurance fraud
  Misstating benefits
  False claims
- Medical claim fraud

- False entries in accounts
  To increase performance reports
  To cover missing assets
- Travel reimbursement abuse
  False expenditures
  Including personal expenditures
  Advances not repaid
- Unauthorized sale of assets
  Inventory
  Equipment
  Scrap
- Computer crimes
  Changing records
  Diverting cash
- Payroll crimes
  Cashing unused paychecks
  Overstating hours
  Ghost employees

Chapter Two

Fraud Perpetrators and Their Motivations
The First Element of The Fraud Triangle: Pressure

Mark Simpson[1] was struggling financially. He was living in his car, had no money to spend, and had no family members or friends to turn to for assistance. Instead of seeking help through legal channels, Mark committed a fraud. His method of deception was *kiting,* meaning that he wrote checks on one bank when there was insufficient money in his account and concealed the fraud by making deposits using worthless checks drawn on a second bank. His victim, the last bank to catch the fraud, lost over $40,000 in less than 2 months. Here, in his own words, is a description of Mark's fraud.

> I, Mark Simpson, am making this statement on my own without threat or promises, as to my activities in regard to the activity of kiting between Bank A and Bank B. As of May 1991, I was having extreme emotional and financial difficulties. I was required to move out of where I was living without notice for religious reasons, and I had no place to go. Also, my grandmother—the only family member I was close to—was dying. I had to live out of my car for 3 and 1/2 weeks. At the end of this time, my grandmother died. She lived in Ohio. I went to the funeral and I returned with a $1,000 inheritance. I used this money to secure an apartment. The entire sum was used up for first month's rent, deposit, and the application fee. From that time, mid-June, until the first part of August, I was supporting myself on my minimum-wage job at the nursery. I had no furniture nor a bed. I was barely making it. I was feeling very distraught over the loss of my grandmother, and problems my parents and brother were having. I felt all alone. The first part of August arrived and my rent was due. I did not have the full amount to pay it. This same week, I opened a checking account at Bank B. I intended to close my

---

[1]Although the case is real and the confession is original, the name of the perpetrator and the setting have been changed to ensure anonymity for those involved.

Bank A account because of a lack of ATMs, branches, and misunderstandings. As I said, my rent was due and I did not know how to meet it. On an impulse, I wrote the apartment manager a check for the amount due. I did not have the funds to cover it. I thought I could borrow it, but I could not. During the time I was trying to come up with the money, I wrote a check from my Bank B account to cover the rent check and put it into Bank A. I did not know it was illegal. I knew it was unethical, but I thought since the checks were made out to me that it wasn't illegal. This went on for about a week—back and forth between banks. I thought I could get the money to cover this debt but I never did. My grandmother's estate had been quite large, and I expected more money, but it was not to happen. After a week of nothing being said to me by the banks, I began to make other purchases via this method. I needed something to sleep on and a blanket and other items for the apartment. I bought a sleeper sofa, a desk, a modular shelf/bookcase, dishes, and also paid off my other outstanding debts—college loans, dentist bill, and credit. I was acting foolishly. No one had said nor questioned me at the banks about any of this. I usually made deposits at different branches to try to avoid suspicion, but when I was in my own branches, no one said a thing. I thought maybe what I was doing wasn't wrong after all. So I decided to purchase a new car, stereo, and a new computer to use at home for work. Still, I did not have a problem making deposits at the banks. But, I was feeling very guilty. I knew I needed to start downsizing the "debt" and clear it up. I began to look for a better paying job. Finally, last week I got a call from Bank B while I was at work: They had discovered a problem with my account. I realized then that the banks had found out. Later that day, I got another call from Bank A. They told me that what I had been doing was illegal and a felony. I was in shock. I didn't know it was that bad. I realize now how wrong what I did was. From the start, I knew it was unethical, but I didn't know it was indeed a crime until now. I have had to do a lot of thinking, praying and talking to those close to me about this. I am truly sorry for what I have done, and I don't EVER plan to do it again. All I want now is to make amends with the banks. I do not have the money to pay back either bank right now. I realize this hurts them. I want to try to set this right whether I go to prison or not. I am prepared to work however long it takes to pay the banks back in full with reasonable interest from a garnishment of my wages from now until the full amount is paid and settled. I committed this act because I was feeling desperate. I was emotionally a wreck and physically tired. I felt I didn't have a choice but to do what I did or return to living in my car. I now know what I did was wrong, and I am very sorry for it. I am attempting to seek psychological counseling to help me deal with and resolve why I did this. I feel I have a lot to offer society once I am able to clean up my own life and get it straightened out. I pray the bank employees and officers will forgive me on a personal level for the hardship my actions have caused them, and I want to make full restitution. I have done wrong, and I must now face the consequences. This statement has been made in my own words, by myself, without threat or promise, and written by my own hand.

Mark Simpson

THE FRAUD TRIANGLE

While there are thousand of ways to perpetrate fraud, Mark's kite illustrates the three key elements common to all of them. The three ingredients that make up the fraud triangle and that came together to motivate and allow Mark to perpetrate his fraud were: (1) strong financial pressure, (2) a perceived opportunity to commit and conceal the fraud, and (3) a way to rationalize or justify the fraud as being OK.

No one likes to live in a car. After moving into an apartment, Mark could not pay the second month's rent. Faced with a choice between being dishonest or going back to living in his car, Mark chose to be dishonest. Every fraud perpetrator faces some kind of *pressure*. Most such pressures involve financial need. However, nonfinancial pressures—such as the need to report results better than actual performance, frustration with work, or even a challenge to beat the system—can motivate fraud. Later in this chapter we will discuss the different kinds of pressures in more detail.

The second element in the fraud triangle is opportunity. Mark perceived a way to commit fraud by repeatedly writing bad checks drawn on one bank to cover bad checks drawn on another bank. He didn't need to gain access to cash, or use force, or even to confront his victims physically. Rather, he wrote checks to himself in the privacy of his own apartment, then he deposited them in the two banks. His weapons of crime were checks from the two different financial institutions and a pen. Whether or not Mark could actually get away with his crime didn't matter. What mattered was that Mark believed he could conceal the fraud—he had a *perceived opportunity*.

The third element in the fraud triangle is some way to *rationalize* the fraud so as to make the illegal actions consistent with the perpetrator's personal code of conduct. Mark's rationalization was twofold: (1) he didn't believe what he was doing was illegal, although he recognized it might be unethical, and (2) he believed he would get an inheritance and be able to pay the money back. In his mind, he was only *borrowing*, and, while his method of borrowing was perhaps unethical, he would repay the debt. After all, almost everyone borrows money.

The three elements of (1) perceived pressure, (2) perceived opportunity, and (3) ability to rationalize are common to every fraud. Neither the pressure nor the opportunity has to be real. An observer may look at this fraud and say, "Mark, you didn't have the kinds of pressure to do something like that, and you should have known you would get caught." However, it doesn't matter what the observer or anyone else besides Mark thinks. If he perceives a pressure and an opportunity and can rationalize his behavior, he is likely to commit fraud.

The Fire Triangle: A Comparison

In many ways, fraud is like fire. In order for a fire to occur, three elements are necessary: (1) oxygen, (2) fuel, and (3) heat. As shown in Figure 2–1, when these three elements come together, there is a fire.

As an illustration of the similarities between the elements in the fire triangle and the fraud triangle, consider the case of one of the author's brothers. Last year he and his family moved into a new home. The home was in a rural neighborhood, and he decided to install a 350-gallon gasoline tank in his backyard so he could refuel his truck and cars without going to a service station. The tank was placed on a 6-foot-high structure with four supporting legs and was first filled in December when the ground was frozen. As the ground started to thaw in the spring, the weight of the gasoline caused the two front legs to sink into the ground.

One afternoon, while the parents were at their son's basketball game and their two daughters, ages 10 and 7, were home alone watching television, the full tank rolled off the structure and fell onto the driveway. When the tank landed on the concrete driveway, the hose jarred lose and gasoline started to run out. The gasoline ran along the sidewalk, down the back steps and into the basement. In the house were not only oxygen but also heat—in the form of a pilot light on the furnace. All that was needed to complete the fire triangle was fuel, which was fast approaching the furnace room.

When the gasoline fumes reached the pilot light, there was an explosion. The girls, thinking the explosion was an earthquake, did as they had been instructed and quickly hid under the kitchen table. No sooner had they gotten under the table than they saw a ball of fire coming up the steps from the basement. The fire was moving through the house like a locomotive looking for oxygen. The girls opened the kitchen door and ran outside. As they jumped outside, the entire house exploded, blowing off the roof and pushing the walls out a full 6 inches. Fortunately, the girls suffered only minor burns and trauma.

The force of the explosion was a blessing in disguise: It consumed all the oxygen and extinguished the fire. After the explosion, gasoline continued to pour into the basement. However, now there was no heat. In fact, the firefighters who soon arrived waded around (wearing masks because of the intense smoke) in over 300 gallons of gasoline, thinking it was water. There was enough gasoline in the home to blow up the entire block on which the house was located.

The fire burned for only four seconds but reached a temperature of over 1,800° Fahrenheit. Nothing in the house was completely burned; rather, everything was melted. The telephone on the wall looked like an icicle. The TV set the girls had been watching was a melted heap of plastic.

FIGURE 2–1
Comparing Triangles–Fire and Fraud

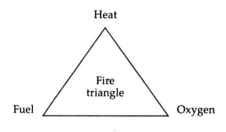

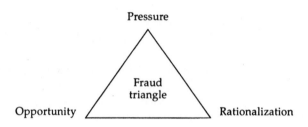

Firefighters are smart. They know a fire can be extinguished by eliminating any one of the three fire elements. Oxygen is often eliminated by smothering, by using chemicals, or by causing explosions, as was the case with the brother's fire and with many of the oilwell fires in Kuwait. Heat is most commonly eliminated by pouring water on fires. Fuel is removed by building fire lines or fire breaks, or by shutting off the source of fuel.

Fraud fighters are generally not as smart. As will be shown in later chapters, people who want to prevent fraud usually work on only one element of the fraud triangle: opportunity. Because they generally believe that opportunities can be eliminated by having good internal controls, they focus all or most of their prevention efforts on implementing controls and ensuring adherence to them. Rarely do they focus on the pressures motivating fraud or on the rationalizations of perpetrators.

As with the elements in the fire triangle, the three elements in the fraud triangle are interactive (see Figure 2–1). With fire, the more flammable the fuel, the less oxygen and heat it takes to ignite. Similarly, the purer the oxygen, the less flammable the fuel needs to be to ignite. With fraud, the greater the perceived opportunity or the more intense the pressure, the less rationalization it takes to motivate someone to commit fraud. Likewise, the more dishonest a perpetrator is, the less opportunity and/or pressure it takes to motivate fraud.

It is interesting to note that almost every study of honesty recently performed in advanced countries reveals that levels of honesty are decreasing. Given the interactive nature of the elements in the fraud triangle, the decreasing levels of honestry present a scary future concerning fraud. (Less honesty makes it easier to rationalize, thus requiring less opportunity and/or pressure for fraud to occur.)

Rationalizations and related honesty levels as well as fraud opportunities will be discussed in later chapters. We now turn our attention to the pressures motivating individuals to commit frauds.

PRESSURES TO COMMIT FRAUD

Fraud can be perpetrated to benefit oneself or to benefit an organization. Employee fraud, in which an individual embezzles from his or her employer, usually benefits the perpetrator. Management fraud, in which an organization's officers deceive investors and creditors, is most often perpetrated to benefit an organization and its officers.

All types of fraud involve pressures. Pressures that motivate individuals to perpetrate fraud on their own behalf can be divided into four types: (1) financial pressures, (2) vices, (3) work-related pressures, and (4) other pressures.

Financial Pressures

Personal studies by the authors have shown that approximately 95 percent of all frauds involve either financial or vice-related pressures. Mark Simpson's financial pressures were that he was living in his car, had no furniture or other living necessities, and was broke. Common financial pressures associated with fraud are:

1. Greed
2. Living beyond one's means
3. High personal debt
4. High medical bills
5. Poor credit
6. Personal financial loss
7. Unexpected financial needs

Certainly, this list is not exhaustive, and these pressures are not mutually exclusive. However, each pressure in this list has been associated with numerous frauds. We know individuals who have committed fraud because they were destitute. We know other fraud perpetrators who were living lifestyles far beyond that of their peers. When one perpetrator was caught embezzling over $1.3 million from his employer, for example, it was learned that he had spent the money on monogrammed shirts and gold cuff links; two Mercedes Benz sedans; an expensive suburban home; a beachfront condominium; furs, rings, and other jewelry for his wife; a new car for his father-in-law; a country club membership; and $50 tips at bars. Most people would say he really didn't have financial pressures.

Financial pressures can occur suddenly or can be long-term. Unfortunately, very few fraud perpetrators inform others when they are having financial problems. As a case in point, consider Susan Jones.[2] Susan worked at the same company for 32 years without her integrity ever being questioned. At age 63, she became a grandmother to two beautiful granddaughters. Immediately, she became a spendaholic. She bought everything she could get her hands on for her two grandchildren, and she became addicted to the Home Shopping Network. During the three years prior to her retirement, Susan stole over $650,000 from her employer. Today, she is serving a one-year prison sentence and has deeded everything she and her husband owned to her former employer. When she is released from prison, she will be required to repay her employer the $250,000 she still owes.

The fact that someone has been an "honest" employee for over 32 years seems to make no difference when severe financial pressures occur or an individual perceives that such pressures exist. Recent studies have found that while approximately 30 percent of employee frauds are perpetrated by employees during their first three years of employment, 70 percent are committed by employees with 4 to 35 years of service.

Financial pressures are usually the most common motivation for deception, such as management fraud which benefits organizations rather than individuals. Most companies that overstate assets on the balance sheet, for example, do so because of financial pressures such as a poor cash position, uncollectible receivables, loss of significant customers, obsolete inventory, a declining market, or restrictive loan covenants that are being violated. Regina Vacuum Company is a case in point. Because the company's vacuum cleaners were defective and had melting parts, thousands were being returned. Recognizing the large amount of sales returns on the income statement would have reduced net income significantly. To hide this financial pressure, Regina's officers did not record sales returns, understated the cost of goods sold, and overstated inventory. Reported cost of sales as a percentage of revenues in the company went from 65 percent to 52 percent in four years.

---

[2]Again, the name and the situation have been changed, although the case is real.

Vice Pressures

Closely related to financial pressures are vices such as gambling, drugs, alcohol, and expensive sexual relationships. As an example of how these vices motivate a person to commit fraud, consider one individual's personal confession of how gambling led to his dishonest acts:

As I sat on the stool in front of the blackjack table I knew I was in trouble. I had just gambled away my children's college fund. I stumbled to my hotel room, hoping to wake up and realize this evening was nothing more than a nightmare. While driving back to San Jose from Reno Sunday morning, I could not face the embarrassment of telling my wife. I had to come up with the money. I was sure that if I had only $500, I could win the money back. But how could I get $500? A short time later at work, an accounts payable clerk came to my office seeking assistance with a problem. The clerk was matching invoices with purchase orders. He had found an invoice for $3200 that did not match the purchase order. Immediately, I realized how I could get the $500 "loan." My company was a fast-growing microchip producer whose internal controls were quite good on paper but were often not followed. The company had a policy of paying, without secondary approval, any invoice of $500 or less. I decided to set up a dummy company that would issue invoices to my employer for amounts up to $500. I was confident my winnings from these "borrowings" would not only allow me to replace the college fund, but would also allow repayment of the "loan." I couldn't believe how easy it was to "borrow" the money. The first check showed up in a PO box I had opened a few days earlier. I called my wife with the bad news. Together with the controller, I would have to fly to Los Angeles over the weekend to meet with lawyers over a company matter. Within minutes, I was on my way to Reno. Upon arrival, I went straight to the craps tables. By four AM, I was not only out of money but was in the hole over $600. I was concerned about the losses, but not as worried as before. I would just submit more fictitious bills to the company. Over the next few months, my fraud progressed to the point where I had set up two more dummy companies and insisted that accounts payable clerks not verify any invoice of less than $750. No one questioned my changing the policy because I had worked for the company for over 14 years and was a "trusted" employee. After 1 year, I had replaced the college fund and purchased a new automobile; I had stolen over $75,000. I was caught when the internal auditors matched addresses of vendors and found that my three dummy vendors all had the same PO box.

Vices are the worst kind of fraud motivators. We have known female employees who embezzled because their children were on drugs and they couldn't stand to see them go through withdrawal pains. We have also known "successful" managers who, in addition to embezzling from their companies, burglarized homes and engaged in other types of theft to support their drug habits. To understand how addictive vices can be, consider the following confessions from reformed gamblers.

Gamblers' confessions

- Gambling was the ultimate experience for me—better than sex, better than any drug. I had withdrawal tortures just like a heroin junkie.
- I degraded myself in every way possible. I embezzled from my own company; I conned my six-year-old out of his allowance.
- Once I was hooked, any wager would do. I would take odds on how many cars would pass over a bridge in the space of 10 minutes.
- When I was at the blackjack table, my wife could have been home dying from cancer, and I could not have cared less.
- When I caught that first whiff of the race track, I was king in my own fantasy world. There was no other high like it.
- I stole vacation money from the family sugar jar. I spent every waking hour thinking about getting to the track.
- After I woke up from an appendectomy, I sneaked out of the hospital, cashed a bogus check, and headed for my bookie. I was still bleeding from the operation.
- I'll never forget coming home from work at night, looking through the window at my family waiting for me, and then leaving to place a couple more bets. I was crying the whole time, but I had simply lost all control.

If someone will steal from his six-year-old child or sneak out of a hospital still bleeding from an operation, he will certainly steal from his employer or commit other types of fraud. The number of embezzlers who trace their motivation for stealing to alcohol, gambling, and expensive sexual relationships is high. However, the motivation to steal for drugs may even be worse. Consider these confessions of former addicted drug users.

Drug users' confessions

- We were the parents of two children, a daughter age seven and a son six months. Yet, the most important thing in our lives was shooting up, sometimes as much as 10 or 15 times a day.
- I began living with a man who was a heavy drug user. We had a child, but the relationship didn't last. By the time it ended, I was high on drugs and alcohol so much of the time I could barely manage to make it to work every day.
- I was the branch manager of a large bank. But secretly I was shooting up in my office all day and stealing money from my employer to finance it.
- On a lark, I snorted heroin. I told myself I could try it and walk away from it. In just five weeks I graduated from snorting to shooting speedballs directly into my veins. I was often too sick to show up for work or to make breakfast for my son.
- One day my daughter stretched out her little arms in front of me. She had made dots with a red pen on each of the creases in her arms. "I want to be just like my mommy," she said proudly.

- My wife and I literally whooped for joy at the sight of our newborn son: a 7-pound baby with big eyes and rosy cheeks—normal and healthy-looking. But we both knew a moment we had been dreading was now just hours away. The baby would be going through withdrawal. We didn't want him to suffer because of our awful habit. And we had to keep the doctors from finding out he had drugs in his system, or he would be taken from us and placed in foster care. We felt we had no choice. When the nurses left the room, I cradled our baby in my arms and clipped a tiny piece of heroin under his tongue.

- I lost my job. I was robbing and stealing every day to support my habit, which cost $500 per day.

- There was no level to which I would not descend in order to get drugs. While I was supposedly a successful businessman, I stole from stores; I broke into homes and stole TVs, VCRs [videocassette recorders], jewelry—anything that would bring cash to support my habit.

- Because I was often incapacitated, my eight-year-old daughter was frequently forced into the role of surrogate parent. When I was sick, she would feed my baby, change his diapers, do the laundry. She would get up in the middle of the night to care for him when I was too zonked out to hear him crying. I only rarely shopped or cooked. Sometimes Jennifer would have her cereal with water because there was no milk.

- One morning in a semiblackout, lonely and depressed, I slashed my wrists with a kitchen knife. When I saw the blood all over, I regained my senses and frantically called the police.

Someone who will clip a piece of heroin under a newborn baby's tongue or burglarize homes to support his habit will surely look for ways to embezzle from employers or commit other types of fraud.

Work-Related Pressures

While financial pressures and vices motivate most frauds, some people commit fraud to get even with their employer or with someone else. Factors such as getting little recognition for job performance, having a feeling of job dissatisfaction, fearing losing one's job, being overlooked for a promotion, and feeling underpaid have motivated many frauds. Here is an example.

I began my career at the XYZ Company as a staff accountant. I am a religious person. In fact, I spent a year volunteering with a nonprofit agency that provided relief to people in need of food and shelter. Because of this experience and because of my six years with the company, I was considered a person of impeccable character and a very trusted employee. The president of XYZ is a workaholic and considers an eight-hour-day to be something a part-time employee works. As a result, I spent six years working in my finance position, putting in between 12 and 14 hours per day. During this period, I was paid a salary, with no overtime compensation. Early in my career, the extra hours didn't bother me; I considered them an investment in my future. In early 1989,

I was named manager of the purchasing department. After two years in that position, I realized that the 12- to 14-hour days were still an expected way of life at the company. I was becoming bitter about the expectation of overtime and felt that the company "owed me" for the time I had worked for "nothing." I decided to get my "pay" from the company. Working with a favored vendor, I accepted kickbacks to allow over $1.5 million in overcharges to the company. I figured the $80,000 I received in kickbacks was compensation that I deserved.

Other Pressures

Once in a while, fraud is motivated by other pressures, such as a spouse who insists (either directly or indirectly) on an improved lifestyle, or a challenge to beat the system. One perpetrator, for example, embezzled $45,000 because his wife demanded a new and bigger home. A woman embezzled over $450,000 so her husband could drive a new car, enjoy a higher lifestyle, and eat steak instead of hamburger. There is a famous computer consultant, described in Chapter 5, who is retained by major companies to help them deter and detect computer fraud. He is famous because he once felt personally challenged to "commit the perfect crime." After purchasing and taking delivery of over $1.5 million in inventory that was paid for by accessing a large company's computer records, he was caught when one of his inventory managers turned him in.

CONCLUDING COMMENTS

Most of us face pressures in our lives. We have legitimate financial needs, we make foolish or speculative investments, we are possessed by addictive vices, we feel overworked and/or underpaid, or we are greedy and want more. We sometimes have a difficult time in distinguishing between wants and needs. Indeed, the objective of most people in a capitalistic society is to obtain wealth. We measure success by how much money or wealth a person has. If you say you have a very successful uncle, what are you really saying? You probably mean that he lives in a big house, has a cabin or a condominium, drives expensive automobiles, and has money to do whatever he wants.

To some people, being successful is more important than being honest. If they were to rank the personal characteristics they value most, being successful would rank higher than having integrity. Psychologists tell us that most, if not all, of us have a price at which we will be dishonest. Individuals with high integrity and low opportunity need high pressure to be dishonest. Most of us can think of scenarios in which we, too, may commit fraud. If for example, our children were starving, we worked in an environment where cash was abundant and not accounted for, and we really believed that we would repay the money taken to feed our children, even we might commit fraud. Honest Abraham Lincoln once threw a man out of his office, angrily turning down a substantial bribe. When someone asked why he was so angry, he said, "Every man has his price, and he was getting close to mine." One thing is for certain, eliminating pressures in the fraud triangle has an effect similar to the removal of heat from the fire triangle. Without some kind of pressure, fraud rarely occurs.

Chapter Three

Internal Control Factors
The Second Element of the Fraud Triangle: Opportunity (Part A)

A perceived opportunity to commit fraud, to conceal it, and to avoid being punished for it is the second element of the fraud triangle that was introduced in Chapter 2. While there are many kinds of such opportunities, in this chapter and in Chapter 4 we discuss six of them. These six do not represent an exhaustive list of the opportunities that allow fraud to be committed but they do provide a sufficient number of settings to illustrate the role of opportunities in the fraud triangle. The six opportunities that will be considered are:

1. Lack or circumvention of controls that prevent and/or detect fraudulent behavior
2. Inability to judge quality of work
3. Lack of disciplinary action
4. Asymmetrical information
5. Ignorance and apathy
6. No audit trail

We will discuss controls in this chapter and the other five opportunities in Chapter 4.

CONTROLS THAT PREVENT AND/OR DETECT FRAUDULENT BEHAVIOR

Having an effective *control structure* is probably the most important step an organization can take to prevent and detect employee fraud. There are three elements in a company's control structure: (1) the control environment, (2) the accounting system, and (3) control procedures or activities. The accounting profession has defined the components of each of these three elements; here we discuss only the components that are the most effective in deterring fraud.

The Control Environment

The control environment is the work atmosphere that an organization establishes for its employees. The most important element in establishing an appropriate environment is *management's role and example*. There are numerous instances on record in which management's dishonest or inappropriate behavior has been learned and modeled by employees. In the famous Equity Funding case, management was writing insurance policies on individuals who didn't exist and selling them to other insurance companies. Seeing this dishonest behavior, one employee said to himself, "It doesn't make sense to have all these fictitious people live forever. I'll knock a few of them off and collect death proceeds. My actions won't be any different from those of the management of this company." In another case, employees who realized that top management was overstating revenues and receivables began overstating expenses on their travel reimbursement forms, billing for hours not worked, and perpetrating other types of fraud.

As stated in Chapter 1, proper modeling (being an example) and proper labeling (training) are the two most important elements in teaching honesty. When management models unacceptable behavior, the control environment is contaminated. Similarly, if management models a behavior that is inconsistent with good control procedures, the integrity of the control system erodes. For example, when a manager says, "Don't loan keys to anyone else and don't share passwords with others," and then shares her password or keys, she is sending mixed signals and her inappropriate behavior will be emulated by other employees. In other words, employees think to themselves, "What you do speaks so loudly we can't hear what you say." Indeed, management's example or model is the most critical element of the control environment. Inappropriate behavior by management allows others to justify overriding or ignoring control procedures.

The second critical element in the control environment that helps to reduce fraud opportunities is *management's communication*. Proper labeling or communicating what is and is not appropriate is critical. Parents who are trying to teach their children to be honest must say things like, "Taking a candy bar off a store shelf without paying for it is dishonest" and "Not returning the extra change when someone overpays you is dishonest." Similarly, organizations that want employees to behave honestly and in ways that are consistent with good control procedures must clearly label what is and is not acceptable. Codes of conduct, orientation meetings, training, supervisor/employee discussions, and other types of communication that distinguish between acceptable and unacceptable behavior are critical.

To be an effective deterrent to fraud, communication must be consistent. Messages that change depending on circumstances and situations serve only to confuse employees and to encourage rationalizations. The reasons so many frauds occur in crash or rush projects are that typical control procedures are not followed and inconsistent messages relating to procedures and controls are conveyed. Strikes, mergers, bankruptcies, and other dramatic events usually result in inconsistent labeling and communication and allow for increased fraud.

The third critical element in creating the proper control structure is *appropriate hiring.* Recent research has shown that nearly 30 percent of all people in the United States are dishonest, another 30 percent are situationally honest (honest where it pays to be honest and dishonest where it pays to be dishonest), and 40 percent are honest all the time.[1] While most organizations are convinced that their employees, customers, and vendors are all among the 40 percent who are honest, this simply isn't the case.

When dishonest individuals are hired, even the best controls will not prevent fraud. Take a bank, for example. There are too many employees who can steal. Tellers, managers, loan officers, and others who have access to funds *can* steal. They may get caught, but they can steal. Banks hope that detective controls, the fear of punishment, and personal integrity will deter theft.

As an example of the consequences of poor hiring practices, consider the case of a famous performer who was raped a few years ago. This performer checked into a well-known hotel. A few hours after her arrival, there was a knock on her door accompanied by the words "Room service." She hadn't ordered anything but thought maybe, because she was famous, the hotel was bringing her a basket of fruit or some complimentary wine. When she opened the door, three hotel custodians burst into her room and raped her. She later sued the hotel for $4 million and won. The basis of her lawsuit was that the hotel did not adequately screen its employees, because all three had previous arrest records and had been fired from previous jobs because of rape.

No matter how good the hotel's controls are, if it hires convicted rapists and allows them access to guests, it will have some problems. Similarly, no matter how good an organization's controls are, if it does not adequately screen its employees, it will have fraud. To understand how good hiring practices can prevent fraud and other problems, consider, for example, a company that decided to take extra precautions in

---

[1]Richard C. Hollinger, *Dishonesty in the Workplace: A Manager's Guide to Preventing Employee Theft* (Park Ridge, Ill.: London House Press, 1989), pp. 1–5.

its hiring practices a few years ago. Their approach was, first, to train all persons associated with hiring decisions to be expert interviewers and, second, to check three background references for each prospective employee thoroughly. Because of these extra precautions, over 800 applicants (13 percent of all hires) who would have been hired were disqualified. These applicants had undisclosed problems, such as having provided false employment information, previous arrest records, uncontrollable tempers, alcoholism, drug addition, and having been fired from previous jobs. Charles Osgood, a radio journalist, on a November 1992 *Osgood File* radio broadcast, stated that one of three résumés of prospective employees contains one or more entries that are not true.

The fourth fraud-deterring element of the control environment is a *clear organizational structure.* When everyone in an organization knows exactly who has responsibility for each business activity, fraud is less likely to be committed. In such situations, it is easier to track missing assets and harder to embezzle without being caught. Strict accountability for job performance and for assets is critical for a good control environment. As an example of how failure to assign custody resulted in a fraud, consider the case of Jane D.[2]

> I was one of eight tellers in a medium-sized bank. Because we all had access to money orders and bank checks, I stole 16 money orders. I didn't use them for two weeks to see if anyone would notice them missing. Then, I used one for $300. After nothing being said during the next two weeks, I used seven more.

The fifth element of the control environment that is critical in deterring and detecting fraud is *an effective internal audit department, combined with security or loss prevention programs.* While most studies have found that internal auditors detect only about 20 percent of all employee frauds (others are detected through tips, by alert employees, and accidentally), the mere presence of internal auditors provides a significant deterrent effect. Internal auditors provide independent checks and cause perpetrators to question whether they can act and not be caught. A visible and effective security function, in conjunction with an appropriate loss prevention program, can help ensure that fraud is properly investigated and that control weaknesses and violations are appropriately published.

Taken together, the five control environmental elements—(1) proper management modeling, (2) good communication or labeling, (3) effective hiring procedures, (4) clear organizational structure and assigned responsibilities, and (5) an effective internal audit department and a workable security function—can create an atmosphere in which fraud

---

[2]Throughout this chapter, the names of the perpetrators have been changed.

opportunities are decreased, because employees see that fraud is not acceptable and not tolerated. Relaxing any one of these five elements dramatically increases fraud opportunities.

The Accounting System

The second element of the control structure that reduces fraud opportunities is a good accounting system. Every fraud is composed of three elements: (1) the theft act, in which assets are taken, (2) concealment, which is the attempt to hide the fraud from others, and (3) conversion, in which the perpetrator spends the money or converts the stolen assets. An effective accounting system provides an audit trail that allows frauds to be discovered and makes concealment difficult. Unlike bank robbery, in which there is usually no effort to conceal the theft act, concealment is probably the major distinguishing element of fraud. Frauds are often concealed in the accounting records. Accounting records are based on transaction documents. In order to cover up a fraud, documents must be altered, misplaced, or made fraudulent. Frauds can also be discovered in the accounting records by examining journal entries that have no support, or by probing financial statements that are not reasonable. Without a good accounting system, distinguishing between actual fraud and unintentional errors is often difficult.

Control Procedures

The third component of the control structure is good control procedures or activities. An individual who owns his or her own business and is the sole worker does not need many control procedures. While such people may have ample opportunity to defraud their companies, they have no incentive to do so. They won't usually steal from themselves, and they never want to treat customers poorly. However, organizations that involve many employees must have control procedures, so that the actions of employees will be congruent with the goals of management or owners. In addition, with control procedures, opportunities to commit and/or conceal frauds are eliminated or minimized. No matter the kind of business—whether it is the business of raising children; operating a financial institution, a grocery store, or a Fortune 500 company; or investing personal assets—there are only five types of control procedures:

1. Segregation of duties, or dual custody
2. System of authorizations
3. Independent checks
4. Physical safeguards
5. Documents and records

There are thousands of variations on each of these five control procedures. As an illustration of how control procedures can be used to
achieve goal congruence, consider the case of a son of one of the authors.

> Mark was a seventh grader. At the annual parent-teacher conferences, we dis-
> covered that he was getting straight A's in all of his classes except one—a Ger-
> man class in which he was getting an F. When we later asked Mark about the
> class, he said, "I hate the teacher. She is a jerk and I refuse to work for her."
> After discussions with the teacher and Mark, we decided to implement three
> controls so that Mark's actions would be consistent with the desires of his par-
> ents. First, we printed up some simple little forms (documents) for the teacher
> to check off each day and send home. These pieces of paper contained two
> simple statements: (1) Mark (was) (was not) prepared for class today, and (2)
> Mark (was) (was not) responsible in class today. The teacher would circle the
> appropriate response to each phrase, initial the paper, and send it home each
> day with Mark. By insisting on reading the note each night, we were perform-
> ing an independent check on Mark's performance. In addition, Mark's roller
> blades were taken away from him until his grade improved. Taking away his
> right to play street hockey on his roller blades was a variation of an authoriza-
> tion control. (He lost his authorized use.) When we invoked the three controls
> of (1) documents, (2) independent checks, and (3) taking away an authorized
> activity, Mark's behavior and performance in German changed, to become
> more in line with the goals of his parents. By the end of the term, his grade in
> German changed from an F to a B.

Segregation of duties and dual custody.   Activities can usually
be better controlled by invoking either segregation of duties, or dual-
custody control. This form of control, like most preventive controls, is
most often used when cash is involved. For example, the opening of incoming cash in a business is usually done in dual custody. The accounting for and the custody of cash are usually separated so that one person
does not have access to both. An example of the ease with which fraud
can be perpetrated when accounting for and custody of assets are not
separated is the fraud of John R.

> John R. worked for a medium-size homebuilder. He was in charge of writing
> checks as well as reconciling bank statements. Over a period of time, John stole
> over $400,000 by manipulating the check register and forcing bank reconcilia-
> tions to balance. If, for example, his employer owed a subcontractor $15,000,
> John would write the check for $15,000 and then write $20,000 on the check
> stub. Then, using the next check, he would write himself a check for $5,000 and
> mark the check stub "voided." When the bank statement was returned, he
> would destroy the checks written to himself and force the reconciliation.

John's fraud could easily have been caught, if not prevented, if someone
besides John had either reconciled the bank statements or written checks.
There are at least three critical functions that even small business owners
should either set up as segregated duties or always do themselves: (1) writing checks, (2) making bank deposits, and (3) reconciling bank statements.

Dual custody is a variation on this type of control procedure, in that it does not allow complete access to a transaction by one employee. Dual custody requires two individuals to work together on the same task, whereas segregation of duties does not allow one person complete control over all aspects of a transaction. Both versions of this control are the same: They do not allow one person to have unchecked access to funds.

Dual custody is very difficult to enforce. When two individuals are working in dual custody, they cannot take their eyes or their minds off the task to answer telephones, use the restroom, respond to a question, or even sneeze. An example of a fraud that was perpetrated in a supposed dual-custody environment is the case of Roger M., who made the following confession:

> On January 2, 19XX, I took the amount of $3,062 in cash, which was contained in a disposable night drop bag. I concealed my actions by putting it inside a night drop envelope that I processed on the same day. I have no real excuse for taking money. I saw an easy way of taking the money, and I took advantage of it. Circumstances that made it seem easy to take the money without being caught or observed were that I was situated on the customer side of the merchant vault, which obscured the view of my dual-custody partner. I have reimbursed the bank today (January 27, 19XX) the amount of $3,062.

System of authorizations.   Authorization control procedures take many forms. Passwords authorize individuals to use computers and to access certain databases. Signature cards authorize individuals to enter safe deposit boxes, to cash checks, and to perform other functions at financial institutions. Spending limits authorize individuals to spend only what is in their budget or approved level. When people are not authorized to perform an activity, the opportunity to commit fraud is reduced. For example, when individuals are not authorized to enter safe deposit boxes, they cannot enter and steal someone else's contents. When individuals are not authorized to approve purchases, they cannot order items for personal use and have their companies pay for them. As the following fraud case shows, the failure to enforce authorization controls makes the perpetration of fraud simple.

> Mary and Ron B. had been customers of a certain bank for many years. Because he owned a jewelry store, they maintained a safe deposit box at the bank to store certain inventory. Most employees of the bank knew them well because of their frequent visits to make deposits and conduct other business. What was unknown to the bank employees, was that Mary and Ron were having marital difficulties, which ended in a bitter divorce. At the time of the divorce, they canceled their joint safe deposit box. The husband came in a short time later and opened up a new box, with his daughter as cosigner. Because the wife was bitter about the divorce settlement, she entered the bank one day and told the safe deposit custodian (who had been away on vacation during the B.'s divorce) that she had misplaced her key to the box and needed

to have the box drilled. Because the custodian knew Mary and didn't know the box had been closed and a new one opened, she arranged to force open the box. Without any problems, the box was drilled and the ex-wife emptied the contents. When the husband tried to enter the box a few days later, he discovered what had happened. Because the wife was not a signer on the account at the time the box was forced open, the bank was completely liable and settled out of court with the jeweler for $200,000. This fraud was allowed to be perpetrated because the authorization control of matching signatures to a signature card was not performed.

Independent checks.   The theory behind independent checks is that if people know that their work or activities will be monitored by others, the opportunity to commit and conceal a fraud will be eliminated. There are many varieties of independent checks. The Office of the Controller of the Currency (OCC) requires that every bank employee in the United States take one week's consecutive vacation each year. While employees are gone, others are supposed to perform their work. If an employee's work merely piles up while he or she is out for the week, this "mandatory vacation" control is not working as it should and the opportunity to commit fraud is not taken away. Periodic job rotations, cash counts or certifications, supervisor reviews, employee hot lines, and the use of auditors are other forms of independent checks. One large department store in Europe has a complete extra staff of employees for its chain of department stores. This staff goes to a store and tells everyone who works there to go on holiday (vacation) for a month. While they are gone, the extra staff operates the store. One of the purposes of this program is to provide complete, independent checks on the activities of store employees. If someone who is committing fraud is forced to leave for a month, the illegal activity will usually be discovered. As an illustration of the creative use of independent checks, consider the case of a Baskin-Robbins ice cream store in Washington, DC.

Upon entering this 31-flavors establishment, the customer is greeted by a smiling cashier. Two large signs hang on the wall behind the cashier. One sign reads, "If you have problems with service, please call the manager at this telephone number." The other reads, "If you get a star on your sales receipt, you receive a free sundae." In an ice cream store, or any retail establishment for that matter, one of the easiest ways to perpetrate fraud is to accept cash from customers and either not ring it into the cash register or ring in a lesser amount. If the store happens to sell ice cream, cones can be made a little smaller so that the extra ice cream used in the cones that are not entered into the cash register is not noticeable. The purpose of these signs is to encourage customers to receive and examine their sales receipts. So that customers can look for a star, sales receipts must be issued. If the cashier charges $2 for an ice cream cone and rings only $1 into the cash register, sooner or later a customer who knows what is happening will call the manager's telephone number, which is listed on the other sign, and inform him or her that the cashier is embezzling funds.

Physical safeguards.   Physical safeguards are often used to protect assets from theft by fraud or other means. Physical safeguards such as vaults, safes, fences, locks, and keys take away the opportunity to commit fraud by making it difficult for people to access assets. Money locked in a vault, for example, cannot be stolen unless someone gains unauthorized access or unless someone who has access violates the trust. Physical controls are often used to protect inventory, which is kept in locked cages or warehouses; small assets such as tools, which are locked in cabinets; and cash, which is locked in vaults or safes.

Documents and records.   The fifth type of control procedure involves use of a document or record to create an audit trail. Documents rarely serve as preventive controls but provide excellent detective control. Banks, for example, prepare kiting suspect reports and large- and unusual-item reports, and monitor the bank accounts of their employees to detect abuse by employees or customers. Most companies require a document such as a purchase order to initiate a purchase transaction or a customer order to initiate a sales transaction. In some ways, the entire accounting system serves as a documentary control. Without documents, no accountability exists. Without accountability, it is much easier to perpetrate a fraud and not get caught.

CONCLUDING COMMENTS

The control environment, the accounting system, and the many variations of the five control procedures work together to eliminate and/or reduce the opportunity for employees and others to commit fraud. A good control environment establishes an atmosphere in which proper behavior is modeled and labeled, honest employees are hired, and all employees understand their job responsibilities. The accounting system provides records that make it difficult to conceal fraudulent behavior. The five control procedures make it difficult for perpetrators to gain access to assets, to conceal frauds, and to convert stolen assets without being discovered. Together, these three elements make up the control structure of an organization.

Unfortunately, most frauds are perpetrated in environments in which controls are supposed to be in place but are not being followed. Indeed, it is the overriding and ignoring of existing controls, not the lack of controls, that allow most frauds to be perpetrated.

Chapter Four

Noncontrol Factors
The Second Element of the Fraud Triangle: Opportunity (Part B)

The focus of Chapter 2 was pressures that motivate people to commit fraud. The subject of Chapter 3 was control structures that deter fraud opportunities. In this chapter, we conclude the discussion of factors that provide opportunities for the perpetration of fraud. The five opportunity-providing factors that will be discussed here are:

1. Inability to judge the quality of performance
2. Failure to discipline fraud perpetrators
3. Lack of access to information
4. Ignorance, apathy, or incapacity
5. Lack of an audit trail

These five factors, even when combined with the control elements discussed in Chapter 3, do not constitute an exhaustive list of all the elements that create opportunities for fraud. These five factors do, however, provide a sufficient number of settings to illustrate noncontrol issues that should be considered when deciding whether a fraud opportunity is present.

INABILITY TO JUDGE THE QUALITY OF PERFORMANCE

If you pay someone to construct a fence, you can probably examine the completed job and determine whether or not the quality of work meets specifications and is consistent with the amount of the contract. If, however, you hire a lawyer, a doctor, a dentist, an accountant, an engineer, or an auto mechanic, it is often difficult to know whether you are paying an excessive amount or receiving inferior service or products. With these kinds of contracts, it is easy to overcharge, perform work not needed, provide inferior service, or charge for work not performed. As an example of fraud perpetrated by a professional whose work quality could not be assessed, consider the following *Los Angeles Times* article, which reported an alleged fraud by a dermatologist who supposedly substituted cancerous tissues for patients' healthy lab samples, in order to collect higher fees for treatment.[1]

A dermatologist who was struck and killed after walking into freeway traffic last week had been under investigation by the state medical board for allegedly faking diagnoses of skin cancer to collect higher fees. Dr. Orville Stone, who once headed the dermatology department at UC Irvine Medical Center, was accused by five former employees of using cancerous patients' skin tissue to fake diagnoses for hundreds of other patients. Those employees named 13 healthy patients who Stone allegedly treated for cancer and accused him of deliberately doing the same to hundreds more. Last Friday, the day after the board served a search warrant at his Huntington Beach practice, Dermatology Medical Group, Stone, 61, walked in front of traffic on the San Bernadino Freeway near Indio, the California Highway Patrol said. "He basically parked his car, walked down to the embankment and walked in front of the path of a truck and was struck by four other cars." The Highway Patrol listed the death as a suicide. Former employees accused Stone of hoarding cancerous moles or skin tissue he removed from at least 3 patients. He then would take healthy tissue from patients, diagnose them as having cancer and switch tissues, sending the diseased tissue to a laboratory for analysis. Stone normally charged about $50 to remove noncancerous skin tissue and about $150 to remove the cancerous one.

In this case, a fraud opportunity was created because patients could not judge for themselves whether or not their skin conditions were cancerous. Many such frauds are committed daily by doctors (the statistics cited in Chapter 1 indicated that 10–20 percent of all medical procedures should not be performed), lawyers, engineers, accountants, and automechanics. A massive example of auto mechanic fraud is the recent case of Sears Automotive in California in 1991 and 1992.

Prompted by an increasing number of consumer complaints, the California Department of Consumer Affairs has recently completed a one-year investigation into allegations that Sears Tire and Auto Centers have been overcharging their customers for auto repair services. The undercover investigation was conducted in two phases. In the first phase, agents took 38 cars known to have defects in the brakes and no other mechanical faults to 27 different Sears Automotive Centers in California during 1991. In 34 of the 38 cases, or 89 percent of the time, agents were told that additional work was necessary, involving additional costs. The average amount of the overcharge was $223, but in the worst case, which occurred in San Francisco, agents were overcharged $585 to have the front brake pads, front and rear springs, and control-arm bushings replaced. Although a spokesman for Sears denies the allegations and says that Sears will fight any attempt to deprive them of their license to do auto repair work in California, the evidence of fraud is substantial. In one case, Ruth Hernandez, a citizen of Stockton, California, went to Sears to have new tires put on her car. While she was there, the mechanic informed her that she also needed new struts, which would cost an additional $419.95. When Mrs. Hernandez sought a second opinion, she was told her struts were fine. The Sears mechanic later admitted to having made an incorrect diagnosis.[2]

In trying to understand why a well-established, well-reputed company might commit such a fraud, it is important to know that Sears had established a quota of parts, services, and repair sales for each eight-hour shift. Allegedly, mechanics who consistently did not meet their quotas either had their hours reduced or were transferred out of the parts and service department. Apparently, faced with the pressure to cheat or fail, and believing that customers could not know for themselves whether or not the parts and services were actually needed, many service centers chose to cheat.

FAILURE TO DISCIPLINE FRAUD PERPETRATORS

It is generally agreed among criminologists that rapists have the highest rate of repeat offenses (recidivism) of all criminals; each offender is likely to commit multiple crimes. Next to rapists in number of repeat offenses are probably fraud perpetrators who are not prosecuted or severely disciplined. An individual who commits fraud and is not punished or is merely terminated suffers no significant penalty and often resumes the fraudulent behavior.

On the other hand, fraud perpetrators who are prosecuted, incarcerated, or otherwise severely punished rarely commit additional fraud offenses. Fraud perpetrators are usually individuals who command respect in their jobs, communities, and churches. They usually suffer significant embarrassment from having family, friends, and business associates know about their offenses. Our experience has been that fraud perpetrators who are marginally sanctioned or terminated rarely inform their families and others of the real reason for their termination or punishment. They cannot avoid having others know if they are prosecuted, and, often, telling their spouses, children, and other associates what they have done is the most difficult punishment they can suffer.

---

[2]Information about this fraud was taken from Kevin Kelly, "How Did Sears Blow the Gasket? Some Say the Retailer's Push for Profits Sparked Its Auto-Repair Woes," *Business Week*, June 29, 1992, p. 38; and Tung Yin, "Sears Is Accused of Billing Fraud at Auto Centers," *The Wall Street Journal*, June 12, 1992, western ed., p. B1.

FIGURE 4–1
John Doe—Employment and Fraud History

Occupation	Job Length	Amount Embezzled
Insurance sales	10 months	$200
Office manager	2 years	1,000
Bookkeeper	1 year	30,000
Accountant	2 years	20,000
Accountant	2 years	30,000
Controller	6 years	1,363,700
Manager	Still employed	?

Because of the expense and time involved in prosecuting, many organizations merely dismiss dishonest employees, hoping to rid themselves of the problem. What these organizations fail to realize is that such action is rather shortsighted. While they may have rid themselves of one fraud perpetrator, they have just sent a signal to others in the organization that fraud perpetrators will not suffer significant consequences for their actions. Indeed, lack of prosecution can give others a "perceived opportunity" that, when combined with pressure and rationalization, will result in additional frauds in the organization. Opportunity is removed when there is a probability that perpetrators will be punished, not just discovered.

In today's society, in which workers are mobile and often move from job to job, mere termination often helps them to build an attractive résumé rather than resulting in eliminating fraud opportunities. A man we'll call John Doe is a classic example of someone whose termination without being punished for fraud allowed him to get increasingly attractive jobs at increased salary levels. Figure 4–1 shows his employment and fraud history for approximately 14 years. (Note that the name was changed, but the facts are real.)

According to one reference that described the fraud, this man was never prosecuted. His victim organizations either felt sorry for him, thought prosecution would be too time-consuming and too expensive, or merely chose to pass the problem on to others. As a result, every succeeding job this perpetrator obtained was better than his previous one until he became a controller and chief financial officer (CFO) making $130,000 a year. By merely terminating the perpetrator, his victims helped him to build a résumé and to secure increasingly attractive jobs.

LACK OF ACCESS TO INFORMATION

Many frauds are allowed to be perpetrated because victims don't have access to telling information possessed by the perpetrators. This fraud opportunity is especially prevalent in many of the large management frauds that have been perpetrated against stockholders, investors, and debt holders. In the famous ESM Government fraud case, for example, the same securities had been sold to investors several times. Yet, because those investment records were only in the possession of the perpetrator organization, victims couldn't know of the fraudulent sales.

A classic example of a fraud in which lack of information allowed the fraud to be perpetrated is the Lincoln Savings and Loan Association case. On January 6, 1992, Charles Keating and his son, Charles Keating III, were convicted on 73 and 64 counts of racketeering and fraud, respectively. Charles Keating had created sham transactions to make Lincoln Savings look more profitable than it really was, in order to please auditors and regulators. He was able to perpetrate the fraudulent schemes because auditors and regulators were not given complete access to transactions. For example, one such transaction, known as the *RA Homes sale*, was structured as follows:

> On September 30, 1986, defendants Keating and others caused a subsidiary of Lincoln Savings to engage in a fraudulent sale of approximately 1,300 acres of undeveloped land northwest of Tucson, Arizona, to RA Homes, Inc., at a price of approximately $25 million, consisting of a $5 million cash down payment and a $20 million promissory note, secured only by the undeveloped land. Defendants Keating and others caused Lincoln to record a sham profit of approximately $8.4 million on the sale. In reality, RA Homes agreed to purchase the land only after Keating orally (1) promised that Lincoln would reimburse RA Homes for the down payment on the purchase, (2) agreed that the Lincoln subsidiary would retain responsibility for developing and marketing the property, and (3) guaranteed that RA Homes would be able to sell the land at a profit within a year following the purchase.[3]

In this case, auditors didn't know about any of the oral commitments, all of which violate accounting standards for a sale of real estate and would not allow the recognition of profit. Subsequent to these oral agreements, in supposedly separate transactions, Keating loaned RA Homes $5 million (to cover the down payment) and then continued to manage, market, and develop the "sold" property. In fact, when a real estate agent, who had listed the property, discovered that the 1,300 acres had supposedly been sold, he contacted Charles Keating and was told that no real

---

[3]Expert witness testimony, June 1990 grand jury indictment, US District Court for the Central District of California.

estate commission was due because the land had just been "parked" with RA Homes. With the higher reported profits, Lincoln was able to appear profitable and further perpetrate its fraud on investors and others. Many other similar transactions occurred at Lincoln Savings and Loan.[4]

Most investment scams and management frauds are dependent on the ability to withhold information from victims. Individuals can attempt to protect themselves against such scams by insisting on full disclosure including audited financial statements, a business history, and other information that could reveal the fraudulent nature of such organizations.

Certain employee frauds are also allowed to be perpetrated because only offenders have access to necessary information. One small business employee, for example, stole $452,000 from her employer by writing checks to herself. Because she both wrote checks and reconciled the bank statement, no one caught her illegal activity. If, for example, a vendor was owed $10,000, she would write a check to that vendor for $10,000 but enter $20,000 in the check register. Then, after writing at $10,000 check to herself, she would write the word "VOID" in the check register next to the $10,000 check number. Her very simple fraud continued undetected because she was the only employee who had access to the checking account, the check register, and the bank statement.

IGNORANCE, APATHY, OR INCAPACITY

Older people, individuals with language difficulty and other "vulnerable" citizens are often fraud victims because perpetrators know that such individuals may not have the capacity or the knowledge to detect their illegal acts. Fraud involves deception by trickery or cunning, and such vulnerable people are easier to deceive. One such fraud is the following:[5]

A nurse with purple hands was charged on Tuesday with embezzling money from patients' rooms at a local hospital. The nurse's hands were purple because invisible dye had been put on money planted in a purse used to trap the embezzler. The nurse was on loan from a temporary-help agency. On September 2, two sisters reported to hospital security that money had been taken from their purses, which had been left unattended in their father's room. A check of the staff roster showed that the nurse had been alone in the room just before the money was discovered missing. A purse containing dye-covered bills was planted in a room on September 4. Later that day, a supervisor reported that the nurse had dye on her hands. When confronted, the nurse first

---

[4]The information on Lincoln Savings and Loan was taken from the June 1990 grand jury indictment, US District Court for the Central District of California.

[5]The facts of this case were taken from a U.S. daily newspaper. To protect the individuals and the hospital involved, the names have been omitted.

said she had accidentally knocked the purse to the floor and her hands had been stained while she was replacing the items. After further questioning, however, the nurse admitted to taking the money from the women's purses.

The nurse had found that elderly patients were an easy target for theft. In a hospital room, where patients are often under the influence of sedating drugs, they may not have the ability to recognize theft.

Notorious frauds called *pigeon drops* are specifically designed to take advantage of elderly victims. In such thefts, perpetrators often pose as bank examiners trying to catch dishonest bankers, or they may use some other scheme to get elderly or non-English-speaking customers to withdraw money from banks. When such a customer leaves the bank with the money, the perpetrators flee with the money instead of examining it as they promised, knowing the elderly person has no chance to catch them.

Many investment scams are also designed to take advantage of elderly victims. In the AFCO case, an investment scam that was perpetrated in Utah, elderly victims were convinced to take out mortgages on their homes. They were persuaded by questions and statements such as:

- Do you know you have a sleeping giant in your home that you are not using?
- Your home is worth $100,000, is completely paid off and you could get $80,000 out of it.
- If you are willing to borrow and invest $80,000, we'll pay the interest on the loan, pay you an additional 10 percent interest and buy you a new luxury car to drive.

A financially aware person would recognize that perpetrators could not possibly pay the 60 percent interest they were promising on the loan (10 percent to the bank, 10 percent to the elderly victim, and a new car costing $32,000 for a total cost of $48,000 ÷ $80,000 = 60%), but many elderly victims found the offer too good to refuse. As a result, several hundred elderly, retired citizens invested a total of over $39 million in the AFCO scam. Inability to understand whether a business transaction makes sense because of incapacity, apathy, or ignorance provides fraud opportunities that are attractive to perpetrators.

LACK OF AN AUDIT TRAIL

Organizations go to great lengths to create documents that will provide an audit trail so transactions can be reconstructed and understood. Many frauds, however, involve cash payments or a manipulation of records that cannot be followed. Smart employee fraud perpetrators understand

that their frauds must be concealed. They also know that such concealment must involve manipulation of financial statements. When faced
with a decision about which financial statement to manipulate, they almost always abuse the income statement, because they understand that
the audit trail will quickly be erased. Here is an example.[6]

> Joan Rivera was the controller for a small bank. Over a period of four years
> she stole more than $100,000 by having an upstream bank pay her credit card
> bills. Each time, she covered her fraud by creating an accounting entry like the
> following:

$$\text{Advertising expense} _____ \text{XXX}$$
$$\text{Cash} _____ \qquad \text{XXX}$$

> Joan used this approach because she knew that at year end all expense ac-
> counts, including advertising expense, would be closed and brought to zero
> balances. If bank auditors and officials didn't catch the fraud before year
> end, the audit trail would be erased and the fraud would be difficult to de-
> tect. On the other hand, she knew that if she covered the cash shortage by
> overstating outstanding checks on the bank reconciliation, for example, the
> cash shortage would be carried from month to month, creating a "perma-
> nent" concealment problem.

In the above example, Joan was not caught until she got greedy and
started using other methods of fraud which were not as easily concealed.

CONCLUDING COMMENTS

Opportunity is the second element in the fraud triangle. Opportunities
are provided by a weak internal control environment, lack of internal
control procedures, failure to enforce internal controls, or other factors
such as (1) inability to judge the quality of performance; (2) lack of punishment; (3) lack of access to information; (4) ignorance, incapacity, or
apathy; or (5) lack of audit trail. Opportunities can be real or perceived.
After investigating a fraud, you may say, "How could you have hoped to
get away with that fraud? You should have known you would get
caught." In the end, it doesn't matter what you or anyone else besides
the perpetrator thinks. If he or she is under pressure and perceives an
opportunity, fraud is likely.

---

[6]The name of the perpetrator has been changed.

Chapter Five

How Perpetrators Explain Their Actions
The Third Element of the Fraud Triangle: Rationalization

On October 24, 1989, Jim Bakker and Richard Dortch were convicted on 23 counts of wire and mail fraud and one count of conspiracy to commit wire and mail fraud. As a result of this conviction, the perpetrators of one of the largest and most bizarre frauds in the history of the United States were sent to jail. In his remarks to the court prior to Jim Bakker's sentencing, prosecutor Jerry Miller summarized this PTL (Praise-the-Lord) fraud with the following comments:[1]

> The biggest con man to come through this courtroom, a man corrupted by power and money and the man who would be God at PTL, is a common criminal. The only thing uncommon about him was the method he chose and the vehicle he used to perpetrate his fraud. He was motivated by greed, selfishness, and a lust for power. He is going to be right back at it as soon as he gets the chance. Mr. Bakker was a con man who in the beginning loved people and used things, but he evolved into a man, a ruthless man, who loved things and used people.

How did Jim Bakker, the beloved TV minister of the PTL network, rationalize the committing of such a massive fraud? Here is his story.

PTL had a modest beginning in 1973 when it began operating out of a furniture showroom in Charlotte, North Carolina. By October 1975, it had purchased a 25-acre estate in Charlotte, North Carolina, and had constructed Heritage Village, a broadcast network of approximately 70 television stations in the United States, Canada, and Mexico on which the PTL ministry's show was aired. PTL's corporate charter stated that the religious purposes of the organization were: (1) establishing and maintaining a church and engaging in all types of religious activity, including evangelism, religious instruction, and

---

[1]Facts about the PTL case were taken from "PTL: Where Were the Auditors?" a working paper by Gary L. Tidwell, Associate Professor of Business Administration, School of Business and Economics, College of Charleston, Charleston, South Carolina.

publishing and distributing Bibles; (2) engaging in other religious publication; (3) missionary work, both domestic and foreign; and (4) establishing and operating Bible schools and Bible training centers. Over the following 11 years, PTL built a multimillion dollar empire which consisted of PTL and a 2,300-acre Heritage USA tourist center valued at $172 million. Specific activities of the organization included Heritage Church with a weekly attendance of over 3,000; Upper Room prayer services where counselors ministered to people; Prison Ministry, with a volunteer staff of over 4,000; Fort Hope, a missionary outreach house for homeless men; Passion Play, a portrayal of the life of Christ in an outdoor amphitheater; a dinner theater; a day care center; Heritage Academy; a summer day camp; the Billy Graham Home; workshops; and a Christmas nativity scene that had been visited by over 500,000 people.

PTL also had a wide range of activities that were ultimately deemed by the IRS to be commercial. In one such venture, PTL viewers were given an opportunity to become lifetime partners in a hotel for $1,000 each. Bakker promised that only 25,000 lifetime partnership interests would be sold and that partners could use the hotel free each year for 4 days and 3 nights. In the end, however, 68,412 such partnerships were sold. Through this and similar solicitations, Jim Bakker's PTL had amassed gross receipts of over $600 million, much of which had been used to support the extravagant lifestyle of Bakker and other officers of PTL. Time and time again, Bakker misled worshippers, investors, and his faithful followers by misusing contributions, overselling investments, evading taxes, and living an extravagant lifestyle.

How could a minister perpetrate such a large and vicious fraud in the name of religion? Most people believe that Jim Bakker's ministry was initially sincere, inspired by a real desire to help others and to teach the word of God. He believed that what he was doing was for a good purpose and rationalized that any money he received would directly or indirectly help others. He even recognized at one time that money might be corrupting him and his empire. In 1985 he said, "I was going to say to listeners, 'Please stop giving.' But, I just couldn't say that." What started out as a sincere ministry was corrupted by money until Jim Bakker rationalized on a television program, "I have never asked for a penny for myself. . . . God has always taken care of me." His rationalizations increased to the point that one of the trial attorneys, in her closing argument, stated, "You can't lie to people to send you money—it's that simple. What unfolded before you over the past month was a tale of corruption—immense corruption. . . . What was revealed here was that Mr. Bakker was a world-class master of lies and half-truths."

RATIONALIZATION

The three elements of the fraud triangle were introduced in Chapter 2. The first two elements, perceived pressure and perceived opportunity, were discussed in Chapters 2 through 4. The last element, rationalization, is discussed in this chapter. Jim Bakker rationalized his dishonest acts by convincing himself that his PTL network had a good purpose and that he was helping others. In a similar way, folklore has it that Robin Hood rationalized his dishonest acts by arguing that he was "stealing from the rich and giving to the poor."

Nearly every fraud involves the element of rationalization. Most fraud perpetrators are first-time offenders who would not commit other crimes. Someway, they must rationalize away the dishonesty of their acts. Common rationalizations used by fraud perpetrators are:

- The organization owes it to me.
- I am only borrowing the money and will pay it back.
- Nobody will get hurt.
- I deserve more.
- It's for a good purpose.
- Something has to be sacrificed—my integrity or my reputation. (If I don't embezzle to cover my inability to pay, people will know I can't meet my obligations, which will be embarrassing because I'm a professional.)

Certainly, there are countless other rationalizations. These six, however, are representative and serve as an adequate basis to discuss the role of rationalization in the perpetration of fraud.

WE ALL RATIONALIZE

It is important to recognize that there are very few, if any, people who do not rationalize. We rationalize being overweight. We rationalize not exercising enough. We rationalize spending more than we should. And most of us rationalize being dishonest. Here are two examples of rationalization of dishonesty.

A wife works hard, saves her money, and buys a new dress. When she puts it on for the first time, she asks her husband, "How do you like my new dress?" Realizing that the wife worked hard for the money and that she must really like the dress or wouldn't have purchased it, the husband says, "Oh, it is beautiful," although he really doesn't like it. Why did the husband lie? He probably rationalized in his mind that the consequence of telling the truth was more severe that the consequence of lying. "After all, if she likes it, I'd better like it, too," he reasons. Unfortunately, the rationalization of not wanting to hurt his wife's feelings results in lying, which is dishonest. In fact, the husband will pay for his dishonesty. His wife will continue to wear the dress because she believes her husband likes it. What the husband could have said is, "Honey, you are a beautiful woman and that is one reason I married you. I like most of the clothes you buy and wear, but this dress is just not my favorite."

You go to your mother-in-law's for dinner. For dessert, she has baked a cherry pie. Even though you don't like the pie, you lie and say, "This pie is delicious." Why did you lie? Because you rationalized that you didn't want to hurt your mother-in-law's feelings and that, in fact, it would make her feel good if you complimented her cooking. As in the dress example, you will pay for your dishonesty because your mother-in-law, believing you like her cherry pie, will serve it again the next time you visit. Dishonesty could have been avoided by remaining silent or by saying, "Mom, you are an excellent cook, and I really like most of the food you cook. However, cherry pie is not my favorite."

These two examples of rationalization involve the dishonesty of lying. The dishonesty is rationalized by the desire to make other people feel good. The same sort of rationalization often allows the perpetration of fraud. Sometimes it's lying to oneself. Sometimes, it's lying to others. The next example of rationalization allows one to be dishonest by breaking the law.

You get in your car and start down the freeway. You see a sign that says, "55 miles per hour." What do you do? Most likely you will go faster than 55, justifying your speeding by using one or more of the following rationalizations:

- Nobody drives 55. Everyone else speeds.
- My car was made to go faster.
- Fifty-five miles per hour is a stupid law. Going faster is still safe.
- I must keep up with traffic or I'll cause an accident.
- It's all right to get one or two speeding tickets.
- I'm late.
- The speed limit is really 62 or 63.

Is it right to break the law and speed just because everyone else is doing it? What if everyone else were committing fraud? If so, would that make it all right for you to commit fraud? Breaking the speed limit may, in fact, result in more social harm than committing fraud.

An example of rationalization more closely related to fraud involves income tax evasion. Many people rationalize cheating and underpaying taxes by using the following rationalizations:

- I pay more than my fair share of taxes.
- The rich don't pay taxes.
- The government wastes money.
- I work for my money.

To understand the extent of income tax fraud, consider the following example:

In 1988, for the first time, the IRS required taxpayers who claimed dependents to list the Social Security numbers of their dependents on their tax returns. In 1987, 77 million dependents were claimed on federal tax returns. In 1988, the number of dependents claimed dropped to 70 million. Fully one-tenth of the dependents claimed, or 7 million dependents, disappeared. Where did they go? They had never existed or they had existed in backyards, run around on four legs, and had names like Fido and Felix. The IRS determined that in 1987, and probably in previous years, over 60,000 households had claimed four or more dependents who didn't exist and several million had claimed one or more who didn't exist.

Claiming dependents who don't exist is one of the most blatant and easiest-to-catch income tax frauds. Yet, rationalizations were strong enough to allow millions of citizens to blatantly cheat on their tax returns.

Finally, consider the following example of rationalization, which has immediate implications for fraud.

A friend of one of the authors has six children—five boys and one daughter, who was born last. If you ask him what is the absolutely most important thing is his life he will quickly say, "My wife and children. Work comes later, church comes later, everything comes later." Yet, he readily admits having had the following conversation with one of this book's authors. The author asked him what kind of father he was. The friend answered, "I think I'm a good father. I coach Little League. I am a scoutmaster. I help with homework. I provide well. Yes, I think I'm a good father." Then the friend was asked, "What do you think it means to be a good father? A good father should spend time with his children, right?" "Right," was the response. "You can't be a good father without spending time with your children." The author then asked, "How much time do you spend with your children." At that point, the friend bowed his head in shame and responded, "Probably not enough." You see, even though he does some good things with his children, the friend is, in many ways, a workaholic. He perceives himself to be a good father because he has been judging himself by his intentions and he "intends" to be a good father. Others don't think he's a very good father, because they are judging him by his actions and they don't believe he is spending enough time with his children.

We all do the same thing. We judge ourselves by our intentions and other people by their actions. For most of us, our intentions are far better than our actions. Most of us "intend" to get up earlier, to exercise more, to eat less, to read more, to be better spouses, to be better parents, to help others more, or not to gossip. This reasoning is probably why so many marriages end in divorce. Both husbands and wives judge themselves by their intentions and judge their spouses by their actions.

How does this relate to fraud? When interviewed, most fraud perpetrators say things like, "I intended to pay that money back. I really did." They are sincere. In their minds, they intended to repay the money, and since they judge themselves by their intentions, they do not see themselves as criminals. On the other hand, victims judge perpetrators by the actions and say, "You dirty rotten crook! You stole money from me, or from my organization."

When people judge themselves by their intentions, it is easy for them to rationalize fraud. They have a pressure, they perceive an opportunity, and they intend to (or rationalize that they will) pay the money back.

RATIONALIZATION AND HONESTY

An interesting question, long debated by psychologists, is whether anyone is completely honest. Is there anyone, who, if faced with enough pressure, opportunity, and a way to rationalize, will always be honest?

In deciding whether of not you are an honest person, consider the following hypothetical situation (which was first introduced in Chapter 2). You have high medical expenses that you cannot pay. You work in an environment where significant amounts of cash are present and unaccounted for. You rationalize that you will pay the money back with next month's pay. Many people might "temporarily borrow" in this situation, especially if there were no other way to get money for the medical bills. Most people do not have such critical pressures. Most of us don't work in environments where the opportunity for fraud is so high.

At the other extreme, some people commit fraud even though no real pressure or opportunity exists. Their frauds are usually caught immediately, but they continue to behave dishonestly. Most people are somewhere in between these two extremes. When the combination of pressure, opportunity, and rationalization becomes severe enough, they cross the line of honesty and commit fraud.

EXAMPLE: THE ROLE OF RATIONALIZATION

Jerry Schneider, at age 21, was the model West Coast business executive, bright and well educated. He was different from his cohorts in only one respect. He embezzled over $1 million from Pacific Telephone Company. Here is the story of his fraud.[2]

> Jerry Schneider's fraud had its genesis at a warm, open-air evening party where he and some friends had gathered for drinks, socializing, and small talk. Schneider was the young president of his own electronics corporation. This night, the talk was of organized crime and whether or not it could be profitable. "All these press stories of the big-time killings, and the crooks who build palaces down in Florida and out here on the Coast, aagh . . . " said a cynical male voice, "they're cooked up for the movies."

---

[2]Information about this fraud was acquired from Donn Parker's computer fraud files at the Stanford Research Institute. Donn Parker personally interviewed Jerry Schneider.

Schneider recognized the speaker as a young scriptwriter whose last outline—a crime story set among the Jewish mafia—had been turned down. "Not so," he said. "Some of them clean up. Some of them walk away clean, with a huge pot. You only hear of the ones that don't. The others become respectable millionaires."

A lawyer asked, "You believe in the perfect crime, do you?"

"Yes, if what you mean is the crime that doesn't get detected. I don't say nobody knows it has been done—though there must be some of those, too. But I'm sure there are crooks clever enough to figure ways to beat the system."

Long after everyone had left the party, Jerry Schneider was still thinking about whether or not there was a perfect crime. He had a great knowledge of computers, and he thought maybe he could use his knowledge to perpetrate the perfect crime. Finally, about two AM he felt sick about the whole idea.

No one knows why Schneider later changed his mind. An investigator with the district attorney's office in Los Angeles believes it was because Jerry got possession of a stolen computer code book from Pacific Telephone Company. Schneider accessed the company's computer from the outside. Exactly how he did it was not fully revealed at his trial. He used a touch-tone telephone to place large orders with Pacific's supply division, inserting the orders into the company's computer. He then programmed Pacific Telephone's computers to pay for the merchandise. After he received it, he sold it on the open market.

Schneider was caught when an embittered employee noticed that much of the stuff Schneider's company was selling was Pacific's and became suspicious. He leaked to the police a hint about how Schneider had acquired the material. An investigation revealed that huge amounts of equipment were missing from Pacific's dispatch warehouse. Invoices showed that the equipment had been ordered and authorized for dispatch. The goods had then been packaged and put out on the loading bays ready for collection. Schneider had collected the goods himself, always early in the morning. To avoid the scrutiny of a gate guard and a tally clerk, who would have required bills of lading, Schneider left home at two and three in the morning, night after night, in a pickup truck painted to look like a company transport.

Jerry merely drove in among the assorted wagons and freight piles. He had somehow acquired keys, and documents issued by the computer gave him access to the yard. The inexperienced night security guards not only let him through but even offered him cups of coffee and cigarettes as he and his men loaded the equipment.

Schneider started to have fears about what he was doing: the morality of it, the cheating it involved. He had intended the theft to be just a brilliant near-scientific feat. Jerry began to realize that the effort of the crime was greater than the reward. In Schneider's words, "It got so that I was afraid of my ex-employees, men I knew were aware of what I was up to because they'd seen the stuff come in, day after day, and go out again as our stuff. I began to feel hunted. Scared." The crime left him short of sleep, exhausted, and feeling guilty. In addition, the value of the stolen material passing into his possession was rising dramatically.

Schneider claims to have "robbed" the company of nearly $1 million worth of equipment. His crime is interesting because his rationalization was "to see if the perfect crime could be committed." In fact, he probably couldn't have rationalized committing a crime for any other reason. When he was asked whether he considered himself an honest man, Schneider responded with a firm yes. When he was asked whether, if he saw a wallet on the sidewalk, he would pocket it or try to return it to the owner, his answer was that he was like everyone else; he'd try to return it if it was at all possible. However, when he was asked whether, if he saw $10,000 lying in an open cash box in a supermarket and nobody was watching him, he would take the money, he answered, "Sure, I would. If the company was careless enough to leave the money there, it deserved to have the money taken."

In other words, Schneider saw a difference between doing harm to individuals and doing harm to organizations. He could justify or rationalize taking from companies but not from people. He saw companies as inanimate and bloodless and, therefore, as completely fair targets.

Schneider's goals were money, retaliation (it was revealed at his trial that he hated Pacific Telephone Company), and a compulsion to prove his superiority. Schneider is a man of inner disciplines. He is a strict vegetarian who does a lot of physical exercise to keep fit. He works hard, brilliantly, and successfully at whatever he undertakes. There is little doubt that he could be a valued and even trusted executive at most corporations.

Today, Schneider is a computer security consultant. Jerry Schneider's "perfect crime" failed. It would have never happened, however, if he hadn't acted on a personal challenge and rationalized that he was only playing a game—a game of intellectual chess with a faceless company.

CONCLUDING COMMENTS

Perpetrators don't commit fraud unless they can rationalize it as being consistent with their own personal codes of ethics. Some frauds are rationalized by an animosity toward specific organizations or individuals. Such was the case with Jerry Schneider. Others are rationalized by a love for organizations or individuals. Such was the case with the owners of AFCO (discussed in Chapter 4), who saw their company and investments going down the drain and resorted to fraud to keep it going. Other frauds are rationalized by perpetrators who convince themselves that they will repay the money. While rationalizations, like pressures and opportunities, vary from crime to crime, one thing is certain: Without some way to justify or rationalize the dishonest act, fraud does not occur.

Probably the greatest example of rationalization was one we read in the *New York Times* a long time ago. It goes like this.

Even thieves are able to rationalize their work. A veteran, a very professional thief who lives in New Jersey, reasons, "What I do is good for everybody. First of all, I create work. I hire men to steal the cars, work on the numbers, paint them, give them paper, maybe drive them out of state. That's good for the economy. Then, I'm helping people to get what they could never afford otherwise. A fellow wants a Cadillac, but he can't afford it . . . I save him as much as $2,000. Now he's happy. But so is the guy who lost his car. He gets a nice new Cadillac from the insurance company. The Cadillac company— they're happy, too, because they sell another Cadillac. The only people who don't do so good is [sic] the insurance company, but they're so big that nobody cares personally. They got a budget for this sort of thing anyway. . . . Come on now—who am I really hurting?"[3]

---

[3]*The New York Times*, June 20, 1971.

PART

II

THE DETECTION OF FRAUD

The detection of fraud includes the steps or actions taken to discover that a fraud has been committed. Detection does not include investigative procedures taken to determine motives, extent, method of embezzlement, or other elements of the dishonest act. Fraud is unlike other crimes, in which the occurrence of the crime is easily recognized, in that one of the most difficult tasks is determining whether or not a fraud has actually occurred.

Detection of fraud usually begins by identifying symptoms, indicators, or red flags that can be associated with fraud. In Chapter 6, we discuss how employee, management, and investment frauds are detected and identify different types of fraud symptoms. Chapter 7 discusses accounting and internal control fraud symptoms. Fraud cases in which symptoms such as missing or altered documents or missing internal controls lead to detection are discussed. Chapter 8 covers analytical symptoms and symptoms involving relationships with others. Chapter 9 discusses common types of symptoms: tips and complaints, lifestyle, behavioral, and demographic. All four chapters use real fraud cases to illustrate how detection takes place.

Chapter Six

Fraud Symptoms
Employee, Management,
and Investment

Fraud is a crime that is seldom seen. If a body is discovered and the person has obviously been murdered, there is no question whether or not a crime has been committed. The dead body can be touched, seen, and even smelled. Likewise, if a bank is robbed, there is no question whether or not a crime has been committed. Everyone in the bank, including customers and employees, witnessed the robbery. In most cases, the entire episode is captured on video and can be replayed for doubters. But with fraud, it is not initially certain that a crime has been committed. Only fraud symptoms, red flags, or indicators are seen.

A person's lifestyle may change, a document may be missing, a general ledger may be out of balance, someone may act suspiciously, a change in an analytical relationship may not make sense, or someone may provide a tip that an embezzlement is taking place. Unlike other types of crimes, however, with fraud these factors are only symptoms rather than conclusive proof. There may be other explanations for the existence of the "fraud indicators." Lifestyle changes may have occurred because of inherited money. Documents may have been legitimately lost. The general ledger may be out of balance because of an unintentional accounting error. Suspicious actions may be caused by family dissension or personal problems. Unexplained analytical relationships may be the result of unrecognized changes in underlying economic factors. A tip may be motivated by a grudge on the part of an envious or disgruntled employee, or someone outside the company, to settle a score.

In order to detect fraud, managers, auditors, employees, and examiners must learn to recognize symptoms and pursue them until convincing evidence is obtained. Investigators must discover whether the symptoms resulted from actual fraud or from other factors. Unfortunately, many fraud symptoms go unnoticed, and even symptoms that are recognized are often not vigorously pursued. Many frauds could be detected earlier if fraud symptoms were pursued. In this chapter, types of fraud symptoms related to employee, management, and investment fraud are introduced.

SYMPTOMS OF EMPLOYEE FRAUD

Symptoms of potential employee fraud can be separated into six groups: (1) accounting anomalies, (2) internal control weaknesses, (3) analytical anomalies, (4) extravagant lifestyle, (5) unusual behavior, and (6) tips and complaints. The next three chapters discuss these six types of symptoms in detail. Here, we provide an example of fraud and illustrate how these types of symptoms could have revealed that fraud was occurring. While the names of the company and the perpetrators have been changed, the description is of a real fraud that occurred in a Fortune 500 company.

Elgin Aircraft had claims processing and claims payment departments to administer its health care plans. The company was self-insured for claims under $50,000. Claims above this amount were forwarded to an independent insurance company. The claims processing department's responsibility was to verify the necessary documentation for payment and then to forward the documentation to the claims payment department. The claims payment department approved and signed the payment.

Elgin employees had a choice between two different types of insurance plans. The first was a health maintenance organization (HMO) plan in which employees went to an approved doctor. Elgin had a contract with a group of medical doctors who treated the employees for a set fee. The second plan allowed employees to go to doctors of their own choice rather than to the HMO, but only 80 percent of their medical bills were paid by Elgin.

Management believed that the company had an excellent internal control system. In addition, the company continually had various auditors on their premises: government contract auditors, defense auditors, outside auditors, and internal auditors. These auditors felt, as did management, that controls over health claims and payments were adequate. Health claims were processed from an extensive form filled out by the attending physician and a statement from his or her office verifying the nature of the dollar amount of the treatment. This form was given to the claims processing department, which would verify the following:

- That the patient was an employee of Elgin Aircraft.
- That treatments were covered by the plan.
- That amounts charged were within approved guidelines.
- That the amount of the claims per individual for the year were not over $50,000; if they were, a claim was submitted to the insurance company.
- Which plan the employee was on, and that the calculation for payment was correct.

After verification of the above facts, the claims were forwarded to the claims payment department, which paid the doctor directly. No payments ever went to employees.

In January 1990, an auditor observed the manager of the claims payment department taking her department employees to lunch in a chauffeured limousine. The auditor was curious about how the manager could afford such expensive occasions and was concerned that the cost of the lunch and the limousine were being paid for by the government. In speaking with the vice president of finance, he learned that the manager was "one of the company's best employees." He also learned that she had never missed a day of work in the last 10 years. She was indeed a very conscientious employee, and her department had one of the best efficiency ratings in the entire company.

Concerned about the limousine and other factors, the auditor began an investigation that revealed that the claims payment department manager had embezzled over $12 million from Elgin Aircraft in four years. Her scheme involved setting up 22 dummy "doctors" who would submit medical bills on employees who hadn't had much medical work during the year. Her fictitious doctors would create claims forms and submit them to the claims processing department. The claims processing department would send the approved forms to the claims payment department, which would then send payment to the dummy doctors.

This massive health payments fraud continued for over four years. Yet, several fraud symptoms existed that could have been recognized by management, auditors, and others.

Accounting Anomalies

There were several *accounting symptoms* that could have alerted auditors to the fraud. The fraudulent claims forms from the 22 phony doctors originated from two locations. One was a PO box, and the other was a business located in a nearby city that was owned by the manager's husband. The checks being paid to the 22 doctors were sent to the same two common addresses. Checks were deposited in the same two bank accounts and contained handwritten rather than stamped endorsements.

The likely reasons none of these accounting symptoms were recognized are that managers trusted the perpetrator and that auditors merely matched claim forms with canceled checks. The auditors did not ask questions such as:

Are these payments reasonable? (For example, there were claims forms for hysterectomies for men.)

Do the endorsements make sense?

Why are the checks going to and the bills coming from these 22 doctors coming from the same two addresses?

A major difference between auditors and examiners who detect fraud and those who don't is that most auditors merely match documents to see whether support exists and is adequate. Auditors and examiners who detect fraud go beyond ascertaining the mere existence of documents to determine whether the documents are real or fraudulent, whether the expenditures make sense, and whether all aspects of the documentation are in order.

Internal Control Weaknesses

There were blatant *control weaknesses* that were ignored by the auditors. First, the manager of the claims payment department hadn't taken a vacation in 10 years. Second, employees of Elgin Aircraft never received confirmation of payments so they could determine whether or not the medical claims being paid on their behalf were incurred by them. Third, payments to new doctors were never investigated or cleared by the company.

Allowing employees to not take vacations is a serious control weakness that must always by questioned. One of the most effective ways to deter fraud is to implement a system of independent checks. Employee transfers, audits, and mandatory vacations are all ways to provide independent checks on employees. As stated in Chapter 3, the Office of the Controller of the Currency requires all bank employees in the United States to take at least a one-consecutive-week vacation each year. Many frauds come to light when employees are on vacation and cannot cover their tracks. In Elgin's case, if another employee had made payments during the manager's absence, the common addresses or the payments being made to a business might have been recognized.

The lack of confirmation to employees of payments that are made is a serious control weakness. In Elgin's case, doctors were being paid for hysterectomies, tonsillectomies, gall bladder surgeries, and other procedures that were never performed. If employees had been aware that payments were being made for these fabricated services, they probably would have complained and the fraud scheme would have been disclosed.

Another problem is that even if most auditors and managers had discovered the internal control weaknesses, they would probably still not have caught the fraud. Most likely, they would have recommended that the control weaknesses by fixed without giving thought to the possibility that the weaknesses might have already been exploited. A major difference between an auditor who catches fraud and one who doesn't is that the first auditor says, "Here is a control weakness. You had better correct it *and determine whether it has been abused*," whereas the second says only, "Here is a control weakness. You had better correct it."

Before doctors were cleared for payment, some kind of background check should have been conducted to determine whether or not they were legitimate doctors. Just as Dun & Bradstreet checks should be performed on companies with which business is conducted, the legitimacy of doctors should be verified by checking with state licensing boards, medical groups, or even telephone books.

Analytical Anomalies

Analytical anomalies are relationships, procedures, and events that don't make sense, such as a change in a volume, mix, or price that is not reasonable. In this case, there were several *analytical symptoms* that could have alerted others to the fraud. The sheer volume of insurance work performed by the 22 fictitious doctors was very high. Why would $12 million be paid to new doctors over a period of four years? None of the phony doctors were licensed by the state. Yet, payments to them exceeded payments to almost all other doctors. Another analytical symptom was that there were no other payments to any of the dummy doctors by outside insurance companies. In other words, none of the payments to these doctors were for employees who incurred over $50,000 of medical expenses in any year. Finally, medical costs for the company increased significantly (29 percent) during the four years of the fraud.

Extravagent Lifestyle

There were several *lifestyle symptoms* that could have been recognized. How common is it for a manager to take employees to lunch in a limousine? An inquiry by the defense department auditor revealed that the manager was paying for the limousine from personal funds and that she was independently wealthy. She had told employees that she had inherited a large sum of money from her husband's parents. All her employees knew that she lived in a very expensive house, drove luxury cars, and wore expensive clothes and jewelry. If she had such wealth, someone should have wondered why she worked and especially why she never took a vacation. While wealthy people may be employed because of love of work, rarely is their love so great as to cause them never to take a vacation for 10 years.

Unusual Behavior

There were several *behavioral symptoms* that could have alerted others that something was wrong. Employees in the department regularly joked that their manager had a "Dr. Jekyll and Mr. Hyde" personality. Sometimes she was the nicest person around, and sometimes she would have periods of unexplained anger. Interviews with employees revealed that her highs and lows had become more intense and more frequent in recent months.

Tips and Complaints

With this fraud, there were no *tips or complaints.* No employees who felt that something was wrong had come forward, and other doctors were still getting all the legitimate business. They had no reason to complain. Indeed, the only party really being hurt was Elgin Aircraft.

SYMPTOMS OF MANAGEMENT FRAUD

Just as employee fraud is best detected by recognizing fraud symptoms, there are symptoms or red flags of management fraud that, if recognized, can signal that something is awry. The red-flag approach to detecting management fraud has been the subject of several professional accounting pronouncements and certified public accountant (CPA) firm publications. Using red flags to assess how risky a client or potential client is has become standard practice in public accounting.

While numerous lists of management fraud symptoms have been identified in the literature, we like to group management fraud symptoms into four categories:

1. Operating performance anomalies
2. Management characteristics that indicate possible motives
3. Organizational structure anomalies
4. Irregularities in relationships with outside parties

Operating Performance Anomalies

Operating performance symptoms include red flags identified by analyzing financial statements and other organization reports. Common operating performance anomalies include:

- Unexplained changes in financial statement balances
- Operating on a crisis basis
- Urgent need to report favorable earnings
- Unusual or large and profitable transactions near the ends of accounting periods
- Deteriorating quality of earnings
- Insufficient capital
- High debt or interest burdens
- Difficulty in collecting receivables, or other cash flow problems
- Expenses increasing faster than revenues
- Dependence on only one or two products
- Significant litigation

An example in which some of these symptoms indicated fraud was the recent financial statement fraud discovered at Comptronix Corporation. The fraud involved misstated financial statements and was supposedly recognized by a college professor who, after analyzing the company's annual report, noticed that sales increased but receivables didn't and that inventory increased but accounts payable and purchases didn't.

These relationships didn't make sense to him. He reasoned that very few customers pay cash, and, therefore, if the amount of sales increases, the accounts receivable balance should also increase. Further, most companies don't pay cash for inventory purchases; therefore, if inventory increases, the accounts payable balance should increase and the reported amount of purchases should also be higher. The professor was absolutely right. These unexplained and irrational changes in financial statement relationships did not make sense. They occurred because the management of Comptronix overstated sales and inventory to increase reported net income.

Another example is the management fraud that occurred at the Regina Vacuum Company, which was mentioned in Chapter 2. Regina went public in 1985, at a price of $5.25 per share. At the time, the company's chief executive officer (CEO), Donald Sheelen, received 40 percent of the stock, thus incurring a strong vested interest in seeing the stock price increase. During the next three years, not only did the stock price go up but other numbers rose as well. Reported sales increased from $60 million to $181 million, reported net income increased substantially, and the cost of goods sold to sales ratio decreased from 65 to 52 percent. The result was a stock price that increased to $27.50 per share. These rapid changes in reported results occurred only because the company: (1) did not record millions of dollars of product returns; (2) recorded sales when orders were received, not when goods were shipped; (3) recorded fictitious sales; (4) reduced cost-of-goods-sold expenses; and (5) altered the accounting records in several other ways. Donald Sheelen's urgent need for earnings resulted in unexplained financial statement changes, in a deteriorating quality of earnings, and in difficulty in collecting receivables on the thousands of vacuum cleaners that were being returned because plastic parts were melting.

A third example of a financial statement fraud that exhibited operational performance symptoms was Lincoln Savings and Loan. Charles Keating, the company's CEO, had a very strong need for Lincoln to appear profitable. If Lincoln were profitable, S&L regulators would stay away, investors would be willing to buy Lincoln's bonds (thus providing a large source of cash), and the company could upstream income taxes on reported profits to the parent company, American Continental. Once the tax payments reached the parent company, Keating and his associates could extract the money from American Continental for personal use. If Lincoln were not profitable, bonds wouldn't sell, regulators would appear, and cash would not be available for personal use. Because of the critical need to report profits near the end of every quarter, Lincoln Savings and Loan entered into real estate transactions with straw buyers that resulted in millions of dollars of reported income.

Management Characteristics that Indicate Possible Motives

Management characteristic symptoms include attributes of executives that signal a strong motivation to be dishonest, or a high risk of fraud. Common fraud indicators of this type are:

- Executives with high personal debt or financial needs
- Executives who are involved extensively in gambling or speculative transactions
- Executives with questionable or criminal backgrounds
- Dishonest or unethical management
- Executives whose financial success is closely tied to the success of the organization
- Executives who don't have lives separate from the organization

Historically, personal information regarding these attributes of management has been difficult to obtain. However, with the increased availability of electronic databases and private investigators who will search backgrounds for nominal fees, fraud symptoms inherent in a CEO's background are now easy to tract. For example, a quick search of the LEXIS/NEXIS® database (a publically available database of major U.S. newspapers) revealed numerous articles about Charles Keating prior to his association with Lincoln Savings and Loan. At least one of these articles associated Charles Keating with a $14 million financial institution fraud in Ohio. Auditors and others who later did business with Keating's Lincoln Savings could have benefited greatly from a quick perusal of this database.

Another way to get information is to identify executives' Social Security numbers from voter registration records or other sources. Once an executive's Social Security number is known, it is easy to access records that indicate whether or not the executive has declared bankruptcy, has incurred large amounts of debt, has liens on real estate and other property, has been divorced, or has been the target of previous civil or criminal action. Personally, the authors would never associate themselves in a significant way with any organization without first doing background searches on its key executives.

Organizational Structure Anomalies

Organizational structure fraud symptoms include attributes of an organization that are unreasonable and/or do not have a legitimate reason for existence. Common symptoms of this type include:

- Unduly complex business structure
- Lack of effective internal audit staff
- High-risk industry

- Severe obsolescence of assets
- Changes in executives or directors
- Significant transactions by related parties

As an example of an organizational structure fraud symptom, consider the case of ESM Government Securities, a brokerage firm in which the management perpetrated a major financial statement fraud and embezzled nearly $400 million. By selling the same government securities several times and deceiving investors in other ways, the company ended up with net receivables from customers of approximately $1.3 billion and with payables to outsiders of $1.7 billion. To cover the $400 million shortfall, the company set up a system of related companies, including a parent company from which ESM showed a net receivable of $400 million. Because the receivable was from an affiliated company, auditors didn't conduct significant audit procedures to determine its collectability and existence. (In fact, they should have conducted more extensive audit procedures because of the related-party nature of the receivable.) The only reason for ESM's complex business structure involving numerous related parties was to mask the huge fraud.

Likewise, to mask his fraud, Charles Keating created a complex business structure at Lincoln Savings, involving over 15 separate business entities. Having, for example, various subsidiaries sell and buy real estate, while other subsidiaries borrowed and loaned money, the impression was created that related transactions were separate from each other.

Irregularities in Relationships with Outside Parties

In today's complex and highly regulated business world, it is impossible for an organization to exist in isolation. Executives who perpetrate management fraud often go to extensive and sometimes expensive lengths to create relationships that will facilitate fraud or make it more difficult for outside parties to detect. Common fraud symptoms involving relationships with other entities include:

- Frequent changes in auditors
- Problems with regulators such as the Securities and Exchange Commission (SEC)
- Reluctance to provide auditors with needed data
- Frequent changes in outside legal counsels
- Use of several different banks
- Pressure to sell, merge, or be taken over
- Adverse political, social, or environmental impact

Lincoln Savings is an excellent example of an organization that worked hard to hide management fraud from outsiders by frequently changing auditors and legal counsels. Arthur Andersen & Co. audited Lincoln through 1985; Ernst & Young audited Lincoln from 1986 to early 1988; and Deloitte & Touche accepted Lincoln as a client in 1988, although the firm never issued an audit opinion on Lincoln's financial statements.

USING FRAUD SYMPTOMS TO PROVE MANAGEMENT FRAUD

Unfortunately, as with employee fraud, without a confession it is difficult to prove that management fraud symptoms actually represent fraud, or irregularity, rather than unintentional errors. To obtain a civil judgment or a criminal conviction for management fraud, in most cases it is necessary to show a repeated pattern of fraud symptoms. In the Lincoln Savings and Loan case, for example, it was necessary for prosecutors to convince jurors that a repeated pattern (large profitable real estate transactions on the last day of successive accounting periods involving related transactions between buyers and Lincoln) was premeditated rather than circumstantial. The case would have been very difficult to prove if only one or two such transactions had been made.

SYMPTOMS OF INVESTMENT FRAUD

In management fraud, executives usually manipulate financial statements to overstate reported profits. The overstated profits are then used to generate interest in the company and its stock. In investment fraud, perpetrators usually make fraudulent promises or misstatements of fact to induce people to make investments. The two types of fraud are closely related, because investments are usually made on the basis of misstated facts. They differ only in the medium of misstatement. With management fraud, the misstatement is usually in financial statements; with investment fraud, the false statements usually involve promised returns made orally or in writing.

Investment frauds can occur either within or outside business organizations. An example of investment fraud in a business was the loans made by General Motors Acceptance Corporation (GMAC) to a Long Island, New York, automobile dealer.

John McNamara, a wealthy car dealer, conned $436 million from GMAC. He first set up a company, Kay Industries, to produce invoices showing he was buying vans. The vans didn't exist. Then he sent invoices to GMAC to get a 30-day loan, worth about $25,000, for each van. Over seven years, he got $6.3 billion in loans; of that, only $250 million was used for real vehicles. As he got new loans, he used most of the money to pay off old loans. He paid back a total of $5.8 billion over the seven years. He pocketed $436 million—about 7 percent of the total loans—and invested it in real estate, gold mines, oil businesses, and commodities brokerages.

While GMAC thought it was loaning money to a legitimate car dealer, what it was really doing was investing in a classic *Ponzzi scheme* (a scheme in which early investments are repaid with subsequent investments; see the discussion in Chapter 1). The only difference between this investment scam and one that is perpetrated outside an organization was that this investment scheme had only one investor, GMAC.

An example of an investment scam that took place outside a business organization and involved numerous investors was the AFCO fraud, which was first discussed in Chapter 4.

AFCO, based in Salt Lake City, Utah, started as a medical–dental equipment leasing business. One owner was a former insurance salesman, and the other was two years out of law school. The company was mildly successful during its first two years. Several new branches were formed, including a land development company. The land development company purchased 1,000 acres of undeveloped property in Sardine Canyon in northern Utah and began to develop an "old English" family resort called *Sherwood Hills*. The resort was intended to include summer and winter sports, making it a year-round enterprise. Although it was reasonably popular in the summer, the heavy winter snows and poor accessibility made it an unappealing winter resort. To raise money for additional development and marketing efforts, limited partnerships were sold, mostly to physicians and dentists.

Other AFCO projects included a shopping center, apartment complexes, a medical center, and a 700-acre site in West Jordan, Utah. This development was known as *Glenmoor Village* and was touted as Utah's biggest real estate development. It was to include 1,400 homes in a totally planned community, an 18-hole golf course, and equestrian facilities.

As with Sherwood Hills, development of Glenmoor Village was extremely expensive. Maintenance of a positive cash flow depended on lot sales, but sales were slow because the area lacked essential services such as roads and utilities. AFCO had borrowed heavily to make these investments, but only 400 of the 1,400 lots were sold. Residents complained that promised improvements were never made.

Because of severe cash shortages and an inability to obtain additional bank financing, AFCO turned to middle-class homeowners to fund the company. The company's salesmen would contact friends, acquaintances, and referrals, and would offer them opportunities to invest. Using elaborate flip charts and relying on the reputation of other investors, salespeople persuaded homeowners to allow the company to borrow on the equity in their homes. If homeowners would allow a second mortgage, AFCO would service the second mortgage and pay the homeowner an additional 10 percent on the money used. Since second mortgage rates were approximately 20 percent, AFCO was, in effect, offering nearly 30 percent for the money. AFCO was very accommodating: If a homeowner didn't want the return in cash, it would lease a BMW or a Mercedes for the homeowner and service the lease.

While the investment sounded legitimate, returns to be made to homeowners were based on inflated financial statements and empty promises. The investment was nothing more than another Ponzzi scheme. Early investors were paid the 10 percent returns from subsequent investments, and the second mortgage payments were never paid. The assistant US attorney in the district of Utah called the president of AFCO "one of the most ruthless swindlers seen in these parts in years." He sweet-talked about 650 people, many of them business people, into investing some $70 million in his schemes. He later declared bankruptcy, foreclosing his investors' chances of getting their money back.

There are numerous red flags or fraud symptoms that signal potential investment fraud. Anyone considering investing money or other assets in any organization, real or fictitious, should watch for the following symptoms, which have been associated with numerous investment scams:

- Unreasonable promised rates of return
- Investments that do not make sound business sense
- Pressure to get in early on the investment
- Use of a special tax loophole or a tax avoidance scheme
- A business that is new in town and does not offer an adequate history of where its principals come from and what their operations were in previous locations
- A business with a history of bankruptcy or scandals
- Appraisal figures and/or financial claims that have not been soundly verified
- Project dependency on kickbacks, complicated marketing schemes, special concessions to people who have money, or unwritten deals that can't be talked about because of domestic or foreign laws
- Unaudited financial reports or adverse opinions given on financial reports
- Investments that assume continued inflation or appreciation in predicting attractive rates of return, that are unrealistic over time
- Investment success that is dependent on someone's "unique expertise" (such as an uncanny ability to predict commodity prices or unusually good salesmanship) for financial success
- Representation of the emotional desirability of holding an investment as its principal attraction
- Insufficient verification or guarantee of an investment
- Dependency on high financial leverage for success
- Investor liability for debts that are not paid
- Luxurious lifestyles of principals, even though the business is relatively new

- An investment that is not suitable for your risk tolerance
- Pressure to put all your savings into a particular investment
- Inability to pull out or liquidate the investment
- Inducements that make investors feel sorry for the principals and/or put in additional money to help them overcome temporary problems

AUDITORS' RESPONSIBILITY FOR RECOGNIZING FRAUD SYMPTOMS

Both the internal (Institute of Internal Auditors, or IIA) and the external (American Institute of Certified Accountants, or AICPA) audit literature recognize the importance of recognizing fraud symptoms as a way of detecting fraud. Statement No. 3, which was issued by the Institute of Internal Auditors (IIA), says the following with respect to auditors' responsibility for recognizing fraud symptoms:

In conducting audit assignments, the internal auditor's responsibilities for detecting fraud are to:

- Have sufficient knowledge of fraud to be able to identify indicators that fraud might have been committed. This knowledge includes the need to know the characteristics of fraud, the techniques used to commit fraud, and the types of frauds associated with the activities audited.

- Be alert to opportunities such as control weaknesses, that could allow fraud. If significant control weaknesses are detected, additional tests conducted by internal auditors should include tests directed toward identification of other indicators of fraud. Some examples of indicators are unauthorized transactions, overrides of controls, unexplained pricing exceptions, and unusually large product losses. Internal auditors should recognize that the presence of more than one indicator at any one time increases the probability that fraud might have occurred.

- Evaluate the indicators that fraud might have been committed and decide whether any further action is necessary or whether an investigation should be recommended.

- Notify the appropriate authorities within the organization if a determination is made that there are sufficient indicators of the commission of a fraud to recommend an investigation.

Similarly, *Statement on Auditing Standards No. 53*, which was issued by the AICPA, identifies the importance of external auditors' recognizing management fraud symptoms. A portion is reprinted here.

The auditor should assess the risk that errors and irregularities may cause the financial statements to contain a material misstatement. Based on that assessment, the auditor should design the audit to provide reasonable assurance of detecting errors and irregularities that are material to the financial statements.

An assessment of the risk of material misstatements should be made during planning. The auditor's understanding of the internal control structure should either heighten or mitigate the auditor's concern about the risk of material misstatements. The factors considered in assessing risk should be considered in combination to make an overall judgment; the presence of some factors in isolation would not necessarily indicate increased risk. Factors such as those listed below may be considered:

Management characteristics

- Management operating and financing decisions are dominated by a single person.
- Management's attitude toward financial reporting is unduly aggressive.
- Management (particularly senior accounting personnel) turnover is high.
- Management places undue emphasis on meeting earnings projections.
- Management's reputation in the business community is poor.

Operating and industry characteristics

- Profitability of entity relative to its industry is inadequate or inconsistent.
- Sensitivity of operating results to economic factors (inflation, interest rates, unemployment, etc.) is high.
- Rate of change in entity's industry is rapid.
- Direction of change in entity's industry is declining with many business failures.
- Organization is decentralized without adequate monitoring.
- Internal or external matters that raise substantial doubt about the entity's ability to continue as a going concern are present.

Engagement characteristics

- Many contentious or difficult accounting issues are present.
- Significant difficult-to-audit transactions or balances are present.
- Significant and unusual related-party transactions not in the ordinary course of business are present.
- Nature, cause (if known), or the amount of known and likely misstatements detected in the audit of prior periods's financial statements is significant.
- It is a new client with no prior audit history, or sufficient information is not available from the predecessor auditor.

The size, complexity, and ownership characteristics of the entity have a significant influence on the risk factors considered to be important. For example, for a large entity, the auditor would ordinarily give consideration to factors that constrain improper conduct by senior management, such as the effectiveness of the board of directors, the audit committee or others with equivalent authority and responsibility,[1] and the internal audit function. Consideration would also be given to the measures taken to enforce a formal code of conduct and the effectiveness of the budgeting or responsibility reporting system. For a small entity some of these matters might be considered inapplicable or unimportant, particularly if the auditor's past experience with the entity has been that effective owner-manager or trustee involvement creates a good control environment.

The auditor should assess the risk of management misrepresentation by reviewing information obtained about risk factors and the internal control structure. Matters such as the following may be considered:

- Are there known circumstances that may indicate a management predisposition to distort financial statements, such as frequent disputes about aggressive application of accounting principles that increase earnings, evasive responses to audit inquiries, or excessive emphasis on meeting quantified targets that must be achieved to receive a substantial portion of management compensation?

- Are there indications that management has failed to establish policies and procedures that provide reasonable assurance of reliable accounting estimates, such as personnel who develop estimates appearing to lack necessary knowledge and experience, supervisors of these personnel appearing careless or inexperienced, or . . . a history of unreliable or unreasonable estimates?

- Are there conditions that indicate lack of control of activities, such as constant crisis conditions in operating or accounting areas, disorganized work areas, frequent or excessive back orders, shortages, delays, or lack of documentation for major transactions?

- Are there indications of a lack of control over computer processing, such as over access to applications that initiate or control the movement of assets (for example, a demand deposit application in a bank), high levels of processing errors, or unusual delays in providing processing results and report?

- Are there indications that management has not developed or communicated adequate policies and procedures for security of data or assets, such as not investigating employees in key positions before hiring, or allowing unauthorized personnel to have ready access to data or assets?

The Nature of the Symptoms

The detection of fraud usually involves recognizing fraud symptoms that *may* signal the existence of fraud. Some frauds, such as kiting between

---

[1]For entities that do not have audit committees, the phrase "others with equivalent authority and responsibility" may include the board of directors, the board of trustees, or the owner in owner-managed entities.

banks, have very distinct fraud symptoms that can't vary much from kite to kite. For example, kiting can always be recognized by identifying the following **SAFE BANK** symptoms.

Signature and maker on kited checks are often the same.

Area abnormalities (many out-of-area checks).

Frequent deposits, checks, and balance inquiries.

Escalating account balance.

Bank abnormalities (checks are usually drawn on the same banks).

Average length of time money is in the account is short.

NSF activity (frequent problems with not-sufficient funds).

Keeps you from recognizing frequency. [Suspect alternates use of automatic teller machines (ATMs) as well as night drops, drive-up windows, and other branches for deposits and withdrawals.]

These eight kiting symptoms can always accurately signal kiting activity. Together, they spell out the acronym SAFE BANK, which would be useful for banks to remember. They are described below in more detail.

1. *Signature and maker the same* is an indicator most often associated with one-person kiters. Single kiters often use two or more different accounts that they own including personal accounts, custodial accounts, and business accounts. To dispel any suspicion, kiters will often make a memo entry on the bottom of checks to provide justification for the increasingly large amounts of the checks. One kiter, for example, made checks out to himself with memo entries for a trip to Spain, the purchase of a car, the purchase of a lift fork, and the purchase of furniture. Bankers who are alert should recognize that individuals who buy a car, for example, will rarely make checks out to themselves but will instead make the checks directly payable to the car dealer.

2. *Area abnormalities* is a symptom that is almost always present because kiters want to allow as much float time as possible. As a result, the banks being used are often in different cities or regions of the United States. Area abnormalities were certainly present in the large EF Hutton check kiting scheme. Bankers should ask themselves whether the deposit of checks from out-of-area banks really makes sense.

3. *Frequent deposits, checks, and balance inquiries* is probably the single most telling indicator of kiting. Because of the nature of the fraud, kiters have to make frequent deposits and write frequent checks. They usually make frequent inquiries about their bank balances in order to understand the time of the float (the amount of time before the check clears and is debited against their account) and to determine whether there is money in their accounts to support checks.

4. *Escalating account balances* is another very telling sign of kiting. Because every subsequent check must be larger than the previous one, especially if money is leaving the banking system, kiter's balances usually escalate very quickly. In one case, kiting resulted in nearly a $1.5 million loss in just over a month. In a smaller kite, which was perpetrated by an individual who opened up an account and indicated his job status as "unemployed," the account escalated from $10 to over $45,000 in just two months.

5. *Bank abnormalities* means that check kiters usually make deposits with checks drawn on the same banks. In conducting normal business or other transactions, it is highly unlikely that all checks being deposited will be from the same few banks. Banks should recognize that such deposits are highly suspicious and should think of kiting as the motivation for such deposits. One $2 million kite, for example, was detected when a depositor made a deposit which included numerous checks, all drawn on the same bank in which the deposit was being made. The bank, realizing that something was strange, photocopied the checks. The kiter later realized that he had deposited the incorrect bag. He telephoned the bank and brought in a substitute bag of checks for deposit; the substitute deposit included a large number of checks that had all been drawn on another bank.

6. *Average length of time money is in the account* is a calculation that many banks make to determine whether money deposited is immediately being withdrawn. Most kiting-suspect reports make this calculation and highlight accounts in which money stays in the account an average of fewer than two or three days. Because kiters are using the float, this symptom is usually very accurate in detecting kiting.

7. *Not-sufficient-funds (NSF) activity* may or may not be present in kiting. If the balances are escalating dramatically, as is often the case, there may be no NSF activity. Professional kiters usually understand banking requirements well enough to know how long uncollected funds (UCF) holds, extended holds, funds sent for collection, and normal clearing times take. However, the accounts of amateur kiters will often show NSF activity because of the kiters lack of knowledge of clearing times.

8. Finally, use of *alternative deposit and withdrawal methods* in an effort to be unnoticeable is a good predictor of kiting but is usually hard to monitor. Most kiters do not want to be seen entering the same bank branch several times a day. Therefore, they will use drive-up windows, other branches, night drops, ATMs, and other alternative access methods to avoid suspicion.

Together, the eight symptoms described above constitute a very accurate signal that kiting is taking place. Unfortunately, most banks focus on only one or two symptoms, or none at all. One kiting-suspect report used by a major bank, for example, focuses only on two symptoms: the average length of time money is in the account and the frequency of deposits and checks. While these two symptoms are good and are easy to track using computers, the kiting suspect reports are not distributed frequently enough (they should be distributed daily). In addition, many of the branch managers and others who read the reports don't understand what they should do if a suspected kiting is highlighted. If a kiting suspect report signals a potential kite, checks and deposits should be pulled and other kiting symptoms in the SAFE BANK strategy should be investigated.

CONCLUDING COMMENTS

Symptoms suggesting various types of fraud are often not predictable or absolute. Sometimes only one symptom is present, and yet fraud is occurring. At other times, numerous "fraud symptoms" exist, and yet fraud is not being perpetrated. One thing that is certain, however, is that identifying and following up on fraud symptoms is usually the most effective way to detect fraud. Chapters 7, 8, and 9 present more detailed discussions of the symptoms introduced in this chapter.

Chapter Seven

Fraud Symptoms
Accounting, Control, and
Organizational Structure

Chapter 6 provided an overview of the detection of fraud based on red
flags or fraud symptoms. The following categories of fraud symptoms
were introduced and related to employee and management fraud:

Employee Fraud Symptoms	*Management Fraud Symptoms*
Accounting	Operating performance
Internal control	Firm structure
Analytical anomalies	Relationships with others
Tips and complaints	
Behavior ⎤ Lifestyle ⎦	Executive characteristics

As shown in the above list, certain employee fraud symptoms are related
to corresponding management fraud symptoms; for example, accounting
symptoms of employee fraud are related to operational symptoms for
management fraud. Internal control symptoms are similar to firm structure symptoms; analytical symptoms are similar to relationship symptoms; and behavior and lifestyle symptoms are similar to executive characteristic symptoms.

In this chapter, we will discuss in more detail accounting and internal
control symptoms of employee fraud, as well as operational and firm structure symptoms of management fraud. Since the focus is on accounting-
related symptoms, this chapter is rather technical in places. Because accounting records track transactions and assets, however, they often provide excellent fraud symptoms and need to be discussed. We have tried
to write the chapter that even individuals without a background in accounting can understand. Chapters 8 and 9, which discuss other types of
fraud symptoms, are not as technical.

THE RELATIONSHIP BETWEEN ACCOUNTING, INTERNAL CONTROL, FIRM STRUCTURE, AND OPERATIONAL SYMPTOMS

In order to provide feedback about performance to management, investors, creditors, regulators, and other interested parties, organizations prepare periodic financial reports. These reports summarize the transactions that have occurred and usually take the form of a balance sheet (or statement of position), an income statement, and a statement of cash flows. In order to prepare these financial statements, information about transactions (such as buying and selling goods and services, paying salaries, borrowing money, and making investments) is captured on documents. Common documents include sales and purchase invoices, checks, purchase orders, shipping invoices, and receiving reports.

Information about transactions captured on these and other documents is entered into the accounting system either by making journal entries or by using an events-based computer system. After the transactions have been entered into the system, transactions affecting similar accounts (such as receivables, cash, inventory, and payables) are summarized in ledgers. Summary totals from the ledgers are then used to prepare the financial statements that are provided to management and interested outside parties. Figure 7–1 provides a graphic illustration of the flow of financial information in a typical organization.

As indicated in Chapter 2, concealment is one of the three elements of fraud. When perpetrators embezzle from their employers or provide fraudulent information to mislead investors, accounting records such as documents, journal entries, ledgers, or financial statements are usually altered, forged, or missing. For example, an employee fraud that involved setting up a dummy company would entail submission of false invoices from the dummy company to the perpetrator's employer. The employer would then send other documents (checks) to the dummy supplier. A fraud that involved an employee's overstatement of travel expenses might involve submission of a fictitious hotel bill (a document) to the employer. The employer would then give the employee a check (another document) for an amount larger than the employee was entitled to.

Other employee frauds are concealed by making fictitious journal entries. For example, a perpetrator might embezzle cash and attempt to conceal the theft by creating a journal entry increasing an expense such as legal or advertising expense. Such a journal entry might look like the following:

Legal expense 5000
        Cash   5000

FIGURE 7–1
Typical Flow of Financial Information

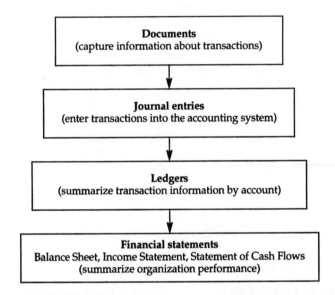

In such a case either there would be an invoice from a fictitious attorney or from an advertising agent to support the journal entry, or support for the entry would be missing.

To conceal management frauds, dishonest executives usually overstate amounts on financial statements, such as revenues on the income statement and accounts receivable, or inventories on the balance sheet. If accounts receivable and revenues are overstated, for example, fictitious sales invoices, shipping records, and other sales-related documents are often created.

In preparing the accounting records, a strong internal control environment, a good accounting system, and specific control procedures should ensure that records and financial statements are prepared with integrity. If, for example, an organization has a good system of authorizations, segregation of duties, independent checks, physical safeguards, and documents, it is difficult to create fraudulent accounting records.

Because accounting records must often be manipulated to conceal fraud, anomalies and problems with the accounting records, as well as weaknesses in the internal control system, provide excellent sources of fraud symptoms.

Sometimes, to conceal fraudulent behavior or sham transactions, perpetrators will create a complex business structure so that entries between various related parties and others will look like independent or arm's-length transactions (transactions in which a buyer and seller, both motivated by their own self-interest, bargain in good faith and reach a mutually agreed-upon price).

Employee frauds are usually not large enough to affect the financial statements. Therefore, employee fraud symptoms usually involve source documents, journal entries, or control weaknesses. Management fraud, on the other hand, is usually so large that symptoms can involve source documents, journal entries, ledgers, financial statements, control weaknesses, or complex business structures that exist for the purpose of concealing illegal actions.

In this chapter, we will first describe fraud symptoms related to source documents. After that, we will describe symptoms related to journal entries, ledgers, financial statements, internal controls, and organizational structure, in this order.

FRAUD SYMPTOMS

Irregularities in Source Documents

Common fraud symptoms involving source documents—such as checks, sales invoices, purchase orders, purchase requisitions, and receiving reports—include:

- Missing documents
- Stale items on bank reconciliations
- Excessive voids or credits
- Common names or addresses of payees or customers
- Increased past due accounts
- Increased reconciling items
- Alterations on documents
- Duplicate payments
- Second endorsements on checks
- Document sequences that don't make sense
- Questionable handwriting on documents
- Photocopied documents

To illustrate how these document symptoms can signal that embezzlement is taking place, we will describe three actual frauds. The first involves the use of photocopied documents; the second, the recognition of increased past due accounts receivable; and the third, excessive voids or credits. While we will discuss only three frauds, we personally know of many frauds that have been detected using each of these symptoms.

Our first example is a fraud that was detected on the basis of an altered document—a photocopied letter from a manufacturer to a vendor suggesting that expensive new equipment be purchased.

A thin line running through a photocopied letter in a vendor invoice file alerted an observant auditor, who had been trained in the recognition of suspicious documents, to probe further. The photocopied letter was from a manufacturer to a vendor, which had suggested the repair of machinery parts as an alternative to the expensive option of replacement, which was also set forth in the letter. By cutting out the paragraph pertaining to the repair of existing machinery, the vendor had substantiated the need for replacing the equipment, thus ensuring a large commission on the sale of new machinery.

This fraud was caught when an alert internal auditor, who had been trained in security-related topics, noticed the thin line in the photocopied letter. He reasoned that the letter must be a copy and decided to pursue the symptom. Further investigation revealed a large, collusive fraud.

In the second example, a fraud was detected by recognizing an increase in past due accounts from customers. This employee fraud was committed against one of the largest Fortune 500 companies in the United States.[1]

Mark Rogers was the accounts receivable department manager at XYZ Foods. In this position, he developed a close relationship with one of the company's largest customers and used the relationship to defraud his employer. For a fee (a kickback), he offered to "manage" his company's receivable from the customer. By "managing" the large receivable, Rogers permitted the customer to pay later than would otherwise have been required. The customer's payable was not recognized as delinquent or past due. Because the receivable involved millions of dollars, paying 30 to 60 days later than was required cost Mark's employer $3 million in lost interest. The accounts receivable manager had received kickbacks totaling $350,000 from the customer.

Mark's fraud was discovered when an alert co-worker realized that the company's accounts receivable turnover ratio was decreasing substantially. The co-worker prepared an aging schedule of individual accounts receivable balances, which identified the customer who was paying kickbacks to Mark as the source of the problem. A subsequent investigation revealed the kickback scheme.

---

[1]Throughout the chapter, the name of perpetrators and companies have been changed.

Our third example is a fraud that was discovered because of excessive credit memos. The case involved a fraud of over $5,000 by a supervisor in the shipping department of a wholesale–retail distribution center warehouse facility.

The supervisor was responsible for the overall operations of the warehouse and had individual accountability for a cash fund that was used for collecting money (usually amounts of $25 to $500) from customers who came to the warehouse to pick up cash-on-delivery (COD) orders. The established procedures called for the supervisor to issue the customer a cash receipt, which was recorded in a will-call–delivery log book. The file containing details on the customer order would eventually be matched with cash receipts by accounting personnel, and the transaction would be closed.

Over a period of approximately one year, the supervisor defrauded the company by stealing small amounts of money. He attempted to conceal the fraud by submitting credit memos (with statements such as "billed to the wrong account," "to correct billing adjustment," or "miscellaneous") to clear the accounts receivable file. The accounts would be matched with the credit memo, and the transaction would be closed. A second signature was not needed on the credit memos, and accounting personnel asked no questions about credit memos originated by the supervisor of the warehouse.

At first, the supervisor submitted only two to three fraudulent credit memos a week, totaling approximately $100. After a few months, however, he increased the amount of his theft to about $300 per week. To give the appearance of randomness, so as to keep the accounting personnel from becoming suspicious, the supervisor intermixed small credit memo amounts with large ones.

The fraud surfaced when the supervisor accidentally credited the wrong customer's account for a cash transaction. By coincidence, the supervisor was on vacation when the error surfaced and was not available to cover his tracks when accounting personnel queried the transaction. Because of his absence, the accounts receivable clerk questioned the manager of the warehouse, who investigated the problem. The manager scrutinized cash receipts and determined that the potential for fraud existed.

Faulty Journal Entries

Accounting is a language, just as English and Japanese are languages. For example, consider the following journal entry:

Legal expense 5000
Cash   5000

In the English language, this entry says "An attorney was paid $5,000 in cash." In the language of accounting, this entry says "Debit legal expense, credit cash." A person who speaks both accounting and English will realize that these statements say exactly the same thing.

The problem with the language of accounting is that it can easily be manipulated to lie. For example, how does one know that an attorney was actually paid $5,000? Instead, maybe an employee embezzled $5,000 in cash and attempted to conceal the fraud by identifying it as a legal expense. Smart embezzlers may conceal their actions in exactly this way, realizing that the fraudulent legal expense will be closed to retained earnings at the end of the accounting period and the immediate audit trail will be gone.

In order to understand whether accounting and journal entries represent truth or fiction, one must learn to recognize journal entry fraud symptoms.

The basic accounting equation states that the sum of all assets must equal the sum of all liabilities plus the sum of all owners' equity or:

Assets = Liabilities + Owners' equity

When perpetrators embezzle, they usually steal assets, such as cash or inventory. (We're still searching for someone to steal our liabilities.) The embezzlement of assets reduces the left side of the accounting equation. In order to conceal the theft of assets, an embezzler must find a way to decrease the right side of the equation (either liabilities or equities); otherwise the accounting records won't balance and the embezzler will be quickly detected. Smart embezzlers understand that decreasing liabilities is not a good concealment method. In reducing payables, amounts owed are eliminated from the books. This manipulation of the accounting records will be recognized when vendors do not receive payments for amounts owed to them. When the liability becomes delinquent, they will notify the company. Subsequent investigation will reveal the fraud.

Smart perpetrators also realize that most equity accounts should not be altered. The owner's equity balance is decreased by the payment of dividends and expenses and is increased by sales of stock and revenues. Perpetrators rarely conceal their frauds by manipulating either dividends or stock accounts, because these accounts have relatively few transactions and alterations are quickly noticed. In addition, transactions involving stock or dividends usually require the board of director's approval and are monitored closely.

By the process of elimination, only revenues and expenses remain as possibilities for decreasing the right side of the accounting equation and making the accounting records balance. Balancing the equation by manipulating revenues would require that individual revenue accounts be reduced. However since organizations either have or do not have revenues (meaning that revenues are increased or remain zero but are rarely decreased), a decrease in a revenue account would not make much sense and would quickly draw attention. Therefore, perpetrators who manipulate accounting records to conceal their embezzlements usually attempt to balance the accounting equation by increasing expenses. Increasing expenses decreases net income, which decreases retained earning and owners' equity, thus leaving the accounting equation in balance. Figure 7–2 illustrates these relationships.

Recognizing an expense to conceal fraud involves making a fictitious journal entry. Managers, accountants, and auditors must be able to recognize fraud symptoms that signal that a journal entry may not be legitimate and may be concealing a fraud. Manipulating expense accounts also has the advantage that expenses are closed or brought to zero balances at year end, thus eliminating the audit trail.

The following are common journal entry fraud symptoms:

- Journal entries without documentary support
- Unexplained adjustments to receivables, payables, revenues, or expenses
- Journal entries that don't balance
- Journal entries made by individuals who would not normally make such entries
- Journal entries made near the ends of accounting periods

To illustrate journal entry fraud symptoms, we will describe two actual embezzlements. The first, a $150,000 embezzlement by the controller of a bank, illustrates journal entries without support.

John Doe was the controller of a small bank. Over a period of several years, he embezzled approximately $150,000 from his employer by telephoning upstream banks and having them pay his personal credit card bills. He concealed his fraud by creating fictitious journal entries to recognize the shortages as advertising expense. Because the total amount of advertising expense was large and the increase in expense resulting from his fraud was relatively small, no one ever questioned the legitimacy of his journal entries. Because he was the bank's controller and in charge of all accounting, he didn't even forge fictitious documentation to support the entries. He was caught when he became greedy and deposited in his own personal bank account a duplicate $10,000 payment from one of the bank's customers. When the customer realized he had paid twice and asked for his refund, the deposit was traced to John's account.

If anyone had questioned the journal entries that were being made without documentary support, John's fraud would have been quickly discovered. In this bank, however, if John had not gotten greedy, his fraud might have continued indefinitely.

Our second example of journal entry fraud symptoms is manipulation of income at Lincoln Savings and Loan. This example illustrates journal entries made at the ends of accounting periods to artificially inflate reported net income. At Lincoln, many large journal entries to create fictitious revenues were made at the end of almost every quarter. A national

FIGURE 7–2
Employee Embezzlement

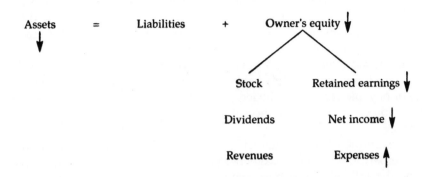

CPA firm that reviewed Lincoln's transactions concluded that Lincoln entered into at least 13 transactions that overstated income by more than $100 million. The auditors from the accounting firm called the transactions the most egregious misapplication of accounting they had ever seen. In almost every case, the journal entries took Lincoln from a net loss to a net profit position. If Lincoln's auditors and regulators had recognized the pattern of successive last-minute entries, Lincoln's massive fraud might have been stopped much earlier and investors would have been saved millions of dollars.

Inaccuracies in Ledgers

The definition of *accounting ledger* is "book of accounts." In other words, all transactions related to specific accounts such as cash or inventory are summarized in their respective accounts in the ledger. The accuracy of account balances in the ledger is often proved by ensuring that the total of all asset accounts equals the total of all liability and equity accounts. Many frauds involve manipulating receivables from customers or payables to vendors. Most companies have master (control) receivable and payable accounts, the total of which should equal the sum of all the individual customer and vendor account balances. Two common fraud symptoms related to ledgers are:

1. A ledger that doesn't balance.
2. Master (control) account balances that don't equal the sum of the individual customer or vendor balances.

The first symptom is indicative of frauds in which cover-up in the accounting records is not complete. For example, a perpetrator may embezzle inventory (an asset) but not record an expense or effect a decrease on the right-hand side of the accounting equation. In this case, the actual inventory balance, as determined by a physical count, is lower than the recorded amount of inventory, and the ledger doesn't balance. Another example of a ledger out of balance would be the theft of cash accompanied by the failure to record an expense. In this case, total assets would be less than total liabilities plus owners' equity.

The second ledger symptom is indicative of manipulation of an individual customer or vendor's balance without altering the master receivable or payable account in the ledger. In this case, the sum of the individual customer or vendor balances does not agree with the master account balance.

An example of fraud characterized by this second ledger symptom was perpetrated by the bookkeeper and proof operator of a small bank. Using the following schemes, she embezzled over $3 million from her bank, which had only $30 million in total assets.

Marjorie E. was the bookkeeper and proof operator at First National Bank of Atlanta. Using two different schemes, she defrauded First National of over $3 million. Her first scheme involved writing personal checks on her bank account at First National to pay for expensive art, jewelry, automobiles, home furnishings, and other expensive acquisitions. Then, when her check would be sent from the Federal Reserve to the bank (in the incoming cash letter), she would allow the overall demand deposit account balance to be reduced but would pull her checks before they could be processed and deducted from her personal account. The result of this scheme was that the master demand deposit account balance was lower than the sum of the bank's individual customers' demand deposits. Her second scheme involved making deposits into her account using checks drawn on other banks and then pulling the checks before they were sent in the outgoing cash letter to the Federal Reserve. Thus, her checks were never deducted from her accounts at the other banks. In fact, her accounts at the banks did not contain sufficient funds to cover the checks if they had been processed. The result of this scheme was that the individual demand deposit balances increased but the master demand deposit account balance did not.

Both of these schemes had the effect of making the master demand deposit account balances lower than the sum of the individual account balances. Over time, as Marjorie wrote checks and made fictitious deposits, the difference between the sum of the individual accounts and the master account balances became larger and larger.

To cover her tracks and prevent the auditors from discovering the fraud, at the end of each accounting period, Marjorie would pull some official bank checks (cashier's checks) that had previously been used and send them in the outgoing cash letter to the Federal Reserve. Because the Federal Reserve procedures were automated, no one there ever personally examined the checks or noticed that they had been processed several times. (In fact, some of the checks were totally black.) Her fraud was assisted by the Federal Reserve's policy of giving immediate credit to First National for the total amount supposedly contained in the outgoing cash letter. The next day, as the checks were processed using bank routing numbers, the Federal Reserve would realize that the official checks were not drawn on other banks but were really First National's own checks and would reverse the credit previously given to First National. The reduction would again throw First National's ledger accounts out of balance. But, for one day—the day the auditors examined the records— the bank's books would be balanced and the shortage would be "parked" at the Federal Reserve. Because the financial statements were prepared for that one day, bank records balanced for the auditors.

This fraud could easily have been discovered if someone had noticed that although the books balanced at month end, they were out of balance for the remainder of the month. Bank managers received daily statements of condition and other reports that showed demand deposit balances significantly different from the balances on the financial statements. They never questioned these unusual balances. This fraud could also have been uncovered if someone had recognized many other symptoms. There were several control weakness symptoms. For example, Marjorie had significant personality conflicts with other employees, and she lived a lifestyle far beyond what her income would have supported. In addition, individual accounting records had been altered, and a previous fraud at the same bank had indicated a need for reports and procedures that, if implemented, would have made the fraud impossible. Surprisingly, the fraud wasn't discovered until a check that Marjorie had reused several times—until it was totally black—was kicked out of a Federal Reserve sorter because it couldn't be read.

UNEXPLAINED CHANGES IN FINANCIAL STATEMENTS

Financial statements are the end product of the accounting cycle. Fraud can be detected through source documents, journal entries based on those documents, ledger balances (which are summaries of journal entries), or the resulting financial statements. Unless a fraud is large, however, it may not affect the overall financial statements significantly enough to be detected. Large frauds may be detected through financial statements; small frauds usually must be detected in the accounting records by focusing on source documents.

Fraud is best detected through financial statements by focusing on *unexplained changes*. For example, in most companies, very few customers pay cash at the time of purchase. Rather, their payments are made by check, based on monthly bills. As a result, it would not usually make sense for revenues to increase without a corresponding increase in accounts receivable. Similarly, if revenues increase, there should probably be an increase in cost of sales and in inventory purchased and accounts payable balances. It would also not make sense for inventory levels to increase while purchases and accounts payable remained constant. In all cases, it is unexplained changes that must be the focus of attention.

To understand how financial statement changes can signal fraud, one must be familiar with the nature of the three primary financial statements. Most organizations publish periodic balance sheets (statements of position), income statements, and statements of cash flow. The balance sheet is a position statement. It shows what an organization's asset, liability, and equity balances are *at a specific point in time* (it is like a snapshot). A balance sheet prepared as of December 31, 1995, for example, reveals what an organization owns and owes on that date only. A balance sheet prepared on January 3, 1996 (three days later), may show drastically different results. Because a balance sheet is a position statement as of a specific date, it must be converted to a *change statement* before it can be used in detecting fraud. The changes can then be analyzed to determine whether or not they make sense or represent fraud symptoms that should be investigated.

An income statement shows what an organization's revenues, expenses, and income were for a period of time. An income statement prepared for the year ending December 31, 1995, for example, would reveal revenues, expenses, and income for the 12 months January through December, 1995. Though an income statement is for a period, rather than as of a specific date, it is not a change statement. Like a balance sheet, it must be converted to a change statement before it can be used effectively as a fraud detection tool.

There are four ways to convert balance sheets and income statements from position and period to change statements: (1) comparing balances in the statements from one period to the next, (2) calculating key ratios and comparing them from period to period, (3) performing horizontal analysis, and (4) performing vertical analysis. The first involves comparing numbers in the statement from one period to the next. For example, the accounts receivable balance of one period can be compared to the balance in a subsequent period to see whether the change is in the expected direction and whether the magnitude of change is reasonable, given changes in other numbers. Unfortunately, because financial statement numbers are often very large and difficult to compare, it may be hard to assess levels of change.

The second method of converting balance sheets and income statements to change statements is to calculate key financial statement ratios and to compare changes in these ratios from period to period. The quick ratio (which is also called the *acid test*) and the *current ratio* assess a company's liquidity. Accounts receivable turnover and inventory turnover ratios assess a company's operational efficiency. *Debt-to-equity* and *times interest earned* ratios assess a company's solvency. *Profit margin, return on assets, return on equity,* and *earning per share* ratios assess profitability. By examining ratios, it is possible to see whether resulting changes in liquidity, efficiency, solvency, and profitability are as expected. Changes in ratios that don't make sense are often the result of fraudulent action by managers.

Detecting fraud through financial statement ratios is much easier than assessing changes in actual financial statement numbers themselves. Ratios usually involve small, easily understood numbers that are sensitive to changes in key variables. In addition, benchmarks for most ratios are well known. Common ratios that can be used to detect fraud are shown in Figure 7–3.

The third way to convert balance sheets and income statements to change statements is to use vertical analysis—a tool that converts financial statement numbers to percentages so they are easy to understand. For a balance sheet, total assets are set at 100 percent and all other balances are a percentage of total assets. Figure 7–4 is a simple example of vertical analysis of a balance sheet.

Vertical analysis is a very useful fraud detection technique, because percentages are easily understood. When we spend $1 or part of $1, we know what it means. If we spend it all, we know we spend 100 percent. Similarly, all through school, we received 70 or 80 or 90 percent on examinations. Everyone understands which of these scores are good, which are bad, and what percentage of the 100 percent possible they represent. Changes in cumbersome financial statement balances can be readily assessed by converting the numbers to percentages. It is much easier to understand that sales increased 20 percent, for example, than to understand the meaning of a sales increase from $862,000 to $1,034,400.

When vertical analysis is used to analyze changes in income statement balances, gross sales are set at 100 percent and all other amounts are converted to a percentage of 100 percent. Figure 7–5 is a simple example of an income statement converted to percentages using vertical analysis.

In this example, cost of goods sold increased from 50 percent of sales in year 1 to 60 percent of sales in year 2. Does this change make sense? Why would cost of sales increase twice as much as sales? Possible explanations include: (1) inventory costs rose faster than sales prices, (2) inventory is being stolen, and (3) there is an error in the accounting records. It wouldn't take much work to determine which of these (or other) factors was the cause of the unusual changes.

The fourth method of converting balance sheets and income statements to change statements is horizontal analysis. Horizontal analysis is similar to vertical analysis in that it converts financial statement balances

FIGURE 7–4

JOHN DOE COMPANY
Vertical Analysis of Balance Sheet
As of December 31, 19x2, and 19x1

	Year 2		Year 1	
Assets				
Cash	$ 50,000	5%	$ 64,000	8%
Accounts receivable	100,000	10	96,000	12
Inventory	200,000	20	160,000	20
Fixed assets	650,000	65	480,000	60
Total assets	$ 1,000,000	100%	$ 800,000	100%
Accounts payable	$ 70,000	7%	$ 16,000	2%
Mortgage payable	120,000	12	80,000	10
Bonds payable	200,000	20	160,000	20
Common stock	400,000	40	400,000	50
Retained earnings	210,000	21	144,000	18
Total liabilities and equity	$ 1,000,000	100%	$ 800,000	100%

FIGURE 7–5

JOHN DOE COMPANY
Vertical Analysis of Income Statement
For the Period Ending December 31, 19x2, and 19x1

	Year 2		Year 1	
Sales	$ 1,000,000	100%	$ 800,000	100%
Cost of goods sold	600,000	60	400,000	50
Gross Margin	$ 400,000	40%	$ 400,000	50%
Expenses:				
Savings expenses	150,000	15%	120,000	15%
Administrative expenses	100,000	10	88,000	11
Income before taxes	$ 150,000	15%	$ 192,000	24%
Income taxes	60,000	6	80,000	10
Net income	$ 90,000	9%	$ 112,000	14%

FIGURE 7–6

JOHN DOE COMPANY
Horizontal Analysis of Balance Sheet
As of December 31, 19x2, and 19x1

	Year 2	Year 1	Change	Percentage Change
Assets:				
Cash	$ 50,000	$ 64,000	$(14,000)	(22)
Accounts receivable	100,000	96,000	4,000	4
Inventory	200,000	160,000	40,000	25
Fixed assets	650,000	480,000	170,000	35
Total assets	$1,000,000	$800,000	$ 200,000	25
Accounts payable	$ 70,000	$ 16,000	$ 54,000	338
Mortgage payable	120,000	80,000	40,000	50
Bonds payable	200,000	160,000	40,000	25
Common stock	400,000	400,000	-0-	-0-
Retained earnings	210,000	144,000	66,000	46
Total liabilities & equity	$1,000,000	$800,000	$ 200,000	25

---

to percentages. However, instead of computing financial statement amounts as percentages of total assets or gross sales, it converts the percentage change in balance sheet and income statement numbers from one period to the next. Figure 7–6 is a simple example of horizontal analysis of a balance sheet; Figure 7–7 illustrates horizontal analysis of an income statement.

Horizontal analysis is the most direct method of focusing on changes. With ratios and vertical analysis, statements are converted to numbers that are easier to understand, and then the numbers are compared from period to period. With horizontal analysis, it is the change in amounts from period to period that is converted to percentages.

As an example of the usefulness of vertical and horizontal analysis, consider the ESM fraud in which one of the authors was an expert witness.

Steve Albrecht was sitting in his office one day when he received a call from an attorney asking him to be an expert witness in a major fraud case that was being litigated. The attorney informed Steve that the case was ESM Government, a securities dealer that had been in the news recently. The attorney indicated that he was defending a large CPA firm that had audited a S&L that had invested in ESM and was now being sued for some $300 million by the insurance commission for negligent auditing. In defense of this firm, the attorney was trying to understand the nature and extent of the fraud as well as to obtain an independent opinion on whether his client was negligent in performing the audit.

FIGURE 7–7

JOHN DOE COMPANY
Horizontal Analysis of Income Statements
For the Period Ending December 31, 19x2, and 19x1

	Year 2	Year 1	Change	Percentage Change
Assets:				
Net sales	$1,000,000	$800,000	$200,000	25
Cost of goods sold	600,000	400,000	200,000	50
Gross margin expenses	$ 400,000	$400,000	$ 0	0
Selling expenses	$ 150,000	$120,000	$ 30,000	25
Administrative expenses	100,000	88,000	12,000	14
Income before taxes	$ 150,000	$192,000	$ (42,000)	22
Income taxes	60,000	80,000	(20,000)	25
Net income	$ 90,000	$112,000	$ 22,000	(20)

The attorney said that he would send the financial statements and requested that Steve analyze them to determine whether or not fraud existed and, if so, in which accounts. In analyzing the financial statements, Steve used horizontal and vertical analysis. His converted financial statements are shown in figures 7–8 (vertical analysis) and 7–9 (horizontal analysis).

Based on his analysis, Steve drew three conclusions. First, if there were fraud, it had to be in either the "securities sold under agreement to repurchase (repo)" account or in the "securities purchased under agreement to resale (reverse repo)" account. Steve was not familiar with either of these accounts but recognized them as being the only accounts large enough to hide massive fraud. Second, he wondered why these two accounts would have identical balances in three of the four years. After he came to understand that these accounts were really only payables and receivables for the company, his concern heightened. It didn't make much sense that a company's receivable balance should exactly equal its payable balance in even one year, let alone three in a row. Third, the numbers in the financial statements seemed to be jumping around almost at random. There were large changes from year to year, and often these changes were in opposite directions. In a stable company, you expect small, consistent changes from year to year.

Steve called the attorney with conclusions based on his analysis. He stated that he wasn't sure that the financial statements were fraudulent but that there were three very significant red flags. He also stated that if fraud were present, it would have to be in the repo and reverse repo accounts.

Based on this analysis, Steve was retained to be an expert witness in the case. He never testified, however, because the case was settled out of court for less than $5 million.

FIGURE 7-8

ESM GOVERNMENT
Vertical Analysis

	$ (Year 1)	%	$ (Year 2)	%	$ (Year 3)	%	$ (Year 4)	%
Assets								
Cash	$ 99,000	0.000	$ 1,767,000	0.001	$ 1,046,000	0.001	$ 339,000	0.000
Deposits	25,000	0.000	25,000	0.000	25,000	0.000	25,000	0.000
Receivables from brokers and dealers	725,000	0.000	60,000	0.000	1,084,000	0.001	2,192,000	0.001
Receivables from customers	33,883,000	0.024	40,523,000	0.027	21,073,000	0.022	16,163,000	0.006
Securities purchased under agreement to resell	1,367,986,000	0.963	1,323,340,000	0.867	738,924,000	0.781	2,252,555,000	0.840
Accrued interest	433,000	0.000	433,000	0.000	1,257,000	0.001	7,375,000	0.003
Securities purchased not sold at market	17,380,000	0.010	161,484,000	0.106	182,674,000	0.193	402,004,000	0.150
Total assets	$1,420,531,000		$1,527,632,000		$946,083,000		$2,680,653,000	
Liabilities and equity								
Short-term bank loans	$ 5,734,000	0.005	$ 57,282,000	0.037	$ 80,350,000	0.085	$ 91,382,000	0.034
Payable to brokers and dealers	1,721,000	0.001	478,000	0.000	3,624,000	0.004	5,815,000	0.000
Payable to customers	2,703,000	0.002	4,047,000	0.003	1,426,000	0.002	3,683,000	0.000
Securities sold under agreement to repurchase	1,367,986,000	0.963	1,323,340,000	0.867	738,924,000	0.781	2,457,555,000	0.917
Accounts payable and accrued expenses	272,000	0.000	796,000	0.000	591,000	0.001	1,377,000	0.000
Accounts payable—parent and affiliates	33,588,000	0.020	127,604,000	0.084	95,861,000	0.101	92,183,000	0.014
Common stock	1,000	0.000	1,000	0.000	1,000	0.000	1,000	0.000
Additional contributed capital	4,160,000	0.040	4,160,000	0.003	4,160,000	0.004	4,160,000	0.000
Retained earnings	4,366,000	0.040	9,924,000	0.006	21,146,000	0.022	24,497,000	0.010
Total liabilities and equity	$1,420,531,000		$1,527,632,000		$946,083,000		$2,680,653,000	

Note: This vertical analysis, based on ESM's actual journal, was prepared by Steve Albrecht.

FIGURE 7–9

ESM GOVERNMENT
Horizontal Analysis*

	Year 1 to Year 2	Year 2 to Year 3	Year 3 to Year 4
Assets			
Cash	1,684%	(40%)	(67%)
Deposits	0	0	0
Receivables from brokers and dealers	(91)	1,706%	102
Receivables from customers	19.5	(48%)	(23)
Securities purchased under agreement to resell	(3)	(44%)	205
Accrued interest	0	190%	487
Securities purchased not sold at market	829	13%	120
Total assets	7.5	(38%)	183
Liabilities and S.E. Equity			
Short-term bank loans	898	40	14
Payable to brokers and dealers	(72)	658	33
Payable to customer	50	(64)	158
Securities sold under agreement to repurchase	(3)	(44)	232
Accounts payable and accrued expenses	192	(100)	55
Accounts payable—parent and affiliates	279	(25)	(4)
Common stock	0	0	0
Additional contributed capital	0	0	0
Retained earnings	127	113	21

*Actual figures are omitted to simplify the presentation.
Note: This horizontal analysis, based on ESM's actual financial statements, was prepared by Steve Albrecht.

Examples of financial statement fraud, some missed by auditors and some caught, that could have been easily detected using horizontal or vertical analysis, are plentiful. In many cases, the unexplained changes are very obvious; in other cases, they are more subtle. Unfortunately, however, managers and even auditors generally use ratios, horizontal analysis, and vertical analysis only as tools for assessing the performance of an organization. Rarely do they use these measures to detect fraud.

The third financial statement is the statement of cash flows. It is already a change statement and does not need to be converted. The statement of cash flows shows the cash inflows and cash outflows during a period. Figure 7–10 is a graphic description of this statement. The format for preparing the statement is shown in Figure 7–11. Because the statement of cash flows focuses on changes, it can answer questions such as:

• Is the increase in cash flow as expected?

FIGURE 7–10
Cash Inflows

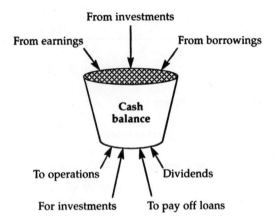

FIGURE 7–11
Statement of Cash Flows—A Change Statement

Net income

± Increase (decrease) in operating accounts
  Increase (decrease) in inventory
  Increase (decrease) in prepaid expenses
  Increase (decrease) in payables
  Increase (decrease) in accrued liabilities
  Increase (decrease) in accounts receivable
= Cash flow from operations

± Increase (decrease) from investing activities
Sales of assets
Purchase of assets

± Increase (decrease) from financing activities
  Payment of debt
  Borrowing
  Issuing stock
  Treasury stock
  Payment of dividends

= increase (decrease) in cash flows

- Why did receivables go up (down)?
- Why did inventory increase (decrease)?
- Why did payables increase (decrease)?
- Why was there an increase in payables when inventory decreased?
- Why were assets sold (bought)?
- Where did the cash come from to pay dividends?

Increases or decreases that do not make sense serve as red flags and can be investigated.

Internal Control Weaknesses

As suggested in Chapter 2, fraud occurs when pressure, opportunity, and rationalization come together. Most people have pressures, and most organizations have pressures. Everyone rationalizes. When internal controls are absent or overridden, everyone has an opportunity to commit fraud.

Internal control was described in Chapter 3 as being composed of the control environment, the accounting system, and control procedures. Common internal control fraud symptoms are:

- Lack of segregation of duties
- Lack of physical safeguards
- Lack of independent checks
- Lack of proper authorization
- Lack of proper documents and records
- Overriding of existing controls
- Inadequate accounting system

Many studies have found that the element most common in frauds is the overriding of existing internal controls. In the proof operator fraud that was discussed earlier in this chapter, there were three glaring internal control weaknesses. Marjorie kept a locked cabinet next to her desk. Only Marjorie had a key to the cabinet, and no one else was allowed access. While the bank had a mandatory, two-consecutive-week vacation policy, Marjorie asked for and received exceptions to the policy. (She used the excuse that her work load would not allow her to be gone that long.) There were also general ledger tickets that had to be signed by two individuals. However, she regularly had subordinates presign these general ledger tickets, using the excuse that she didn't want to "have to bother them if they were busy." All three of these control weaknesses were instrumental in the perpetuation of her fraud.

Two other examples of control weaknesses that allowed fraud to occur are discussed below. In the first, a control weakness allowed a customer to defraud a bank of over $500,000. In the second, a significant internal control weakness allowed a fraud to continue over several years.[4]

Lorraine W. was a customer of Second National Bank. She had opened her account 16 months previously, and she often made deposits and withdrawals in the hundred of thousands of dollars. She claimed to be a member of a well-known, wealthy family. She drove a Porsche, dressed very nicely, and was able to earn the trust and confidence of the bank's branch manager. One day, she approached the manager and said that she needed a cashier's check in the amount of $525,000. The manager, realizing that she had only $13,000 in her account, first denied the request. Then, deciding that she was a valued customer, not wanting to lose her business, and based on her promise to cover the shortage the next day, he gave her the cashier's check. It turned out that she was not who she claimed to be. In fact, she was an embezzler who had stolen over $5 million from her employer; all the funds that had gone through her bank account were stolen. Her employer had caught her and promised not to seek prosecution if she would pay the company back. She was stealing from Second National to repay the money.

As it turned out, Second National had a control requiring two signatures on all cashier's checks exceeding $500,000. However, the bank manager, who was an imposing figure, had ordered his assistant to sign the cashier's check. Without making an independent decision and because the manager told him to sign, the assistant had merely followed the manager's order. Thus the control that required two independent signatures was compromised. There were two signatures, but they were not independent. Both the assistant and the manager, who are now unemployed, later wished the assistant had made an independent decision.

The second example of a glaring internal control weakness fraud is the famous Hochfelder case, which went all the way to the US Supreme Court before it was decided that Ernst & Ernst, a large CPA firm, had not been negligent in performing the audit.

Lestor B. Nay, the president of First Securities Co. of Chicago, fraudulently convinced certain customers to invest funds in escrow accounts that he represented would yield a high return. There were no escrow accounts. Nay converted the customers' funds to his own use.

The transactions were not in the usual from of dealings between First Securities and its customers. First, all correspondence with customers was done solely by Nay. Because of a "mail rule" that Nay had imposed, such mail was opened only by him. Second, checks of the customers were made payable to Nay. Third, the escrow accounts were not reflected on the books of First Securities, nor in filings with the SEC, nor in connection with customers' other investment accounts. The fraud was uncovered only after Nay's suicide.

Respondent customers sued in district court for damages against Ernst & Ernst as aiders and abetters under Section 10b-5 of the 1933 SEC Act. They alleged that Ernst & Ernst had failed to conduct a proper audit, which would have led them to discover the mail rule and the fraud.

The court reasoned that Ernst & Ernst had a common-law and statutory duty of inquiry into the adequacy of First Securities' *internal control system*, because the firm had contracted to audit First Securities and to review the annual report filings with the SEC.

The US Supreme Court reversed the decision of the court of appeals, concluding that the interpretation of Section 10b-5 required the "intent to deceive, manipulate or defraud." Justice Powell wrote, in the Supreme Court's opinion: "When a statute speaks so specifically in terms of manipulation and deception, and of implementing devices and contrivances—the commonly understood terminology of intentional wrongdoing—and when its history reflects no more expansive intent, we are quite unwilling to extend the scope of the statute to negligent conduct."

The Supreme Court pointed out that in certain areas of the law, recklessness is considered to be a form of intentional conduct for purposes of imposing liability.

In this case, the mail rule that required that no one except Lester B. Nay open the mail was an internal control weakness. Had this weakness not been allowed, Nay's fraud would probably have been revealed much earlier and investors wouldn't have lost nearly so much money.

Overly Complex Organizational Structures

Organizational structure symptoms involve any organizational structure that seems to exist without a real business purpose. In several major fraud cases, complex business structures have masked financial statement frauds by not allowing auditors and other outsiders to understand that transactions were not arm's-length and that substantial amounts of revenues and income were not legitimate.

A good example of an unduly complex business structure fraud is offered by Lincoln Savings and Loan. The organizational structure of American Continental, of which Lincoln Savings was a subsidiary, included 55 distinct but related companies. Some of the companies were developers, others were lenders, some were investment organizations, and still others entered into real estate transactions. An example of the kinds of transactions that took place between the various subsidiaries and straw buyers created by the organization was the sale of property to West Continental Mortgage. Figure 7–12 shows a schematic description of this transaction.

This case involves Lincoln Savings and Loan's sale of 1,000 acres of Hidden Valley Ranch to West Continental Mortgage on March 31, 1987. West Continental gave Lincoln a $3.5 million down payment, as well as a

FIGURE 7–12

Lincoln Savings and Loan Association's Sale to West Continental Mortgage, March 31, 1987

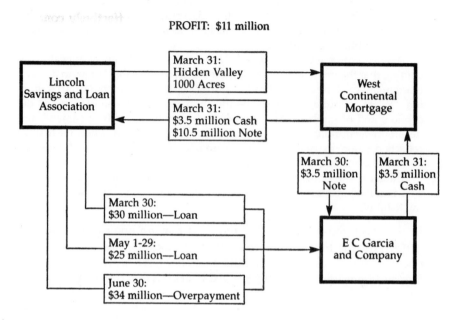

note for $10.5 million for the property. However, a company known as EC Garcia & Company loaned West Continental Mortgage $3.5 million in cash on March 31. On March 30, Lincoln loaned EC Garcia $30 million; another $25 million was loaned on May 1, and a final $34 million was loaned on June 30, 1987. Lincoln Savings booked a profit of $11 million on the transaction. Who really made the down payment, and was there really a sale?

The trend in business today is to simplify. Companies are scaling back to the core products that made them successful and are streamlining management and organizational lines. In this environment, the fraud investigator must question why an organization is so complex that it is hard to understand and it seems to exist without a well-defined business purpose.

CONCLUDING COMMENTS

Accounting, control, and organizational anomalies often provide symptoms that fraud is being perpetrated. The accounting system provides checks and balances that, if understood, can be used to detect both small and large frauds. By nature, the symptoms described in this chapter are quite technical. In order to use these symptoms, it is necessary to have a good understanding of both fraud and accounting. When symptoms are observed, the accounting system provides an excellent audit trail that can be used to determine whether symptoms represent actual fraud or accidental errors.

Anyone can embezzle, and anyone can convert or spend stolen funds. Many people, however, do not understand how to effectively conceal frauds. Because concealment is a major element of most frauds, and because concealment most often affects the accounting records, it is no wonder that most frauds are committed by accounting and finance personnel. One study, for example, found that 73 percent of all perpetrators had backgrounds in accounting and finance.

Searching a company's accounting system for the many symptoms described in this chapter is one of the most useful ways to detect fraud. Unfortunately, most people who understand accounting use it only to track operational results and to provide feedback about how an organization is doing. Rarely do they use it for what it is—one of the most effective tools for recognizing and investigating fraud.

Chapter Eight

Fraud Symptoms
Analytical Procedures and
Relationships with Other Parties

In Chapter 7, accounting and control symptoms were discussed. Other fraud indicators are analytical symptoms, unusual relationships with others that suggest fraud, tips and complaints, behavioral symptoms, and lifestyle changes. In this chapter we discuss analytical symptoms and unusual relationships with others. The remaining three classes of symptoms are left for Chapter 9.

ANALYTICAL FRAUD SYMPTOMS

Several years ago, two partners of a national CPA firm conducted research in which they analyzed frauds that their auditors had discovered. Their research objective was to discover which audit techniques were most effective in detecting fraud. They examined various detailed tests of balances, control tests, analytical procedures, and other audit tasks. The results indicated that most financial statement frauds are detected by recognizing analytical symptoms.

Analytical fraud symptoms are procedures or relationships that are too unusual or too unrealistic to be believable. They include transactions or events that happen at odd times or places; that are performed by or involve people who wouldn't normally participate; or that include odd procedures, policies, or practices. They also include transactions and amounts that are too large or too small, that are performed or occur too often or too rarely, that are too high or too low, or that result in too much or too little of something. Basically, analytical symptoms represent anything out of the ordinary. They are the unexpected.

Common examples of analytical symptoms include:

- Unexplained inventory shortages or adjustments
- Deviations from specifications
- Increased scrap
- Excess purchases
- Too many debit or credit memos
- Significant increases or decreases in account balances
- Physical abnormalities
- Cash shortages or overages
- Excessive late charges
- Unreasonable expenses or reimbursements
- Strange financial statement relationships such as:
  Increased revenues with decreased inventory
  Increased revenues with decreased receivables
  Increased revenues with decreased cash flows
  Increased inventory with decreased payables
  Increased volume with increased cost per unit
  Increased volume with decreased scrap
  Increased inventory with decreased warehousing costs

An example of fraud detected by considering analytical relationships was the Mayberry fraud.[1]

The internal auditors for the Mayberry Corporation, a conglomerate with about $1 billion in sales, were auditing the company's sheet metal division. Every past audit had resulted in favorable outcomes with few audit findings. This year, however, something didn't seem right. Their observation of inventory had revealed no serious shortages, and yet inventory seemed dramatically overstated. Why would inventory increase fivefold in one year? Suspecting something was wrong, the auditors performed some "midnight auditing." Their investigation revealed that the sheet metal inventory was grossly overstated. The auditors had almost been deceived. Local management had falsified the inventory by preparing fictitious records. The auditors had verified the amount of inventory shown on the tags and had deposited their verifications in a box in the conference room they used during the audit. A manager had added spurious tags to the box at night. However, since there was not enough time to fabricate a large number of reasonable tags, some were made to show very large rolls of sheet metal. The manager had also substituted new inventory reconciliation lists to conform with the total of the valid and spurious tags.

---

[1]Throughout this chapter, the names of the perpetrators and the companies have been changed.

The magnitude of the fraud was discovered when the auditors performed some analytical tests. First, they converted the purported $30 million of sheet metal inventory into cubic feet. Second, they determined the volume of the warehouse that was supposed to contain the inventory. At most, it could have contained only one-half the reported amounts; it was far too small to house the total. Third, they examined the inventory tags and found that some rolls of sheet metal would weigh 50,000 pounds. However, none of the fork lifts that were used to move the inventory could possibly lift over 3,000 pounds. Finally, the auditors verified the reported inventory purchases and found purchase orders supporting an inventory of about 30 million pounds. Yet, the reported amount was 60 million pounds.

Faced with this evidence, managers admitted that they had grossly overstated the value of the inventory to show increased profits. The budget for the sheet metal division called for increased earnings, and without the overstatement, the earnings would have fallen far short of target.

In this case, it was the relationship between amounts recorded and the weight and volume that the recorded amounts represented that did not make sense. Unfortunately, few managers or auditors ever think of examining physical characteristics of inventory. Sometimes, it is not unusual relationships that signal fraud but transactions or events that don't make sense. Such was the case with the following fraud:

Don R. was the business manager of Regal Industries. In this position, he often arranged and paid for services performed by various vendors. An alert accountant caught Don committing a fraud. The first symptom observed by the accountant was payments being made to an Oldsmobile dealership though the company only had a few company cars and all were Cadillacs. The accountant thought it strange that company cars were being serviced at an Oldsmobile dealership rather than at a Cadillac dealership. He knew that both cars were made by General Motors (GM) but still wondered about the transactions. Maybe the Oldsmobile dealership was closer, he reasoned. Upon checking, he discovered it was not. Further investigation by the accountant revealed that although payments had also been made to the Oldsmobile dealership for body damage on company cars, no claims had been filed with insurance companies. Then, the accountant noticed that payments of exactly the same amount were being made to the Oldsmobile dealer every month. The combination of Oldsmobile dealer, body damage without corresponding insurance claims, expenditures every month, and expenditures of the same amount did not make sense. He concluded that the only legitimate explanation for all these anomalies would be a fixed-fee maintenance contract with the Oldsmobile dealer to service the company's Cadillacs. An investigation revealed that no such maintenance contract existed. Further investigation confirmed that Don R. had a girlfriend who worked at the Oldsmobile dealership and that he was buying her a car by having the company make the monthly payments.

In this case, an alert accountant saved his company approximately $15,000. Unfortunately, many accountants and auditors would have missed this fraud. They would probably have seen the check being paid to the Oldsmobile dealer, matched it with the invoice that Don's girl-friend supplied each month, and been satisfied. They would not have asked whether the expenditure made sense or why Cadillacs were being serviced at an Oldsmobile dealership.

Recognizing analytical symptoms has always been an excellent method of detecting fraud. A successful fraud investigator revealed to us that he became interested in investigation when he discovered his first fraud back in 1956. This discovery, which determined his lifelong career, is one of the best examples of use of analytical symptoms we are familiar with. Here is the career-changing experience:

It was the summer of 1956. That's what I remember, at least, though it was a long time ago and things get distorted when you look back. And, I have looked back quite a bit since then, for the entire episode was quite an eye-opener for an 18 year-old kid. I was a "numbers man" then and still am. Mathematics is an art to me. I find a beauty in pure numbers that I never see in the vulgar excesses that most of society chases after. You might wonder, then, what I was doing working in a movie theater that summer—the summer that Grace Kelly became a princess and the whole country seemed to worship the cardboard stars on the silver screens. Well, the truth is I spent the summer in a movie theater because I needed employment. I'd just graduated from South High and was waiting to begin college. To earn money, I took a job as ticket taker at the Classic Theater. As movie theaters go, the Classic was con-sidered one of the best. Not in terms of elegance: it wasn't one of those gilt and velvet-lined monstrosities with fat plaster babies and faux chandeliers. No! What the Classic had was a certain charm in the same way that drive-in hamburger joints of the decade did. I think the style was called *deco-modern* and it made me feel a bit like I was rushing toward the 21st century. So the place wasn't all bad, though it wasn't the kind of job that a dedicated numbers man usually sought. But as it turned out, my numbers did come in useful. For that's how I caught on to him, you see; it was because of the numbers.

Ticket taking is not the most exciting job there is and I didn't find it a real intellectual challenge. My mind was free to wander, and I got in the habit of noting the number of each ticket that I tore: 57, 58, 59, 60. The numbers would march to me in a more or less consecutive order as they came off the roll that the ticket seller sold from: 61, 62, 63, 64. But sometimes, I noticed, the se-quence would be off. A whole chunk of numbers would appear that should have come through earlier: 65, 66, 40, 41, 42. It would happen almost every time I worked. I thought it was odd and was curious about what could be dis-turbing the symmetry of my numbers. The world of numbers is orderly and logical; for every apparent irrationality, there is an explanation. I began to use the puzzle as a mental game to occupy my working hours. Noting each time the sequence was off, I came to realize that it always happened after my daily break. The manager, Mr. Smith, would relieve me while I was on break. I watched closer and noticed another fact: the numbers would always be off while the ticket seller, who had the break after mine, was being relieved. Mr. Smith filled in for the ticket seller too.

Until this point, this amateur detective work had been merely a way to pass the time. Now, I began to suspect that something wrong was going on and it made me uncomfortable. After more observation and thought, I solved Mr. Smith's scheme. When he relieved me as ticket taker during my break, he would pocket the tickets instead of tearing them in two. Then, when he relieved the ticket seller, he would resell the tickets he had just pocketed and keep the cash. Thus, the ticket numbers that I saw coming through out of sequence were really coming through for the second time. The numbers gave him away.

Although this is small fraud that took place in a little theater, it illustrates that when things don't look right, they probably aren't right. If the ticket taker had not been fascinated with numbers, the manager probably wouldn't have been detected. The manager was trusted more than other workers. The number of tickets he pocketed was small in relation to the total number of tickets sold in a day, and so management didn't see a large drop in profits. Every night the bookkeeper computed the total number of tickets sold, using the beginning and ending ticket numbers, and compared the total to the cash taken in, but the balance wasn't off. The theater hired separate people to sell and take tickets specifically to avoid this type of fraud. But Mr. Smith was the manager and no one perceived a problem with letting him do both jobs while others were on break. There is probably no way Mr. Smith's fraud would have been caught if it hadn't been for a "numbers man" who saw relationships in the numbers that didn't make sense.

This same kind of relationship between numbers is available in financial statements. To individuals who really understand accounting, financial statements tell a story. The elements of this story must be internally consistent. Many large financial statement frauds could have been discovered much earlier if financial statement preparers, auditors, analysts, and others had understood numbers in the financial statements the way our friend the ticket taker understood his numbers.

One of the best examples of numbers that didn't make sense were the numbers in MiniScribe Corporation's financial statements. MiniScribe was a Denver-based producer of computer disk drives. Here is a description of the MiniScribe fraud and an analysis of the numbers in the firm's financial statements that didn't make sense.[2]

---

[2]Details of this fraud were taken from a number of articles, including "The Case of the Delayed Deliveries,"CFO, *The Magazine for Senior Financial Executives* 9, April 1993, p. 32; Cooking the Books," *The Wall Street Journal*, Sept. 18, 1989, p. A1; Brian Deagon, "Inventory Problems Hit MiniScribe," *Electronic News* 35, Feb. 6, 1989, p. 11; "Fraud Is Cited at MiniScribe," *The New York Times*, Sept. 13, 1989, p. D22; "MiniScribe Calls Data Not Reliable," *The New York Times*, May 20, 1989, p. A37; "MiniScribe, Citing Lawsuits, Makes Bankruptcy Filing," *The New York Times*, Jan. 3, 1990, p. D4; "MiniScribe Corp., Interim Report," *Standard & Poors Corporate Updates*, 1990, pp. 2107, 2463; "MiniScribe Files for Bankruptcy," *Electronic News* 36 Mar. 26, 1990, pp. 1, 54; "MiniScribe Takes a $40 Million Charge to Earnings," *The Wall Street Journal*, Dec. 4, 1989, p. A4; Stuart Zipper, "MiniScribe Execs, Others to Pay $128 Million in Colorado Settlement," *Electronic News* 38, June 8, 1992, p. 7; Stuart Zipper, "SEC to Ex-MiniScribers: Pay $10 Million," *Electronic News* 37, Aug. 19, 1991, p. 1 and Andy Zisper, "MiniScribe's Investigators Determine that Massive Fraud was Perpetrated," *The Wall Street Journal*, Sept. 12, 1989, p. A6.

On May 18, 1989, MiniScribe Corporation announced that the financial statements that had been issued for 1986, 1987, and the first three quarters of 1988 could not be relied upon because sales and net income had been grossly overstated.

In 1988, MiniScribe was voted the most "well-managed" personal computer (PC) disk drive company. The company had experienced an increase in sales from $113.9 million in 1985, a year in which it lost International Business Machines (IBM)—its largest customer—to a reported $603 million in 1988. In April 1985, Quentin Thomas Wiles was appointed CEO and director of the company, with the hope that he might lead the company, which was operating in the red, out of financial trouble. Under his management, the company's sales and profits seemed to increase, even though downturns in the market and severe price cutting were taking place within the industry. Unfortunately, the financial statement numbers were fraudulent.

Wiles had a reputation for using a strict, overbearing management style to reach his goal of turning failing companies into successes. At MiniScribe, he set stringent goals for each manager to increase sales and income and did not tolerate failure to reach these goals. In an effort to please Wiles, reports were forged and manipulated throughout the company. One marketing manager revealed that division managers were told to "force the numbers" if they needed to. Thus, the fraud began with managers simply touching up internal documents as they moved up the line. Wiles continued, however, to push for increases in sales, even during times of recession and price cutting within the industry. This pressure led managers to invent various schemes to make the company look better than it really was. Some of the schemes used were:

- Packaging bricks, shipping them, and recording them as sales of hard drives.
- Dramatically increasing shipments to warehouses and booking them as sales.
- Shipping defective merchandise repeatedly and booking the shipments as sales.
- Shipping excess merchandise that was not returned until after the financial statements had been released.
- Understating bad debts expense and the allowance for doubtful accounts.
- Changing shipping dates on shipments to overseas customers so that revenues were recognized before sales were made.
- Changing auditors' working papers.

The result of these and other schemes was a significant overstatement of net income and sales. Inventory records at the end of 1987 revealed $12 million on hand; in reality, it was more like $4 million. In 1989, the company booked a $40 million charge to income to offset these overstatements. On January 1, 1990, the company filed for bankruptcy, listing liabilities of $257.7 million and only $86.1 million in assets.

Several analytical symptoms indicated that things were not right at MiniScribe. First, MiniScribe's results were not consistent with industry performance. During the period of the fraud, severe price cutting was going on, sales were declining, and competition was stiff. MiniScribe Corporation reported increases in sales and profits, while other companies were reporting losses. MiniScribe had very few large customers and had lost several major customers, including Apple Computer, IBM, and Digital Equipment Corporation (DEC). MiniScribe was also falling behind on its payments to suppliers, indicating a severe cash flow problem. The company even began returning virtually all the merchandise it purchased from suppliers. Returns to suppliers forced the bankruptcy of MiniScribe's major supplier of aluminum disks, Domain Technologies.

In addition, numbers that were reported at the end of each quarter were amazingly close to the projections made by Wiles. Financial results were the sole basis for management bonuses. There were significant increases in receivables, and yet the allowance for doubtful accounts was far less than the industry average. An aging of receivables revealed that many accounts were old and would not be collectible. A simple regression analysis relating inventory to sales would have revealed that while reported sales were increasing, inventory was not increasing proportionately. Indeed, financial statement numbers did not make sense. Relationships within the statements, relationships with industry standards, and an examination of Miniscribe's customers provided analytical symptoms that suggested that something seriously wrong was occurring. Unfortunately, by the time these symptoms were recognized, investors, auditors, lawyers, and others had been fooled, and many people had lost money in the scam.

FRAUD SYMPTOMS INVOLVING RELATIONSHIPS WITH OTHER PARTIES

In today's complex world, an organization cannot exist without interacting extensively with other organizations, governmental agencies, and individuals. Sometimes, these interactions and relationships are of a nature that is symptomatic of fraud. Listed below are specific fraud symptoms involving relationships with others.

- Relationships with lawyers:
  Significant litigation.
  Frequent changes in legal counsel.
- Relationships with auditors:
  Frequent changes in outside auditors.
  Reluctance to give auditors needed data.
  Lack of internal auditors.
  Adverse opinion or disclaimer of opinion on financial statements.

- Relationships with board members:
  Unexplained resignation of board members.
  Frequent turnover of board members.
- Relationships with regulators and the IRS:
  Revoked licenses.
  Frequent reviews by regulators.
  Identification by regulators as being high-risk.
  Significant or frequent tax adjustments.
  Continuing problems with the IRS.
- Relationships with management:
  High turnover of management.
  New management.
- Relationships with banks and other lenders:
  High debt.
  Violation of debt restrictions.
  Use of several different banks.
  Inability to borrow, or poor credit.
  Existence of large contingent liabilities.
- Relationships with related parties:
  Existence of related-party transactions.
- Relationships with other companies:
  Pressure to merge, sell, or be taken over.
  Restructuring.
- Relationships with vendors or customers:
  High-volume new customers or vendors.
  Vendors or customers without Dun & Bradstreet reviews.

Change of Auditors

Examples of frauds that have involved one or more of these relationship symptoms abound. Many major management frauds, for example, have been discovered in companies that frequently changed their outside auditors. Most of these auditor changes occurred because of disagreements between companies and their auditors. Some firms have changed auditors when they thought their auditors were getting close to discovering a fraud.

An example of management fraud punctuated by a change in auditors was Lincoln Savings and Loan Association. As described previously, three different CPA firms were associated with Lincoln during the period 1985–88—Arthur Anderson & Co., Ernst & Young, and Deloitte & Touche. Lincoln Savings and Loan also was characterized by two other significant relationship symptoms. They were constantly on the S & L regulators' problem list, and the Ernst & Young partner in charge of the Lincoln account left Ernst & Young and accepted employment with Lincoln Savings and Loan, substantially increasing his salary. Even before leaving Ernst & Young, he wrote letters to regulators and others defending Lincoln and stating that his client was being harassed by regulators.

An example of a fraud involving an adverse audit opinion was the AFCO case which was described in Chapter 6. In this case, the outside CPA firm issued an adverse opinion because some of the assets on AFCO's financial statements had been stated at fair market value instead of at cost and because a large portion of AFCO's assets were comprised of a receivable and related interest due from the sale of property to a related party. Because of the related-party nature of the sale, the CPA firm could not determine whether or not the transaction was arm's-length.

In AFCO's case, the adverse opinion was a significant warning signal that something was wrong. As it turned out, the sale of land to the related company, the income from this sale, the receivable arising from that transaction, and the interest on the receivable were all misstatements that resulted from a phantom transaction. When the phantom sale and its impacts were subtracted from AFCO's balance sheet, all that remained was $1,299 in cash and some real estate that financial statement readers couldn't evaluate because it was recorded at market value. Total assets were far less than the $21 million represented by the company. AFCO's balance sheet and income statement, as originally issued, and as revised by an expert witness in the fraud trial, are shown in Figure 8–1.

The ZZZZ Best case is an example of a fraud that characterized the relationship symptom of "reluctance to give auditors needed data." (Note that the full company name was ZZZZ Best, but people refer to it as Z-Best, as we shall do here.)

> Barry Minkow grew up living with his family in one of the poorest sections of Reseda, in California's San Fernando Valley. At a young age, Minkow began accompanying his mother to work at the carpet cleaning business which she managed. At age 9, he started soliciting jobs by phone, and by age 10, he was cleaning carpets. During the next four to five years, he worked evenings and summers, and saved $6,000.[3]
>
> At age 14, Barry met 30-year-old Tom Padgett in a San Fernando gym. Padgett was unhappy with his life. Barry charmed Padgett and convinced him to take out a personal loan of $4,500. Barry used his savings of $6,000, Padgett's loan of $4,500, and another weight lifter's $1,500 to buy steam-cleaning equipment. Working out of his parents' garage, Minkow began a carpet cleaning

---

[3]Kevin Kelly, "Wall-To-Wall Trouble for the Carpet-Cleaning King," *Business Week*, July 13, 1987, p. 83.

FIGURE 8–1

AFCO
Balance Sheet and Statement of Income; and Retained Earnings

Balance Sheet

	Originally Issued		Restated
Assets			
Current assets:			
Cash	$1,299		$1,299
Current portion of contract receivable	276,084		-0-
Interest receivable	124,197		-0-
Total current assets		401,580	$1,299
Contact receivable long-term portion		8,373,916	-0-
Investment property:			
Real estate Jackson Village (at market)	$10,832,480		
Real estate Mountainland Hills	1,800,000		?
Total assets		12,623,480	?
		$21,398,976	$1,299 + ?
Liabilities and stockholder's equity			
Current liabilities:			
Accounts payable to related parties	$27,000		$27,000
Accrued interest	176,965		176,965
Current portion of long-term debt	902,944		902,944
Total current liabilities		1,106,909	$1,106,909
Long-term debt less current portion		12,781,688	12,781,688
Deferred income taxes		3,041,729	3,041,729
Contingencies			
Stockholder's equity:			
Common stock, par value $1.00, authorized 50,000 shares issued and outstanding, 1,000 shares	1,000		1,000
Appraisal increase	1,663,606		0
Retained earnings	2,804,044		?
		4,468,650	
		$21,398,976	

FIGURE 8–1 *(concluded)*

	Originally Issued		Restated
Gain on sale of Mountain Hills	$4,887,000		-0-
Interest income	324,197		-0-
Total income		5,211,197	-0-
Interest expense	627,796		627,796
General and administrative expenses	27,190		27,190
		654,986	654,986
Income before income taxes		4,556,211	($654,986)
Provision for federal and state income taxes		2,258,855	-0-
Net income		2,297,356	($654,986)

Note: These published financial statements were used in the prospectus and adjusted by Steve Albrecht for use in his expert testimony.

business, Z-Best.[4] When business improved, he hired his mother as office manager and employed his father in sales.[5] He seemed to be the model entrepreneur, except that he never actually made an annual profit.[6]

Initially, Z-Best was a legitimate enterprise. However, cleaning carpets was to become only a small part of the company's business. From the beginning, Minkow's desire to succeed led him to obtain capital by whatever means necessary. He arranged burglaries of his own home and car, so as to collect insurance money. He stole his grandmother's pearls after receiving a $2,000 loan from her. In 1984, he forged $13,000 in money orders from a Reseda liquor store.[7]

Minkow's appetite for money was insatiable. In 1985, a local bank issued him a merchant's account which allowed him to accept credit cards. During the next few years, whenever he was short of cash, Minkow would add false charges to customers' credit card fees. When complaints arose, Minkow would claim that dishonest employees or subcontractors were responsible. He would readily agree to return stolen funds to the customers and then would continue perpetrating his fraud. In the meantime, he would have the free use of customers' money for up to 3 months at a time.[8]

Minkow's dishonest activities escalated, involving more and more individuals. In one instance, Minkow established Interstate Appraisal Services, a fictitious company used to verify Z-Best's business dealings to potential investors. Tom Padgett was hired as the supposed owner and operator of Interstate.

[4]Kim Murphy, "ZZZZ Best: How the Big Bubble Burst," *The Los Angeles Times*, Mar. 30, 1989, sec. I, pp. 1, 21.

[5]Phillip Elmer DeWitt, "ZZZZ Best May Be ZZZZ Worst," *Time*, July 20, 1987, p. 56.

[6]Joanne B. Ciulla, "Nothing but ZZZZ Best," *The New York Times*, Feb. 25, 1990, sec. 7, p. 20.

[7]Ibid.

[8]Ibid.

Minkow used Interstate to convince bankers and investors that Z-Best had won large contracts from insurance companies to restore fire- and water-damaged buildings. In addition, Padgett forged documents and contracts to make Z-Best revenues look legitimate.

The company's situation worsened. New loans were signed just in time to cover payments coming due on existing loans. Because of his poor cash flow, Minkow resorted to borrowing money from a reputed mobster and convicted counterfeiter, at "loan-shark rates of 2 to 5 percent a week".[9] Z-Best also continued to fabricate restoration jobs to convince creditors and investors that the company had strong cash flows. Minkow and his associates felt confident that eventually they would be able to cover their tracks.

In December 1986, Z-Best made an initial public offering, generating $11.5 million in cash. As required by the offering, an audit of Z-Best's financial statements by an auditor in New Jersey was included in the prospectus. A limited review of the financial statements for one quarter was also included, using new auditors. To deceive their auditors and securities lawyers, Minkow even leased a building that was supposedly being restored in Sacramento to create the illusion of a Z-Best restoration job. Even though the auditors and lawyers actually inspected the building, they didn't see past the facade Minkow and Z-Best had created.[10]

After the public offering, Z-Best's credibility soared and banks became increasingly willing to extend loans. Z-Best's stock price skyrocketed. By March 1987, Minkow's shares were worth $64 million; a month later they had increased in value to $110 million.[11] With all the excitement on Wall Street, shares quadrupled from their offering price of $4 per share.[12] Barry Minkow was personally worth a purported $109 million.

Although Wall Street success assisted Z-Best during difficult times, the company still could not meet its debt obligations.

In spring 1987, Drexel Burnham Lambert agreed to underwrite a $40 million junk bond offering to allow Z-Best to acquire KeyServ, a nationwide carpet cleaning chain that generated its business through the country's premier retailer, Sears, Roebuck and Co. Minkow and Padgett counted on KeyServ's legitimate business to rescue Z-Best from its repayment burdens. It was to be the "big cure." However, before the deal with Drexel was closed, word of Z-Best's fraud was exposed, and Z-Best's new auditors and Drexel resigned. This spelled the end for Z-Best.[13]

In the author's opinion, two events led to the demise of Z-Best. First, on May 22, 1987, Daniel Akst, a reporter for *The Los Angeles Times*, published an article titled, "Behind 'Whiz Kid' is a Trail of False Credit Card Billings." The article revealed that during 1984 and 1985, Z-Best had accumulated $72,000 in false credit card charges. The article also reported false credit card charges at a flower shop owned by Z-Best's chief operating officer, totaling $91,000.[14]

---

[9]Jeff B. Copeland and Michael A. Lerner, "A Whiz Kid Goes Wrong," *Newsweek*, July 20, 1987, p. 40.

[10]Daniel Akst, "How Barry Minkow Fooled the Auditors," *Forbes*, Oct. 2, 1990, p. 129.

[11]Ciulla, op. cit.

[12]Alan Abelson, "Up and Down Wall Street," *Barron's*, May 25, 1987, pp. 27, 37.

[13]Murphy, op. cit., p. 21.

Minkow again blamed dishonest employees and subcontractors. He again re-paid customers. Despite Minkow's claim, the day after *The Los Angeles Times* article appeared, Z-Best stock lost 38 percent of its value.[15]

Second, an accountant who rented office space from Interstate approached Z-Best's new auditors and informed them that the restoration job in Sacramento was not legitimate. After investigating, the new auditors resigned.

Because the fictitious restoration projects accounted for 80 percent of reported revenues, Minkow had to hide the jobs from his outside auditors. Even though the new auditors had been engaged to performed only a review of one quarter rather than a full audit, the partner in charge of the engagement insisted on seeing some of the restoration projects. Because the projects did not exist, Minkow was hesitant. He finally agreed to allow the new auditors to see a major project if they would examine the property on a weekend and promise not to talk to others about it. He insisted that the reasons for these restrictive conditions were that he didn't want to interrupt construction work and he didn't want to give his competitors an advantage by revealing information about his projects. The new auditors agreed to both conditions for purposes of their limited review. Minkow then leased a building, quickly tore it apart to make it look as though it was under construction, placed "ZZZZ Best" construction signs all over the walls, and successfully fooled the auditors. If the original auditors had insisted on seeing construction projects on their own terms or on an unannounced basis during the full audit, it would have been very difficult for Minkow to hide his fraud.

Management Turnover

High management turnover and management new to the company are relationship symptoms that have been associated with numerous frauds. Regina Vacuum Company, for example (see Chapter 6) became a completely different company when Donald Sheelen became CEO. Nearly all the S & L's that failed during the late 80s and early 90s were firms that had changes in management and ownership during the 1983–85 period. Most of the new owners were real estate developers who used the acquired thrifts as their own personal banks. In most cases, the new owners and managers, who had little or no financial institution experience, got their thrifts started on a course of high direct investments in real estate and other assets, along with less reliance on

[14]Abelson, op. cit., p. 37.
[15]Ciulla, op. cit.

traditional home lending. Charles Keating III, who became CEO of Lincoln Savings and Loan, for example, had no financial institution experience. The job he held immediately before he became CEO of Lincoln Savings was as a busboy at a country club. His father purchased Lincoln Savings and made him CEO.

Probably the best example of a fraud perpetrated by new owners occurred in a company called AMI.

> AMI was a sleepy little old firm, just barely making it, when a man named Roy Ash took charge. He said, "I'm going to make this a go-go company. And pretty soon, instead of earnings per share (EPS) of 10:1, it's going to be 40:1. We're all going to get rich." To turn AMI around, he brought in a bunch of high-powered managers. The company as a whole, not just Ash, adopted a policy called *NBO*. Essentially, NBO meant that managers and Ash agreed on the goals for each division for the next period, and then Ash left managers alone to manage toward these goals. Implied in NBO was the idea that the goals were fair to begin with. However, as it turned out, Ash leaned on each manager at the start of each period and said, "Look, the company is going to earn $1.90 a share next year. Your share of that total is $0.42." As the year went along, periodic meetings between the manager and Ash occurred. If the manager was not on target to reach $0.42 a share, he or she would be told, "If you can't find a way to manage that goal, we'll find someone else who can."
>
> One of the ways AMI managers met their targets was to say, "Who cares when you cut the books off? A sale is a sale, right? Does it really matter whether we reach a little bit into next week and take some of the sales we ship next week and record them this week? After all, they were all made during this month anyway." Soon, one week stretched into two weeks, then three, until eventually is wasn't too hard for managers to say, "We know that customers are going to buy our products eventually; let's book the sales now." Consequently, AMI managed toward imposed objectives rather than toward reality. Finally, managers were reporting sales that were so far beyond reality that the company collapsed.

Related-Parties Transactions

Many frauds have been characterized by dishonest dealings between related parties. The Lincoln Savings and Loan case was one. Another was AFCO, which was referred to earlier in this chapter. The case of ESM Government Securities, a fraud that was discussed in Chapter 7, is probably the best example of a fraud involving related parties.

> ESM Government Securities was incorporated in 1975. The name was taken from the initials of the last names of its owners: Ronnie R. Ewton, Robert C. Seneca, and George G. Mead. ESM was established as an unregistered broker–dealer that traded mainly in repurchase and reverse repurchase agreements of government securities. A *repurchase*, or *repo*, involves selling government securities to a

customer and agreeing to buy them back later at a higher price. In effect, a loan is given to the dealer by the customer, who hopes for a higher return than the securities could have provided. A *reverse repurchase*, or *reverse repo*, involves purchasing government securities and agreeing to sell them back later at a fixed price—in effect, giving a loan to the customer.[16] Typically, the customer sells the securities because he or she anticipates being able to invest the cash from the loan at a higher rate than the securities are yielding. In either case, the securities are collateral for the loan. In order to make money, dealers must receive a higher rate of return than the interest rate that they are paying on loans. ESM did not receive higher rates. However, the company's public financial statements continued to appear strong.

ESM was losing money in very large amounts. In order to keep the financial statements strong, the losses, along with large amounts of cash, were transferred via fictitious intercompany transactions to another, unconsolidated company that was wholly owned by Ewton. The cash that was transferred to the second company immediately flowed to the pockets of Ewton and other ESM investors. However, not only ESM's purported financial position but also much of its collateral was illusory. ESM was able to stay in business only because the cash inflows from repos exceeded the cash outflow from reverse repos and drawings by the owners. Also, many of ESM's repo customers did not require delivery of the securities. The securities that ESM continued to hold were pledged repeatedly as collateral for loans from several different customers. "The net result of Government's transaction was substantial borrowing through term repos (liabilities) far in excess of money loaned through reverse repos (assets).[17] In fact, ESM had perpetuated this scam for at least six years before it was closed down on March 4, 1985. By then the fictitious transactions amounted to over $300 million.

The nature of these related parties was well known by anyone who read ESM's financial statements. The company's 1983 annual report contained the following footnote:

Note D—Security transactions

The company entered into repurchase and resale agreements with customers whereby specific securities are sold or purchased for short durations of time. These agreements cover securities, the rights to which are usually acquired through similar purchase/resale agreements. The company has agreements with an affiliated company for securities purchased under agreements to resell amounting to approximately $1,308,199,000 and securities sold under agreements to repurchase amounting to approximately $944,356,000 at December 31, 1983. Accrued interest receivable from and payable to the affiliated company at year end were $6,932,000 and $16,454,000 respectively.

---

[16]Dan Cook and other, "The Rise and Fall of Marvin Warner," *Business Week*, May 6, 1985, p. 105; Dan Cook and others, "Marvin Warner: The Man in the Middle of the ESM Collapse," *Finance*, Mar. 25, 1985, p. 63; and Robert J. Sack and Robert Tangreti, "ESM: Implications for the Profession," *Journal of Accountancy*, April 1987, p. 95.

[17]Sack and Tangreti, ibid.

The receivable from the related party, totaling $1,308,199,000, exceeded the payable to that same related party by $363,843,000. This raises serious questions about whether the receivable can ever be collected. Because total receivables and total payables on the financial statements were the same amount, this footnote means that receivables from outsiders were $363,843,000 less than payables to outsiders. There was no way ESM could have paid off this net liability, especially since it was short-term.

Unusual Relationships with Customers

There are many fraud symptoms involving relationships between a company and its customers. The following is a good example of fraud involving a strange and new relationship with a customer.[17]

John Richards entered the First National Bank of New York one day and opened up a checking account. In establishing the account, John presented three checks totaling $102,907.62 drawn on a German bank and denominated in German deutsch marks. The new accounts officer of the bank, realizing that the relationship with the customer was new, placed an "uncollected funds (UCF) hold" on the deposit. Unfortunately, UCF holds are valid only on checks drawn on US banks in US currency. The officer should have sent the checks to Germany for collection, which could have taken months, before giving the customer access to the funds. As it turned out, the checks were uncollectible. Five days later, the customer entered the bank and withdrew over $102,000 from the account.

In this case, John Richards embezzled over $102,000 from First National Bank. Since the average bank robber gets $2,300 per incident, John's theft was the equivalent of approximately 44 bank robberies. In essence, when he opened his account, he gave First National three worthless pieces of paper which the new accounts officer thought were checks. Five days later Richards walked out of the bank with $102, 000 in cashier's checks.

There were several red flags in this case. First, the relationship with the customer was new. Second, the amount involved was large. Third, the checks were drawn on a foreign bank. All three of these red flags are relationship symptoms that should have encouraged the bank officer to exercise extreme care.

A second fraud involving an unusual relationship with a customer also occurred in a bank.

A business that had been an account holder for four years made a deposit in Second National Bank consisting of one check for $31,358. The deposit was approved by the branch manager, and immediate credit was granted. A review of the account holder's history would have indicated that this was an unusually large transaction. In fact, due to recent returned items on the account, the branch was suspicious about the business. Deposits by this customer were normally under $4,000, and the branch had been placing UCF holds on the firm's deposits.

With this deposit, the manager recognized the account holder but did not question the large dollar amount. In fact, the check being deposited had been altered—raised by $30,000. The manager did not see this alteration on the check. The item was subsequently returned, and the bank lost over $30,000.

Unusual Relationships with Vendors

Unusual relationships with vendors have allowed many frauds. In most cases, the frauds have been punctuated by obvious red flags. In fact, there is probably no one area in which fraud is more prevalent and in which red flags are more obvious than the procurement area.

The three types of procurement fraud are: (1) frauds in which the buyer and the supplier act in collusion, (2) frauds in which the supplier acts alone, and (3) frauds in which the buyer acts alone. Two examples of the first type are a bank vice president who was charged with approving over $1 billion in bad loans in exchange for $585,000 in kickbacks and the CPA firm partner in charge of the ESM audit. ESM encouraged the audit partner to put pressure on another client who was doing business with ESM and was planning to discontinue the relationship. When he refused, ESM's management informed him of a major fraud the company was committing which his audits had missed. Rather than revealing his client's fraud, the audit partner accepted a $150,000 kickback from ESM's management as payment for concealing the fraud and putting pressure on his other client. With the audit partner's help, ESM was able to conceal a $300 million fraud for over seven years.

Red flags that indicate procurement fraud in which buyers and suppliers act in collusion are:

- Increasing costs due to paying too high a price.
- Customer complaints about receiving inferior products.
- Not receiving goods or services ordered.
- Buying unnecessary goods or services.
- Bid rigging.
- Courtesy billing.
- Employee complaints.

When a buyer becomes involved in fraudulent activities with a vendor, control of purchase transactions is transferred from the buyer to the vendor. Because perpetrators usually get even more greedy over time, prices usually increase, product quality decreases, or the volume of purchases from the favored vendor increases. An example of the transferring of control is evident in the following fraud:

The purchasing agent of a midsize municipality in the South was responsible for acquiring a long list of janitorial supplies, including mops, pails, soap, plywood, rakes and paper goods. Area paper jobbers, who were experienced connivers, approached the civil servant with a deal. "Without changing our invoice price," they told him, "if you agree, we can deliver a cheaper brand of paper towels. Half the extra is for us; the other half is for you." Once the purchasing agent had accepted a lesser brand, the supplier raised the price on the invoice and billed for five times the amount of merchandise actually shipped. What could the buyer do?

In this case, the buyer was trapped. He couldn't go to his supervisors and inform them that there was a fraud going on and that he was a participant in that fraud. Rather, he was forced to sit by and watch the paper jobbers become more and more greedy until they were finally caught.

Symptoms of procurement fraud in which a buyer is acting alone include:

Altered copies of company contracts, bills, etc.

Goods ordered for personal use.

Invoices from unapproved (fictitious) vendors.

Purchases of unneeded items.

An example of this type of procurement fraud is one committed by an employee of a retail company.

John Jones, 61 years old, was indicted for defrauding ABC Company of more than $2 million. When caught, he had been an employee for over 15 years and was responsible for leasing buildings to house ABC stores. On 22 occasions, he altered leases and forged letters billing ABC for fictitious legal and building maintenance services. He altered ABC's copy of the leases so that the company overpaid, and then he collected the excess payments.

Two additional cases of procurement fraud involving only company employees are described below.

Bill Brown, head of XYZ's public relations department, was indicted for defrauding the company of $1.1 million over four years. During the four years, he approved more than 150 invoices for services that were never rendered in connection with a newsletter XYZ considered publishing. Mr. Brown, who had a salary at the time of $124,000 per year, helped set up two dummy printing companies that bilked XYZ by submitting fraudulent invoices.

Dave Dunn, a $35,000 middle manager at LMN Company, embezzled $1 million over a 6-year period. The scam began when he decided to see whether he could get a fake invoice through the system. His job was to process bills from painters and carpenters who kept the company's headquarters sparkling. He forged the signature of a superior on an invoice for painting that was never done, submitted it to accounts payable, and told the clerk not to mail the check but to give it to him because the painter needed it in a hurry. Dunn then forged the painter's endorsement on the check and deposited it in his own account. So easy was his scam that he continued it for five years. He used the money to buy a $416,000 contemporary house, five cars, and an expensive motorboat.

The third type of procurement fraud, in which a supplier acts alone, is also usually punctuated by obvious red flags. Some of the more common symptoms of this type of fraud are:

- Substitution of lower-quality products or services.
- Billing for work not performed or hours not worked.
- Short shipping.
- Providing more goods or services than required.
- Using client facilities or products and charging for them.
- Padding overhead charges.
- Courtesy billing with other contractors.

An example of procurement fraud involving supplier only was the case of DEF Oil Company, which overbilled for fuel oil and delivered lower-quality fuel to one of its principal customers.

RST Chemical contracted with DEF Oil Company, a local wholesale dealer, to supply fuel oil for the company on a cost-plus contract. DEF overpriced its oil and also mixed sludge with the fuel oil to reduce its costs, but continued to charge RST the premium price. In addition to overpricing oil actually delivered, DEF also included charges on its invoices for oil that was never delivered. These charges were made to appear legitimate by regularly driving empty trucks to RST's location to give the impression that deliveries were being made. The fraud continued for four years and resulted in losses of $2.5 million to RST.

In each of these procurement fraud cases, relationships with real or fictitious vendors provided clues that, if understood, could have signaled that fraud was occurring. Even when the frauds involved buyers or suppliers acting alone, a hypothetical relationship was present. Sometimes that fictitious relationship involved a dummy company; at other times it involved a real company with unreasonable terms.

CONCLUDING COMMENTS

Analytical symptoms and unusual relationships with other entities and individuals often signal that fraud is present or that something is wrong. In fact, analytical anomalies, if they are understood, probably provide the single most reliable source of fraud symptoms for large management frauds and for investment scams. Relationships within financial statements follow certain logical patterns. When the patterns vary, it is usually because someone has manipulated numbers, balances, or relationships.

Like analytical symptoms, relationships between companies and individuals usually follow defined patterns. It is expensive to deal with lawyers, auditors, regulators, banks, and other parties. Costly changes in these relationships made without obvious reasons often signal some kind of problem.

With both analytical and relationship symptoms, it is *changes* that provide clues to fraud. Auditors, managers, investors, and others who recognize unusual or unexplained changes as fraud symptoms will not be victimized nearly as often as those who don't.

Chapter Nine

Fraud Symptoms
Tips and Complaints, Changes in Behavior or Lifestyle, and Demographics

This chapter concludes our discussion of fraud symptoms. Here we cover four well-known classes of fraud indicators: (1) tips and complaints, (2) changes in behavior, (3) changes in lifestyle, and (4) demographic indicators.

FRAUD SYMPTOMS

Tips and Complaints

Auditors are often criticized for not detecting more frauds. Yet, because of the nature of fraud, auditors are often in the worst position to detect its occurrence. The factors that make fraud possible were depicted in Figure 2–1 as a triangle consisting of pressure, opportunity, and rationalization. Interestingly, fraud can also be illustrated as a triangle, as shown in Figure 9–1.

The theft act involves the actual taking of cash, inventory, information, or other assets. Theft can occur manually, by computer, or by telephone. Concealment involves the steps taken by the perpetrator to hide the fraud from others. Concealment can involve altering financial records, miscounting cash or inventory, or destroying evidence. Conversion involves selling or transferring stolen assets into cash and then spending the cash. If the asset taken is cash, conversion means merely spending the stolen funds. As we have noted previously, virtually all perpetrators spend their stolen funds.

Fraud can be detected at all three stages: first, at the theft act stage, by witnessing someone taking cash or other assets; second, at the concealment stage, by recognizing altered records or miscounts of cash or inventory; and third, at the conversion stage, by focusing on the lifestyle changes that perpetrators almost inevitably make when they convert their embezzled funds.

FIGURE 9–1
The Three Elements of a Fraud

Who in an organization is in the best position to recognize fraud at each of these stages? Certainly, at the theft act stage, it is not the auditors. Auditors are rarely present when funds are stolen. Rather, they spend one or two weeks on periodic audits and thefts usually stop during the audit periods. Instead, it is co-workers, managers, and other employees who are usually in the best position to detect fraud at the theft act stage.

At the concealment stage, auditors do have a chance to detect fraud. If audit samples include altered documents, miscounts, or other concealment efforts, auditors may detect fraud at this stage. However, company accountants and even co-workers are probably in a better position to detect fraud at the concealment stage.

At the conversion stage, the auditors are definitely not in the best position to detect fraud. There is no way, for example, that auditors could recognize certain changes, such as when an employee who used to drive a used Ford Pinto, begins to drive a new BMW or Lexis. Likewise, auditors won't recognize as unusual activities such as wearing Gucci socks, taking expensive vacations, buying expensive jewelry, or buying a new home with stolen funds. Auditors don't have a reference point from which to see these *changes* in lifestyle. Again, it is co-workers, friends, and managers who should detect fraud at the conversion stage.

In all three of the fraud elements, it is co-workers and managers who are in the best position to detect fraud. Unfortunately, co-workers and managers are usually the least trained to recognize fraud or even be aware that it can exist. Even so, many frauds are detected when an employee, a friend, a manager, a customer, or another untrained person provides a tip or complaint that something is wrong. One large company, for example, that uncovered over 1,500 individual frauds during 1992, discovered 43 percent of them on the basis of customer complaints or employee tips.

Complaints and tips are categorized as fraud symptoms rather than actual evidence of fraud because many tips and complaints turn out to be unjustified. It is often difficult to know what motivates a person to complain or provide a tip, but customers, for example, may complain because they feel they are being taken advantage of. Employee tips may be motivated by malice, a desire to even a score, personal problems, or jealousy. Tips from spouses and friends may be motivated by anger, divorce, or blackmail. Whenever tips or complaints are received, they must be treated with care and considered only as fraud symptoms. Individuals should always be considered innocent until proved guilty and should not be unjustly suspected or indicted.[1]

> As an example of a spurious tip, consider the one provided by Joan M., who worked in a bank. After work one day Joan approached the branch's operations manager and informed her that two weeks ago she had seen Jean C. place a bundle of bills (currency) in her blouse. She said that for two weeks she had not been able to sleep and so she had finally decided to inform the bank. For two weeks, auditors and security people scoured the bank's records and cash vault. Employees cried, and suspicion and distrust abounded. Finally, it was discovered that Jean had been sleeping with Joan's boyfriend and Joan's tip was false and motivated by jealousy. When the truth was learned, Joan quit. Because of the nature of the event that aroused the jealousy, branch management couldn't inform all employees about what had happened. Jean was never again fully comfortable working in the bank but could not afford to quit.

In most organizations, there are co-workers and others who have knowledge or suspicions that fraud is occurring but do not come forward with their information. Here are five reasons for this hesitancy. First, usually it is impossible to know for sure that fraud is taking place. Fraud is unlike murder or bank robbery, in that there are no dead bodies or videotapes of the crime. All the potential informants see is symptoms. They may see someone who is living a changed lifestyle, behaving strangely, or stashing company inventory in a garage. Because they recognize that they are seeing only symptoms, they don't want to take the chance of accusing the other person wrongly. Even when their suspicions are strong, the possibility exists that there is a legal and legitimate reason for the symptom.

The second reason most informants are hesitant to come forward is that they have read or heard horror stories about what happens to whistleblowers. Even though such reports are usually anomalies and are often exaggerated, people do fear that they will suffer by losing their jobs or undergoing some other kind of reprisal if they become informants.

Third, employees and others are often intimidated by perpetrators. Especially when the perpetrator is a superior, subordinates are afraid to come forward with their suspicions. For example, one fraud continued for

---

[1]Throughout this chapter the names have been changed.

six years even though several co-workers knew about it, because the per-petrator had such a dominant personality. He literally made others afraid of him, and he fired people who questioned his integrity.

Fourth, most of us have been conditioned to believe that it is not good to squeal on others, even when they are doing something wrong. Techni-cally, one who has been taught not to squeal is an *ethnological liar*. Not squealing is the creed of the Mafia. As an illustration of people's general reluctance to squeal, consider the following actual event that happened to one of the book's authors.

Scott Albrecht is Steve's oldest son. When he was a junior in high school, he en-rolled in a word processing class. He was informed that students' grades for the class would be mostly determined by how many processed projects they com-pleted. Students were informed by the teacher that they must work alone and, in fact, that working together constituted cheating and would result in an F grade for the course. One night, Scott informed his dad that the best grade he could get in word processing was a B unless he cheated, and then he could probably get an A.

"What do you mean," Steve asked?

"Well," said Scott, "our grades are mostly based on the number of jobs we complete. And while we have been told we must work alone, a number of stu-dent groups have formed in the class. Within these groups, each member com-pletes a certain number of projects and then they all copy each other's disks as though they had completed the projects themselves. There is no way I can complete an many projects alone as a group of three or four students can. I have been invited to work in a group but I don't know whether I should. What do you want me to do, Dad? Should I cheat and get an A or settle for a B?"

Needless to say, Steve was quite upset. While he didn't want Scott to cheat, he didn't want him to be disadvantaged and earn a B either. His counsel to Scott was to do neither but to go to the teacher and inform her what was hap-pening. Scott's quick reply was "I can't." Steve then asked Scott if he was afraid to inform the teacher. Scott pointed out that he was an all-state quarter-back and convinced his dad that he wasn't afraid. Rather, "these are my friends," he said, "and it wouldn't be right to squeal on them."

"But they are hurting your grade and possibly putting you at a disadvan-tage in getting into college." Steve argued.

"Still, I can't turn them in," Scott maintained.

As it turned out, Steve and Scott discussed this issue until 3:00 A.M. before Scott finally agreed that he should approach the teacher with his knowledge that cheating was occurring. Once informed, the teacher took appropriate action.

A fifth reason most employees and others don't come forward with their suspicions or knowledge of fraud is that organizations don't make it easy for them to do so. In most organizations, employees don't know whom they should talk to if they suspect fraud, how the information should be conveyed, or what the consequences will be if they do come forward. In addition, they don't know whether their tips will remain anonymous or their squealing will be exposed.

Organizations that are effective in using tips and complaints as fraud symptoms have learned that they need to nourish and encourage employees in order to receive tips. They have learned that employees must be given easy avenues for whistleblowing and be encouraged to come forward. Domino's Pizza, for example, has a hot line for drivers to call if managers send them out with so little time that they would have to speed and break the law to get the pizza delivered within the allotted 30 minutes. Complete anonymity is guaranteed. Another company has packaged fraud with other undesirable actions such as drug use, safety violations, discrimination, and harassment, and has trained all employees what to do if they see any of these. In this company, the training has taken the form of seminars for new hires; posters and other periodic reminders; a billfold card that is given to each employee, which lists alternative actions they can take if they witness violations; and videos that are periodically shown as reminders of the program. Employees are told, and the information is reinforced on the billfold card, that they have five options if they suspect problems in any of these areas: (1) they can talk to their manager or to their manager's manager; (2) they can call corporate security at a specified number; (3) they can call internal audit at a specified number; (4) they can call a companywide ombudsman, who will forward the complaint or tip; or (5) they can call an 800-number hot line that connects them to an outside answering service, which screens the calls, guarantees anonymity, and forwards the information to relevant company individuals who can deal with the problem.

The hot line should not be considered a substitute for maintenance of an open environment in which employees can feel comfortable about reporting known or suspected fraudulent activities. Employees should be encouraged to first consider reporting such activities to someone in their management chain, to an internal auditor, or, to corporate security, or to legal counsel. They should, however, be kept aware of the hot line option and encouraged to use it if they are not comfortable with other options.

Companies that provide hot lines have detected numerous frauds annually which would not otherwise have been detected. These companies have also reported use of the hot line as erratic, including periods of considerable use and periods of very little use. What is important is to make an option available to employees who would not otherwise report suspected activities.

Many organizations use hot lines that are managed by third parties. Other organizations have gone so far as to reward employees for legitimate tips. While we strongly endorse hot lines and while the research evidence suggests that they are an excellent fraud detection tool, the evidence and our personal experience on rewarding employees for tips is mixed at best. However, the following companies do offer rewards and do believe that their rewards have paid significant dividends:

- Bloomingdales awards employees $2,500 for valid tips.
- Alexander's awards employees $1,000 for valid tips.
- Another company offers one year of chances in New York's twice-weekly lottery.
- Marshall Field's doubled its reward to $500 from $250 and saw the number of rewards increase by 70 percent, the number of thieves caught increase to over 500 per year, and inventory losses drop from 3.3 percent to 2.1 percent.

Two frauds that have been detected by tips and complaints are the GE fraud and the Revere Armored Car Company fraud. GE's fraud went as follows:[2]

In 1982, John Michael Gravitt, a machine foreman at GE, stood up at an assertiveness training session and told the class that GE was ripping off the government. He told approximately 30 colleagues that the time cards going into supervisor's offices weren't the same ones coming out. Within a few minutes several other foremen stood up to confirm Gravitt's story. Even after his outburst in the assertiveness class, Gravitt's superiors still pressured him to coax his subordinates to cheat on their time cards. Gravitt was told that if his subordinates would not alter their own time cards, he was to do so. When Gravitt refused, his supervisors altered the cards for him. According to Gravitt, the process was hardly subtle. "With black or blue felt-tipped pens, they (the supervisors) altered the billing vouchers. Usually they scrawled the number of a project safely within cost constraints over the number of a job that was already running over budget. Foremen who refused to falsify vouchers had their vouchers sent to the unit manager, Robert Kelly. Kelly would then complete the blank vouchers himself. When Kelly died, his successor, Bill Wiggins, continued the falsification of time cards and billing vouchers. At one time, Wiggins told Gravitt that GE was like a great big pie and that everyone who participated (in cheating) got a piece; those who didn't participate didn't get a slice.

Falsifying at GE became a way of life. One foreman confessed to personally altering 50 to 60 percent of his subordinates' time cards during an eight-month period. Once, when Gravitt told his foreman that he could go to jail for altering cards, the foreman replied that he was only carrying out orders and that there wasn't any chance of getting caught.

---

[2]The description of this fraud was taken mostly from an article entitled "Bounty Hunter: Ex-Foreman May Win Millions for His Tale about Cheating at GE," which was written by Gregory Stricharchuk and published in *The Wall Street Journal* on June 23, 1988 (p. A1).

Finally, Gravitt decided he needed to alert someone who could do something about the problem. One weekend he slipped into a secretary's office and photocopied about 150 altered time cards and billing vouchers. He wrote an eight-page letter explaining what had been going on. The next week, delivered the letter and the photocopies to Brain H. Rowe, the senior vice president in charge of the engine plant. The same day, Gravitt was dismissed from GE.

A subsequent investigation by the FBI and the Defense Contract Audit Agency revealed that $7.2 million of idle time had been falsely billed to the US government. They also found that 27 percent of the time-sheet vouchers in the shop where Gravitt worked had been falsified during the three years Gravitt worked at GE.

In this case, John Gravitt's tips were the sole reason fraud was detected. Certainly GE didn't make it easy for Gravitt to come forward. GE's fraud highlights many of the mistakes that companies make regarding informants. Even though Gravitt knew with certainty that fraud was occurring, the firm's punishment and intimidation of whistleblowers and their not making it easy to come forward concealed the fraud for a long time.

A second fraud that was revealed by tips was the Revere Armored Car case, in which the informants were competitors.[3]

The revelation of fraud at Revere Armored Car began when some competitors, tired of losing customers to Revere's cutthroat prices, employed a video camera. The competitors taped a Revere delivery in December 1992 of $100 million to the NY Federal Reserve Bank's Buffalo branch. They were hoping for evidence of shoddy security. They got it. In the parking lot of a highway restaurant, the tape showed the driver and a guard leaving the truck locked but unguarded, its engine running, while they went inside to eat. The competitors presented their tape to Lloyds of London, the underwriting group that had insured Revere for $100 million. The tape was aimed at demonstrating to Lloyds the "ease with which someone could whack'em." The videotape prompted Lloyds to hire an investigator to check out Revere. Among other things, the investigation turned up evidence of past wrongdoings. Based on the evidence, federal authorities launched a predawn raid on Revere headquarters and found what could be the biggest scandal ever in the armor-truck industry: millions of dollars missing, allegedly pilfered by Revere owners Robert and Susanna Scaretta. Of the $84.6 million that banks say they had in storage at Revere, only $45 million was discovered. Apparently the Scarettas had run up significant gambling debts; they may have been using Armored Car as a money-laundering operation for illegal gambling proceeds. Several banks lost considerate amounts of money in this fraud. Citicorp's Citibank lost more than $11 million, and Marine Midland Bank lost nearly $34.8 million.

---

[3]The description of this fraud was taken from Fred R. Bleakley, "Suspicions of Rivals Open Up a Scandal at Armored-Car Firm," *The Wall Street Journal*, Feb. 17, 1993, p. A1.

This fraud was allowed to continue because banks and Lloyds of London didn't perform adequate due diligence. Neither the banks nor Lloyds were regularly monitoring Revere's operations. If it hadn't been for the tip from competitors, this fraud might still be going on today. Revere had been commingling funds of different banks rather than keeping each bank's funds separate. Even though large amounts had been stolen, it was always able to have enough money on hand to satisfy auditors of any one bank at a given time.

Changes in Behavior

Research in psychology reveals that when a person (especially a first-time offender, as many fraud perpetrators are) commits a crime, he or she becomes engulfed by emotions of fear and guilt. These emotions express themselves in an extremely unpleasant sensation called *stress*. The individual then exhibits unusual and recognizable behavior patterns to cope with the stress, as shown in Figure 9–2.

Some recognizable behavior changes are: insomnia; increased drinking; the taking of drugs; unusual irritability and suspiciousness; inability to relax; lack of pleasure in things the person usually enjoys; fear of getting caught; inability to look people in the eye; showing embarrassment around friends, co-workers, and family; defensiveness or argumentativeness; unusual belligerence in stating opinions; confessing (either to a religious figure or to a psychologist or other professional); obsessively contemplating possible consequences; thinking of excuses and finding scapegoats; working standing up; sweating; and increased smoking. It is not any particular behavior that signals fraud; rather, it is *changes* in behavior. People who are normally nice may become intimidating and belligerent; people who are normally belligerent may suddenly become nice.

We have seen several cases of changed personalities in fraud perpetrators. A woman who stole over $400,000 said, "I had to be giving off signals. I couldn't look anyone in the eye." A man who embezzled over $150,000 said, "Sometimes I would be so wound up I would work 12 or 14 hours a day, often standing up. Other times I would be so despondent I couldn't get off the couch for over a week at a time." Eddie Antar, mastermind of the Crazy Eddie fraud, became very intimidating and then finally vanished. His fraud went as follows:

> Crazy Eddie, Inc., a 42-store retail company located in New York, New Jersey, Connecticut, and Pennsylvania, sold entertainment and consumer electronic products. After hiring as officers his father, his brother, his uncle, his cousin, and his father's cousin, he allegedly overstated inventory by over $65 million. As the fraud progressed, he was said to become increasingly overbearing.

FIGURE 9–2
The Psychological Aftermath of Crime

Finally, overwhelmed by fears that he would be caught and prosecuted, he skipped the country and ended up in Israel. He has since been extradited back to the United States and is now facing charges for his fraud.

Two other examples of changes in behavior motivated by the stress caused by committing fraud were the behaviors of both Donald Sheelen, CEO of Regina Vacuum Company and Lester B. Nay, CEO of First National of Chicago. Although their actions were different, neither was able to cope with the stress. Although his fraud had not been discovered, Donald Sheelen went to his priest and confessed his entire scheme. Lester B. Nay's actions were even more dramatic. After penning a suicide note detailing how he had defrauded investors of millions of dollars, he took his life. However a perpetrator copes with the stress caused by guilt—by being intimidating, by confessing, or by committing suicide—stress always seems to be present.

This tale of a fraud that occurred in a small company provides sufficient detail to illustrate how stress can change the behavior of a perpetrator.

Johnson Marine is an industrial diving company that services marine-related problems all over the eastern United States. The firm salvages downed aircraft in oceans, lays submarine pipelines, inspects dams, conducts insurance recoveries, and performs search-and-rescue missions. Johnson's part-time accountant, Rick Smith, uncovered a serious fraud that had been perpetrated by Joseph Simons, vice president of the company. Rick had been hired by Johnson's office manager. His first encounter with Joseph Simons involved an argument between Simons and the office manager; Simons was angry because the office manager had hired an accountant without his permission. Joseph Simons was the accountant's immediate supervisor. Joseph basically told the accountant that he was to report *only* to Joseph, to pay bills *only* when Joseph asked, and to ask *only* Joseph whenever he had a question. It was apparent to Rick that the office manager was heavily intimidated by Joseph. Joseph not only treated the office manager like a slave but also continually reminded him that if he didn't mind his own business, he would no longer be with the company.

The accountant's first job was to update all the balances in accounts payable. Upon close inspection, he found very few of the 120 accounts payable balances to be correct. He spent a week fixing them on the computer, only to be criticized by Joseph. Joseph said that the accountant should spend his time on more productive work and not worry about trivial things. When the accountant opened the petty cash box and tried to identify the petty cash system, he found none. He found that no petty cash reconciliation had been done in over five months and that a negative difference of $13,600 existed between checks written to replenish the cash box and total receipts in the cash box. Rick immediately went to Joseph to tell him what he had found and was told to make an adjusting entry on the computer to fix the problem.

The accountant talked to the company president that afternoon and explained the situation. The president confronted Joseph, but Joseph explained that the office manager should have been keeping tabs on the petty cash fund. Joseph also assured the president that any money he had used had been properly accounted for. During the accountant's first two weeks, Joseph asked Rick to hold his (Joseph's) paycheck and said that he would accept his pay when the company was doing better. The third week, when the president was out of town, Joseph told Rick to pay him for this week and for the last two weeks. Rick thought this order was strange, since the company was not doing noticeably better. When he went to the payroll setup menu, the accountant noticed that Joseph's salary was *higher* than the president's. When the president returned a few days later, the accountant asked the president why the vice president was making a higher salary than he was. The president exploded and called Joseph into his office. Heated words were exchanged. Joseph weaseled his way out of being fired. He then pulled Rick aside and chewed him out for telling. Since Rick was only a part-time accountant and figured he should be more loyal to the president than to Joseph, he started telling the president about every little discrepancy he discovered.

Rick's next discovery came when he reviewed the company's life insurance policies, two of which were for over $1 million. Joseph Simons was listed as the beneficiary. Next, Rick noticed that large balances were being accrued on the company's American Express card. Although overdue notices were being received, Joseph forbade Rick to pay the bill. When Rick asked the president about it, the president informed Rick that the company did not have an American Express card! Yet, the balance was over $5,500. A similar problem was occurring with the Phillips 66 bill. Again, Joseph told Rick not to pay the bill, even though final notices were being sent. Rick later learned that the company used only Chevron cards.

Looking back over the accounts payable balances, Rick noticed an account with TMC Consulting that had an outstanding balance over 90 days old. He tried to find out more about the account, but there was nothing on file. By coincidence, while he was looking at the account information, Rick noticed that the address was 10 Windsor Circle, the same address to which Rick had sent a diving catalog that was addressed to Joseph two weeks previously. Upon printing out a history of the company's transactions with TMC Consulting, Rick found a series of five $2,000 payments on the account spread over a period of several months. He presented this information to the president, who confronted Joseph. Joseph stalled the president until the next day but never came back. Investigation revealed that he had moved to California, leaving no forwarding address.

In this case, Joseph's intimidating personality had kept the office manager and others at a distance. Although the office manager seemed to know something was wrong, he had never been given the chance to find out. The office manager had always been blamed by Joseph when petty cash was out of balance, yet he had never been allowed to balance it. In fact, Joseph had constantly blamed others for problems. In retrospect, employees understood that Joseph's intimidating behavior was his way of keeping the fraud from being discovered and of dealing with the stress he felt because he was committing the crime.

Once in a while, someone commits a fraud or other crime and does not feel stress. Such people are called *sociopaths* or *psychopaths*. They feel no guilt because they have no conscience. Fortunately, psychopaths are rare. The following individual was one.

> Confessed killer Marvin Harris's ability to pass a lie detector test left two nationally known polygraph experts baffled and anxious to question the dealer in bogus documents on how he passed the test.
>
> Harris pleaded guilty to the bombing deaths of two people, which he said he had carried out to avoid exposure of his fraudulent documents dealings. He had been judged truthful during an earlier polygraph test and had denied his involvement with the slayings. The two nationally known polygraph experts who declared Harris truthful wondered how he had beat the test.
>
> For planting the bombs that killed two people, Harris received a prison sentence of five years to life. By entering into the plea-bargain, he may have avoided the death penalty the original first-degree murder counts could have carried. As part of his plea-bargain, Harris promised to provide details of the crime.
>
> What was most puzzling to the polygraph experts was that Harris didn't just sneak by on the tests. On the plus-minus scale used to gauge truthfulness, a score of plus 6 would have been considered a clear indication the subject was not lying; but Harris had scored twice that—plus 12. The experts were simply wrong.
>
> Apparently, Marvin Harris had no conscience—and because he had no conscience, he felt no guilt about creating bogus documents, and he felt no guilt about killing people.

Extravagant Lifestyle

Most people who commit fraud are under financial pressure. Sometimes the pressures are real; sometimes they represent mere greed. Once perpetrators meet their financial needs, they usually continue to steal, using the embezzled funds to improve their lifestyles. Often they buy new cars. They may buy other expensive toys, take vacations, remodel their homes or move into more expensive houses, buy expensive jewelry or clothes, or just start spending more money on food and other day-to-day living. The authors have met very few perpetrators who saved what they stole. Indeed, most immediately spend everything they steal. As they become more and more confident in their fraud schemes, they steal and spend increasingly larger amounts. Soon they are living lifestyles far beyond what they can reasonably afford. To illustrate how people's lifestyles change when they embezzle, consider the following three examples (The third was first cited in an earlier chapter).[6]

> Kay E. embezzled nearly $3 million from her employer. She and her husband worked together to perfect the scheme over a period of seven years. Because they knew they might someday get caught, they decided explicitly not to have children and bring them into the fraud. With their stolen funds, they purchased a new, expensive home (supposedly worth $500,000) and five luxury cars—a Maserati, a Rolls Royce, a Jeep Cherokee, and two Audis. They filled their home with expensive artwork and glass collections. They bought a boat and several expensive computers, and they paid cash to have their yard extensively landscaped. They invited Kay's co-workers to frequent parties at their home and served lobster and other expensive foods. Yet, none of the employees pursued the change in lifestyle. They didn't note, for example, that Kay drove a different car to work every day of the week and that all her cars were extremely expensive.

> Randy W. stole over $600,000 from the small company he worked for, which was owned by a friend of his. The business constantly had cash flow problems, but Randy drove a Porsche, bought a cabin in the mountains, and took expensive vacations. At one point, he even loaned his friend, the owner of the business, $16,000 to keep the business going. Never once did the owner question where the money was coming from, even though Randy W. was being paid less than $25,000 per year.

> Irma J. worked as a new-accounts clerk for First National Bank for 37 years. During the first 33 years, she was an honest employee. Then, something changed in her life: She became a grandmother to two beautiful children. Irma became engulfed in the desire to provide material gifts for her two grandchildren. She started buying them everything. Soon, she became a TV home shopping addict, buying thousands of dollars worth of merchandise every week. To support her habit, she embezzled money, using customers' certificates of deposit (CDs). She would issue 1099 forms to the customers, using her home computer. Over a period of four years, Irma embezzled over $650,000. When she was caught, she had no money in her bank account. She had spent every penny. Today, Irma is in prison. The bank now owns her home, her retirement savings, and even her husband's retirement savings from another employer. Irma still owes the bank over $200,000. When she gets out of prison in a year, she must go to work and start making restitution payments to the bank. If she fails to make regular payments, she will violate the conditions of her parole and will go back to jail.

A smart crook would save embezzled money for several years before spending conspicuously. However, very few crooks, at least among the ones who are caught, are smart. The same motivation that encourages them to steal seems also to impel them to seek immediate gratification. Embezzlers are people who take shortcuts to appear successful. An embezzler who steals and saves is almost an oxymoron. People who can delay gratification and spending rarely also possess the motivation to be dishonest.

Lifestyle changes are often the easiest of all symptoms to detect. If managers, co-workers, and others would pay attention, they would notice embezzlers living lifestyles their incomes don't support. While lifestyle symptoms provide only circumstantial evidence of fraud, it is evidence that is easy to corroborate. Bank records, investment records, and tax return information are difficult to access, but it is easy to check property records, Uniform Commercial Code (UCC) filings, and other records to determine whether assets have been purchased or liens have been removed.

Demographic Indicators

The final category of fraud indicators discussed in this book is demographic symptoms. While many perpetrators are first-time offenders, some have criminal records or tainted backgrounds that, if known, would signal caution. Unfortunately, because of strong privacy laws in the United States, it is often difficult to discover information about a person's background.

Every day we seem to read of a medical doctor or some other "qualified" individual who has perpetrated a major fraud by claiming to have education or training that he or she simply didn't have. One such fraudster was John C. Nelson.[4]

Philip Crosby, author of the book *Quality Is Free* and a former vice president of International Telephone & Telegraph (ITT), started Philip Crosby and Associates, Inc. (PCA), in 1979. The company was based in Winter Park, Florida. Through his company, Crosby preaches to Fortune 500 executives and others about the necessity of producing quality, error-free products, so as to remain competitive in the world market. Indeed, his firm is one of the largest quality consulting firms in the world. Crosby wove his own values into PCA, creating a supportive and communicative environment. Crosby expressed his philosophy by saying, "If people have pride in working for the company and feel that the company is open and honest with them, they

---

[4]The following description was taken from Hoshua Hyatt, "Easy Money," *Inc.*, February 1988, pp. 19–96.

don't steal from it." PCA was growing fast. In 1985, an office was opened in Brussels. This expansion into foreign markets made it necessary to hire a financial expert who had a knowledge of foreign reporting rules and who could translate the foreign figures into a US accounting system. PCA hired John C. Nelson to fill this role. Nelson was described by references as "rock-solid reliable, with a keen mind to boot." One company reference said that it was sorry to lose him and told PCA how lucky it was to have him. It was later discovered that this reference was written by Nelson's wife, who was an employee of the referring company. Nelson supposedly had an MBA degree and a perceptive understanding of the foreign marketplace. He seemed like an honest, qualified individual.

Nelson's responsibility was to develop financial controls for PCA's international operations and to facilitate the flow of data from foreign units into the parent company, so that the data could be consolidated into PCA's financial statements. He was to provide a balance sheet and a P&L (profit and loss) statement for each office. He flew to Brussels to meet with some of the officers and staff there and to familiarize himself with the system. He bought some software which he claimed would facilitate the smooth flow of data, hung an Illinois CPA license on his office wall, and then went to work.

Nelson's boss, James Gunshanan, noticed that Nelson was slow in converting the foreign figures into US currency (usually not a difficult task for a CPA) and that his monthly reports were up to three weeks late. Nelson took another trip to Belgium, but the trip didn't seem to help.

The employees in Brussels described Nelson as being distant and difficult to build rapport with. When he was in Winter Park, he rarely attended company activities and never invited other employees to his home. He just kept to himself.

In September 1986, the deadline for the third-quarter numbers for the Belgium division passed. Nelson kept on coming up with seemingly feasible excuses, blaming the Brussels bookkeepers and the computer. The reports weren't ready until just before the SEC deadline. It wasn't PCA's style to allow upper management to step in. The company philosophy was that such interference would mess up the operation of a group. The managers assured one another that Nelson was doing a better job on other projects. Nelson came across as learning very quickly.

At the end of 1986, Nelson's bookkeeper quit. This put Nelson solely in charge of all the money that came through the international subsidiary. Nelson fell further and further behind in the bookkeeping. He was coming to work less and less often missing up to a week at a time. Finally, Gunshanan confronted Nelson about his poor work performance. Nelson told Gunshanan that he had a personal problem and that he would talk to him later. Later he did go into Gunshanan's office, broke down, and cried. He told Gunshanan that he had cancer and only had three months to live and that he wanted to spend the time he had left with his son. When Gunshanan asked Nelson what he was going to do about finances during that time, Nelson's reply was "Don't worry about me. I've always believed in socking something away."

For two consecutive quarters, PCA had trouble in producing the kind of earnings it had achieved in the past. PCA stock plunged from $20 to about $12.

On March 2, 1987, the controller of PCA, Pam Forrest, tried to make a transfer of about $500,000 from one account to another. The banker informed Forrest that there was not enough money in the account to complete the transaction. Forrest immediately started scanning the ledgers of wire transfers, looking for irregularities. She found an unposted transfer of about $82,000 to a US company named Allied Exports for shipping products to Brussels. The transaction just didn't look right. Wire transfers are not usually made to domestic companies, and also the money went through South Bend, Indiana, on its way to Brussels. Forrest had heard Nelson talk of South Bend as his home town. Something seemed fishy. Forrest looked through the files to find documentation of the transaction. Neither a contract nor a purchase order was found.

Forrest continued her search for unusual wire transfers and found several others to South Bend. Allied Exports, Allied Services, Allied Management, and other companies (all variations on the name "Allied"), were engaged in the mysterious wire transfers. Every transfer was made to a bank in South Bend.

PCA called the state of Indiana to investigate the incorporation papers and find out who the president of Allied was. The president was someone named Patricia Fox. Nelson's wife was named Patricia Fox Nelson. Nelson's name was immediately taken off the company's accounts, and the overseas managers were told to check bank documentation for irregularities.

Nelson had succeeded in fooling the bookkeeper—PCA's only check on him—by copying Gunshanan's signature on authorization documents and contracts and photocopying the documents. Nelson had shown the bookkeeper the photocopies and assured him that originals were in his files.

By the time Nelson's fraudulent activities were discovered, he had successfully embezzled nearly $1 million from PCA.

Nelson's wife called and attempted to remove $230,600 from Allied's bank in South Bend, but PCA was able to put a freeze on all Allied's accounts for 10 days. A search warrant was obtained, and the investigators proceeded to search Nelson's house for further evidence. A lockbox was found containing Allied's canceled checks, monthly statements, and incorporation papers. An Air Force discharge form was also found, with the name painted out. Nelson's wife was arrested on probable cause of grand theft, but her husband escaped.

Two weeks into the investigation the detective on the case ran across information that John C. Nelson had just received a driver's license in a Winter Park suburb. The detective called Nelson, and the man who answered the phone said he was a loan officer at a bank. Gunshanan went to this man's home to investigate and found that the man was indeed named John C. Nelson, but he was not the right John C. Nelson. The detective showed this man mug shots, and the real John C. Nelson correctly identified the accused Nelson as his old boss—Bruce Fox. Fox had been fired from the Indiana bank because it was discovered that he served an 18-month jail sentence for embezzling $400,000. He apparently had stolen John C. Nelson's personnel file and assumed his name and identity.

The police lab uncovered the name on the Air Force discharge form; it was Robert Walter Liszewski. The Air Force verified the name and matched the fingerprints. "Bruce Fox" was an assumed name.

In hiring employees, it is very important to thoroughly check a person's background. Instead of calling only one previous employer, two or three should be called. In addition, if positive information isn't conveyed, gratuitously, this should probably be interpreted as a negative signal. In addition, people who hire should be trained in interviewing techniques. They should know, for example, that it is legal to ask about past convictions. Unfortunately, most people are afraid to ask tough questions; they do not conduct thorough background checks because they don't want to take the time. Because of the increasing number of dishonest people, this lackadaisical attitude will result in more and more fraud losses in the future. Many organizations do not seek prosecution but merely terminate fraud perpetrators; thus there are large numbers of current employees who have embezzled from previous companies. One such employee is John Doe, whose frauds were briefly described in chapter 4 (see Figure 4–1, p. 39). Stealing from a succession of companies that merely terminated him, John perpetrated increasingly large frauds, as shown in Figure 9–3.

While information about an individual's past is difficult to find, it is not impossible. A growing number of databases can be quickly checked to see whether a person has had negative publicity. As stated in Chapter

FIGURE 9–3
John Doe, the Repeat Offender

Company (Position)	Job Tenure		Amount Embezzled
Life insurance company (salesperson)	10 months		$200
Bakery (office manager)	1–2 years		? (Repaid $1,000)
Manufacturing company (bookkeeper)	1 year		$30,000
Service company (accountant)	1–2 years		? (Repaid $20,000)
Manufacturing company (accountant and office manager)	2 years		$31,000
Communications company (controller, then CFO; salary $130,000/yr)	6 years	Year 1	$49,700
		Year 2	96,200
		Year 3	155,100
		Year 4	327,300
	Presently	Year 5	289,900
Communications company (manager)	employed	Year 6	445,500
		Total	$1,363,700

6, NEXIS, for example, is a database containing newspaper articles from major US newspapers. The Prentice-Hall Legal and Financial Services database is another great source of information on whether individuals have had past legal or other problems. Moody's and other financial sources can provide information on how long a company has been in existence and who its auditors are. There are many ways to discover adverse information on individuals or organizations one is contemplating hiring or doing business with. Unfortunately, most people and most companies do not make the effort or are too naive to go to the trouble of checking the available sources.

We conclude this section on demographic symptoms by considering the following lawsuit (first described in Chapter 3), which was filed a number of years ago.

> A famous singer checked into a hotel run by a well-known chain. After becoming comfortable in her room, she heard a knock at the door. Following the knock came the words, "Room service." She knew she hadn't ordered anything but thought that since she was famous maybe the hotel was giving her flowers, wine, or a basket of fruit. When she opened the door, three custodians of the hotel barged into her room and raped her. The singer sued the hotel for $4 million and won. She donated the proceeds to charity. The basis of her lawsuit was that the hotel had not done a good job of screening its employees. All three had previous arrest records and had been fired from previous jobs because of rape.

Anyone who has studied criminology knows that rapists have a very high rate of recidivism. In fact, as mentioned in Chapter 4, one source stated that rapists commit an average of 170 rapes during their lifetimes. If the actual number is anywhere close to 170, problems at this hotel were predictable. When a hotel hires convicted rapists and allows them to have contact with hotel guests, sooner or later there will be problems. The same is true of fraud perpetrators. If an organization hires dishonest employees or does business with individuals who have dishonest backgrounds, sooner or later it will have problems. Fraud perpetrators who are not forced to confess their dishonesty to family members and others close to them or who are not forced to face justice have a high rate of recidivism.

Not long ago a friend telephoned one of this book's authors. He said, "You remember Marla my bookkeeper." "Yes," we replied. "Well," the friend said, "she stole $1,000 from me. What should I do?" "Fire her and seek prosecution," was our answer. "I couldn't do that; she is a wonderful employee," came the response. "If you don't, she will steal from you again," we told him.

Needless to say, the friend continued to employ Marla. After three months she stole again. This time, however, the amount was $22,000, not $1,000.

CONCLUDING COMMENTS

A friend told us the following story.

> Once there was a wealthy old man. This man loved his money so much that he had very few friends. In fact, he only had three. One was his lawyer, who helped him take advantage of other people. The second was his minister, whom he went and confessed that he had taken advantage of other people. The third was his accountant, who helped him keep track of his money. The old man, knowing he would soon die, called his three trusted friends together. "Listen," he said, "I am getting old. Soon I will die. I have been wealthy all my life and I can't stand going to the grave poor. I am going to give you each an envelope with $50,000 in it. When you come to my funeral and viewing, I want you to put these envelopes into my casket. I want to take some of my money with me to the grave." The three friends agreed to accommodate their wealthy friend.
>
> Soon, he died. They each went by the casket and deposited their envelopes. The casket was sealed and his body was interred.
>
> A short time later, the minister called the other two. "We've got to get together and talk," he said. "I've got a guilty conscience."
>
> At the meeting, the minister said, "I thought about the poor members of my congregation and I thought about that money rotting down there in the grave and I just couldn't do it. I put only $25,000 in and kept $25,000 for my poor members."
>
> After a brief pause, the lawyer spoke up. "Well," he said, "that rich fool asked me for free legal advice so often I felt he owed me. I, too, put only $25,000 in."
>
> "I can't believe you would do it. I can't believe you would be so dishonest," said the accountant. "I want you to know that in my envelope was a check for the full $50,000."

Was the accountant dishonest or was he just smart? Did he commit a fraud, or was he more clever than the other two? Such ambiguities are part of the nature of fraud. Sometimes we don't know whether fraud has occurred or whether losses and other symptoms stem from an honest mistake or an unintentional error. Unlike murder cases, in which a dead body is found and there is no question whether a crime has been committed, there are no dead bodies in fraud cases. All we see are symptoms. We may see the accountant in the above case acting strangely. We may see him change his lifestyle and buy an expensive automobile. In other cases, we may see other symptoms. Fraud is detected by recognizing and pursuing *symptoms!* We have used a lot of space in this book to explain fraud symptoms, because recognizing symptoms is the most important part of detecting fraud. When symptoms aren't recognized, fraud goes undetected. When symptoms are recognized, there is at least a chance that dishonest acts will be discovered. Managers, employees, investors, and others need to be trained to watch for and recognize fraud symptoms. It is the only way to make a dent in the growing problem of fraud in this country.

PART

III

THE INVESTIGATION OF FRAUD

Once fraud is suspected, an investigation is often undertaken to determine whether or not a fraud actually occurred, as well as the who, why, how, when, and where of the fraud. There are four classes of investigative procedures. The first class, theft act investigative procedures, is discussed in Chapter 10. Chapter 11 covers concealment investigation techniques, including computer searches. Conversion investigative techniques, including public records searches and the net worth method, are presented in Chapter 12. Chapter 13 covers inquiry investigative methods, including honesty testing, interviewing, and interrogation. Chapter 14 concludes the investigation section by providing a complete fraud report documenting the investigation of a kickback-type fraud.

Chapter Ten

Theft Act Investigative Methods
The Fraud-Triangle-Plus Approach

Fraud symptoms were discussed in Chapters 6 through 9. When symptoms are observed, a decision must be made whether or not to investigate. The purpose of investigation is to find the truth—to determine whether the symptoms actually represent fraud or whether they represent unintentional errors or other factors. Fraud investigation is a complex and sensitive matter. If it is improperly conducted, innocent individuals can be irreparably injured, guilty parties can go undetected and be free to repeat the act, and the offended entity can be left with incomplete information as a basis for prevention of similar incidents or recovery of damages.

The investigation of fraud symptoms within an organization must have management's approval and can be quite expensive. Investigation should be pursued only when there is reason to believe that fraud has occurred or when "predication" (affirmation) is present. The overall purpose of an investigation is to determine the truth. More specifically, the objectives are to determine:

- Who? The possible perpetrators and their levels of complicity in the fraud.
- Why? The motivation for the dishonest acts.
- How? The way in which the fraud was perpetrated.

TWO APPROACHES TO FRAUD INVESTIGATION

There are many fraud investigation methods. In the past, when conducting fraud training, the authors have classified types of fraud investigative methods in two different ways. The first was to separate investigative techniques into four categories based on the types of evidence they

FIGURE 10–1
The Evidence Square

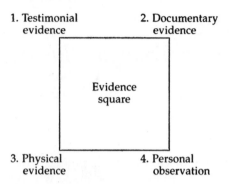

1. Testimonial   2. Documentary
   evidence   evidence

Evidence
square

3. Physical   4. Personal
   evidence   observation

produced. Using this approach, we refer to the *evidence square*, shown in Figure 10–1. This square shows that four types of evidence can be accumulated in a fraud investigation, as follows:

1. *Testimonial evidence* is gathered from individuals. Specific investigative techniques used to gather this sort of evidence are (a) interviewing and (b) honesty testing, such as graphology or polygraph examination.[1]

2. *Documentary evidence* is gathered on paper, via computer, and from other written or printed sources. Specific investigative techniques for gathering documentary evidence include (a) document examination, (b) public records searches, (c) audits, (d) computer searches, (e) net worth calculations, and (f) financial statement analysis.

3. *Physical evidence* includes fingerprints, tire marks, weapons, stolen property, identification numbers on stolen objects, and other tangible evidence that can be associated with the dishonest act. The gathering of physical evidence often involves forensic analysis by experts.

4. *Personal observation* involves evidence that is sensed (seen, heard, felt, etc.) by the investigators themselves. Personal observation investigative techniques involve (a) invigilation (which is described below) and (b) surveillance and covert operations.

---

[1]The authors do not necessarily advocate either type of honesty testing. They are included here in order to comprehensively cover all options.

FIGURE 10–2
The Three Elements of a Fraud

Another, and we believe preferable, way to classify investigative techniques is to use the fraud triangle, which has already been discussed in Chapter 9. As you will recall, the three elements of a fraud are the theft act, concealment, and conversion (see Figure 10–2).

Using this approach, investigative techniques are classified into those that focus on (1) *the theft act,* (2) *concealment efforts,* and (3) *conversion methods.* A fourth classification of investigative techniques is labeled *inquiry methods.* Theft act investigative methods involve efforts to catch one or more perpetrators in the embezzlement acts or to gather information about the actual theft acts. Common theft act investigative techniques include (1) serveillance and covert operations, (2) invigilation, and (3) physical evidence. Concealment investigative methods focus on the cover-up attempts of the perpetrator. Common concealment investigative techniques include (1) document examination, (2) audits, (3) computer searches and queries, and (4) physical counts of assets.

As noted previously, very few fraud perpetrators embezzle and save. Rather, they quickly spend their stolen assets. Conversion investigative techniques focus on the spending of stolen cash or on the conversion of other stolen assets into cash and then the spending of the cash. Common conversion investigative techniques involve (1) public records searches and (2) net worth analysis.

While the fraud triangle is a convenient way to classify most investigative techniques, it leaves out two of the most commonly used methods. Both of these methods involve querying people—witnesses, informants, sources, and suspects—in one way or another. The most common inquiry investigative techniques are (1) interviewing and (2) various forms of honesty testing, including polygraphs, graphology, and paper-and-pencil honesty tests.

In summary form, then, the four investigative methods are classified as shown in Figure 10–3. We will use the fraud-triangle-plus approach in discussing investigative techniques in this book.

FIGURE 10–3
*Classification of Investigative Methods: The Fraud-
Triangle-Plus Approach*

1. Theft act investigative methods
    1. Surveillance and covert operations
    2. Invigilation
    3. Physical evidence

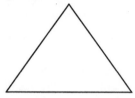

2. Concealment investigative methods
    1. Document examination
    2. Audits
    3. Computer searches
    4. Physical asset counts

3. Conversion investigative methods
    1. Public records searches
    2. Net worth analysis

Inquiry investigative methods
    1. Interviewing and interrogation
    2. Honesty testing

THEFT ACT INVESTIGATIVE METHODS

In deciding which investigative methods to use, it is important to focus on
the strongest type of evidence for the specific fraud being investigated. For
example, because inventory frauds involve the transporting of stolen goods,
it is often easiest to investigate such frauds by using theft act investigative
techniques. On the other hand, payroll frauds, such as charging excess overtime or adding ghost employees to the payroll, can usually be most easily
investigated by focusing on concealment efforts. Such frauds must be concealed in the records of an organization, and it is usually quite easy to gather
documentary evidence. With collusive or kickback-type frauds, however,
there is usually no documentary evidence except maybe purchasing records
showing increasing prices or increasing work by a particular vendor. As a
result, theft act and concealment investigative techniques usually don't
work well in kickback investigations. With such frauds, it is often necessary
to gather circumstantial public record evidence showing a lifestyle beyond
what the perpetrator's known income can support. Inquiry investigative
methods are usually helpful in investigating all types of frauds.

In investigating frauds it is usually best to begin by using investigative techniques that will not arouse suspicion and, most important, will not wrongly incriminate innocent people. Therefore, initially it is probably best to involve as few people as possible, to avoid using words such as "investigation"(words like "audit" and "inquiry" are more acceptable), and to start the investigation by using techniques that will not likely be recognized. As the inquiry proceeds, investigative methods will work inward toward the prime suspect, until finally he or she is confronted in an interview.

For example, if a purchasing employee is suspected of taking kickbacks, the investigation might proceed through the following seven steps.

1. Check the employee's personnel records for evidence of liens or other financial difficulties, or for previous problems.
2. Perform a "special audit" of the purchasing function, to examine trends and changes in prices and purchasing volume from various vendors.
3. Search public records and other sources to gather evidence about the suspect's lifestyle.
4. Perform surveillance or other covert operations.
5. Interview *former* buyers and *unsuccessful* vendors.
6. Interview *current* buyers, including the suspect's manager, only if no collusion with management is suspected.
7. Simultaneously interview the suspected buyer and the suspected vendor.

Several of these steps can be performed without arousing suspicion. For example, security personnel, auditors, and fraud examiners commonly examine personnel records during normal audits. Similarly, purchasing records and public records searches usually don't create suspicion, because they are normal audit procedures or because they can be performed off site.

Surveillance, when properly performed, is done without the perpetrator's knowledge. Only when interviews begin is the suspect likely to become aware of the investigation. Even then, interviews should normally be conducted first with individuals who are objective and are not currently associated with the suspect, and should work inward until the suspect is finally interviewed. The purposes of starting tangentially and working inward are to avoid alerting suspects that they are under investigation too early and to avoid creating undue stress or suspicion among other employees. In addition, this process best protects the subject of the investigations, especially if evidence later reveals that the individual was not, in fact, involved.

Coordinating an Investigation

When beginning a fraud investigation, it is often helpful to prepare a *vulnerability chart* as a method of explicitly considering the most likely suspects. A vulnerability chart coordinates the various elements of the possible fraud, including (1) assets that were taken or are missing, (2) individuals who have theft opportunities, (3) theft act methods, (4) concealment possibilities, (5) conversion possibilities, (6) symptoms observed, (7) pressures of possible perpetrators, (8) rationalization of perpetrators, and (9) key internal controls that had to be compromised for the theft to occur. For example, assume that a bank customer complained that a deposit she made last month was not credited to her account. If it were determined that fraud by an employee was a possibility, a vulnerability chart might be prepared similar to the one in Figure 10–4. A vulnerability chart involves coordinating the various aspects of fraud to determine possible suspects, thus forcing the investigator to consider *all* fraud elements.

As shown in the top section of this vulnerability chart, the assets that may have been taken included the customer's deposit. Theft opportunities may have been available to the teller who processed the transaction, to an operations officer who supervised the teller, or to the proof operator who processed the credit to the customer's account. Movement of the assets was easy and could have occurred by entering a credit into the wrong account, placing the checks (if the deposit involved checks) in the cash drawer and withdrawing cash, stealing cash, or falsely endorsing checks. Concealment was possible by destroying the customer's deposit slip, creating a new deposit slip, or forging a signature. Since the stolen funds involved cash, conversion opportunities were unlimited. Symptoms observed might include changed behavior, an improved lifestyle, or another customer complaint. Pressures motivating the fraud could have involved a tax lien against the teller's property, an expensive new home purchased by the proof operator, or a recent divorce by the operations officer. Rationalizations could have involved past feelings by any of the possible perpetrators of being underpaid or treated poorly. Key internal controls that would have had to be overridden could have involved not allowing an employee to enter credits into his or her own account, use of processing jackets in the proof department, teller omits certification, or restricted access to the computer system.

Similar vulnerability charts can be prepared for any potential fraud. For example, frauds involving stolen inventory and overcharged goods are also shown in Figure 10–4. The advantage of using a vulnerability chart is that it forces investigators to explicitly consider all aspects of a fraud.

FIGURE 10–4
Vulnerability Chart

Assets that Were Taken	Persons to Whom Theft Opportunities Were Available	Ways in Which Movement Was Possible	Concealment Method	Conversion Possibilities	Symptoms Observed	Motive		Key Internal Controls
						Pressures	Rationalization	
Customer deposit	Teller Operations officer Proof operator	Entering verified credits Stealing check; endorsing it	Destroying deposit slip Forged signature Entering credit in own account	Unlimited	Changed behavior Changed lifestyle Customer complaint	Tax lien New home Divorce	Feels underpaid or poorly treated	Use processing jacket Certification Teller counts customer receipts
Goods delivered	Receiving Trucker	Not received Truck	Night Including with trash	Fenced Used personally	Control not followed Goods not counted	New car Spouse laid off	Passed over for promotion	Receiving report
Overcharged for goods	Purchasing agent	N/A	Kickback	Cash Hire spouse	Extravagant lifestyle Asset sold inexpensively	Maintain lifestyle	Greed	Bids

Surveillance and Covert Operations

Surveillance is a theft act investigation technique that relies on the senses, especially hearing and seeing. Technically, there are three types of surveillance: (1) stationary or fixed point, (2) moving or tailing, and (3) electronic surveillance. In covert or undercover operations an agent is placed in an undercover role that is not disclosed to the suspect. Surveillance and covert operations are legal as long as they don't invade a person's reasonable expectation of privacy under the Fourth Amendment to the Constitution ("the right of a person against unreasonable searches shall not be violated").[2] Simple fixed-point or stationary observations can be conducted in routine fashion by anyone and are effective. Observation means watching and recording (on paper, film, or magnetic tape) the physical facts, acts, and movements which form part of a fraud. In conducting a static or fixed-point observation, the investigator should locate the scene that should be observed, anticipate the action that is most likely to occur at the scene, and either keep detailed notes on all activities involving the suspect or record them on film or tape. The detailed records should include the date and day of observation, the name of the observer, the names of corroborating witnesses, the position from which the observation was made and its distance from the scene, and the time the observation began and ended, along with a detailed time log of all the movements and activities of the suspect. Figure 10–5 shows the surveillance log of an investigation of someone who was suspected of taking kickbacks from a vendor.

Mobile observation, or tailing, is much more risky than stationary surveillance. In fact, we personally know of an internal auditor who was shot at while tailing a suspect. While the potential rewards for this type of surveillance are high and may include identifying the receiver of stolen goods or the payer of bribes or kickbacks, the chances of failure are high. We recommend that tailing be done only by professionals.

Electronic surveillance of employees with video cameras is another form of surveillance that is frequently used. It is often of limited value in the investigation of fraud and other white-collar crimes, and its use also raises concerns regarding employees' privacy whether it is used in the workplace and or outside the office or plant. One corporation we know of has instituted strict controls over all forms of electronic surveillance, including video, electronic mail (E-mail) privacy, and access to PCs, to name a few potential forms of surveillance. We recommend that legal counsel and human resources always be consulted before any form of surveillance takes place. In addition, all corporations and institutions should implement strict protocols regarding the use of any form of

---

[2]There are also some state privacy laws that limit the use of surveillance and other court operations.

FIGURE 10–5
Surveillance Log

Time/Date	Event
January 29, 1994	
6:30 PM	Instituted surveillance at Flatirons Country Club, 457 W. Arapahoe, Boulder, CO.
6:40 PM	Alex Tong and unidentified white male seen leaving racquetball courts and entering locker rooms.
7:00 PM	Both men seen leaving locker room.
7:05 PM	Tong and white male enter club restaurant and order drinks. White male orders beer, Tong orders orange liquid drink.
7:10 PM	Twosome order dinner.
7:25 PM	Dinner arrives. Tong has white, cream-based soup and club sandwich. White male has steak and potatoes.
7:30 PM	Break: Surveillance terminated.
7:36 PM	Surveillance reinstituted. Twosome still eating at table.
7:55 PM	Tong goes to rest room. White male remains at table.
8:00 PM	Tong returns to table.
8:15 PM	Twosome order two drinks.
8:25 PM	White male requests check.
8:30 PM	Check arrives and is presented to white male. White male hands credit card to waitress without examining check.
8:35 PM	Waitress returns, gives bill to white male, who signs bill. Waitress gives yellow slip to white male. No indication of Tong attempting to pay check.
8:40 PM	White male removes envelope from portfolio and gives it to Tong. Tong looks pleased and places envelope in his pocket. Twosome leave and are seen getting into a Mercedes Benz and a 1993 Lexus, respectively, and driving away.
8:45 PM	Waitress is interviewed. She displays a copy of a Citibank Gold Mastercard charge slip in the name of Christopher D. Ballard, account number 5424-1803-1930-1493, in the amount of $47.89. Waitress is given $20 cash tip for information.
9:00 PM	Surveillance terminated.

surveillance, to ensure that controls are in place and that a "reasonable person" test is given to any application. The net value of surveillance can be more than offset by employee problems caused by inappropriate or improper application of surveillance.

Undercover operations, in which the true role of an operative or an agent is undisclosed to the suspect, are both legal and valid, provided they are not used as fishing expeditions. Undercover operations are extremely costly and time-consuming and should be used with extreme care. We recommend using undercover investigations only when (1) large-scale collusive fraud or crime is likely, (2) other methods of fraud investigation fail, (3) the investigation can be closely monitored, (4) there is significant reason to believe the fraud is occurring, (5) the investigation is in strict compliance with the laws and ethics of the organization, (6) the investigation can remain secretive, and (7) law enforcement authorities are informed as soon as possible.

Recently, the authors have been involved in three undercover operations. One had to do with suspected collusive fraud, and the other two were concerned with suspected drug dealing at manufacturing facilities. (Drug dealing is an activity which no organization can tolerate, because if an employee purchases and uses drugs on the job and then is involved in an automobile accident on the way home from work, for example, the organization may be legally liable for damages.) Of the three operations, only one was successful. The undercover agent was able to get valuable evidence that led to the conviction of several individuals. In the second operation, the agent became scared and quit. In the third, the agent became sympathetic to the suspects and was not helpful. These incidents highlight some of the risks involved in undercover operations.

Invigilation

Invigilation is a theft act investigative technique that involves close supervision of suspects during an examination period. In invigilation, such strict temporary controls are imposed on an activity that, during the period of invigilation, fraud is virtually impossible. As we have already indicated, opportunity is one of the three conditions that must exist before fraud can occur. When controls are made so strict that opportunities to commit fraud are nonexistent, a fraud-free profile can be established. If detailed records are kept before, during, and after the invigilation period, evidence about whether fraud is occurring can be obtained. The following diagram outlines an invigilation:

Before invigilation (detailed records are maintained)	*Invigilation period (detailed records are maintained)*	*After invigilation (detailed records are maintained)*
14–30 days	*14–30 days*	*14–30 days*

The following is an example of use of invigilation to detect a fraud involving inventory losses:

An oil distributor was experiencing inventory losses of 0.23 percent of the inventory. The manager suspected that fraud was taking place but was not sure how or when. Observation and other investigative methods failed to produce evidence. For a 30-day period, the installation was saturated with security guards and auditors. Every movement of goods both in and out was checked, all documents were verified, and inventory and equipment were regularly checked. During the period of invigilation, losses ceased. After the invigilation, records kept at the plant were examined for absolute, proportional, and reasonableness changes during the invigilation period. It was noted that two service stations—which before the exercise had bought an average of only 2,000 gallons of gasoline a week—suddenly doubled their orders. During the 30 days, in fact, each received more than 19,000 gallons. It was further discovered that a shift foreman who in 23 years of service had taken no sick leave was away from work on 19 of the 30 days. Two or three months were allowed to elapse, and during this time, covert observation was kept on the service stations, whose orders by this time had reverted to 2,000 gallons per week. Using night vision equipment and cameras, unrecorded deliveries to the service stations were detected. The owners were interviewed, and their books were examined. They were subsequently charged with fraud extending back two years and involving 62,000 gallons of gasoline. The shift foreman was not involved. Inquiries suggested that he was a loyal and trustworthy employee. His absence had been caused by the serious illness of his wife.

This example of invigilation took place in a large company and involved losses in inventory. Invigilation can also be used as a fraud investigation tool in smaller organizations and when cash is the stolen asset. The following example illustrates such a scenario:

Mark W. owned an auto tune-up shop. The company had 12 bays, 12 mechanics, and one accountant, John S. Mark trusted John completely. John handled all accounting duties, including cash receipts, bank deposits, the writing of checks, payroll, and taxes. Each year, Mark's business serviced more cars, but each year cash flows became worse. Not knowing what to do, Mark consulted a friend, who was a CPA. The friend performed various cost, volume, and profit analyses and informed Mark that he should be profitable. He suggested to Mark that maybe someone was embezzling money. Mark's reply was that the only one that was in a position to embezzle was John and he was sure that John, his good friend, was honest. The CPA friend encouraged Mark to try an experiment which was essentially an invigilation. He suggested that Mark first make copies of all bank statements and other cash records for one month. Next, Mark should tell all employees, including John, that he was thinking about selling the shop and that the prospective buyer insisted on daily audited records for one month. During this month, an outside CPA would come daily to count cash receipts, to make bank deposits, to write all checks, and to check on parts and inventory. After one month, Mark was to inform all employees that the sale had fallen through and that it was business as usual. Following the invigilation period, Mark was again to copy bank statements and other cash records for one month.

To Mark's surprise, cash paid by customers as a percentage of total receipts (customers either paid by check, credit card, or cash) was 7 percent before the invigilation period, 15 percent during the one-month invigilation period, and again approximately 7 percent in the month following the invigilation period. Mark became a believer quickly. Faced with the evidence, John admitted that he had been embezzling cash from Mark's business. A subsequent analysis revealed that the total amount he had stolen exceeded $600,000.

Invigilation is a fraud investigative technique that can be expensive; it should be used only with top management's approval. It is important when using invigilation to restrict it to a discrete and self-contained area of business. Most commonly, it is used in such high-risk areas of expensive inventory, areas with poor controls over the receipt and loading of goods, and areas with poor controls over accounting records.

When using invigilation, it is important to decide on the precise nature of the increased temporary controls necessary to remove fraud opportunities. It is also important to analyze past records to establish an operating profile for the unit under review. This profile must include such things as normal losses, the number and nature of transactions per day, the number and type of exceptional transactions, and the number of vehicle movements in and out of the facility. In order to get an accurate reading, it is generally agreed that the invigilation period must be at least 14 days in length. In individual cases, however, the optimal duration will depend on the frequency and nature of transactions.

Once in a while, invigilation backfires. One company, for example, was suffering significant small tool losses from its manufacturing plant. In order to determine who was taking the tools, the company decided to check all workers' lunch boxes as they exited the facility. The practice so upset employees that they caused a work slowdown which was more expensive than the fraud losses.

Physical Evidence

The final theft act investigation technique is the use of physical evidence. While physical evidence can be used in fraud cases, it is more commonly associated with other types of crimes, such as property crimes, murder, rape, and robbery. This technique involves analysis of objects such as inventory, assets, and broken locks; substances such as grease and fluids; traces such as paints and stains; and impressions such as cutting marks, tire tracks, and fingerprints. Physical evidence was used to discover who was involved in the 1993 bombing of the World Trade Center in New York City. The vehicle identification number engraved on the axle of the rented van that contained the explosives made it possible to discover the guilty parties by tracing the van to a rental agency. When the perpetrator came back to the rental agency to recover his deposit and make a claim that the van had been stolen, the FBI was waiting and arrested him.

Another example of the use of physical evidence involved the famed detective William J. Burns, who once solved a counterfeit currency conspiracy by tracking down a single clue to its source. Here is how he used the clue to solve the case.[3]

The clue used by Burns was a four-digit number preceded by "xx," which was imprinted on a burlap covering to a sofa shipped from the United States to Costa Rica. In the sofa were hidden nearly 1 million counterfeit pesos. By tracing the clue to its source, Burns gained a great deal of evidence, blew the case wide open, and was instrumental in sending the counterfeiters to Sing Sing State Prison. The steps that Burns took in making the investigation are listed below.

1. He located and called on burlap manufacturers.
2. He learned the significance of the imprinted number on the burlap covering, and how it might help in tracing the specific piece of burlap to its purchaser.
3. He dug for the precise four-digit order number in a pile of old, discarded order forms.
4. He located the retail dry goods store that had sold the particular piece of burlap.
5. He asked a retail clerk about the specific purchase and obtained a description of the person who had purchased the burlap: a little old lady dressed in black and wearing a shawl.
6. He located the purchaser. (Burns later learned that she had bought the burlap for her son-in-law.)
7. He invented a pretense to take the young retail clerk with him to call on the lady, so that the clerk would later be able to identify her.
8. He checked out a number of furniture moving companies to locate the one that had moved the old couch containing the pesos to the docks.
9. He questioned a succession of dockhands until he found one who remembered loading the sofa. The dockhand also remembered the undue concern of a dark, handsome man, who constantly urged the dock hands to handle the sofa with care. The dockhand said he was sure he could identify the man.
10. He located the man who had been so concerned for the safe shipment of the sofa.
11. He discovered that the man, whose name he now knew, had made a trip to Costa Rica shortly before the shipment of the peso-packed sofa. He had been accompanied by a beautiful woman who traveled under her real name.
12. He learned who had engraved the counterfeit plates used to print the pesos. The engraver turned out to be the son of a lithographer in a plant owned by the two people who had traveled to Costa Rica. The chief product of the plant was revolutionary literature that tied in with the plot to overthrow the Costa Rican government.

---

[3]This case was taken from G Caesar, *Incredible Detective: The Biography of William J. Burns*, Prentice-Hall, Englewood Cliffs, NJ, pp. 39–43.

CONCLUDING COMMENTS

Theft act investigation methods are used less often than other methods in the investigation of fraud. They tend to be more expensive and to require more expertise than other investigative techniques. For certain frauds, however, especially those involving the theft of tangible assets, they often offer the best evidence available.

Chapter Eleven

Concealment Investigative Methods
The Fraud-Triangle-Plus Approach

In this chapter we discuss investigative techniques that focus on concealment efforts. Most frauds are concealed by manipulating source documents, such as purchase invoices, sales invoices, credit memos, deposit slips, checks, receiving reports, bills of lading, leases, titles, sales receipts, money orders, cashier's checks, or insurance policies. Most concealment-based investigative techniques involve ways to gather these documents. In this chapter, we will discuss five investigative techniques that are used to gather documentary evidence: (1) chance and tips, (2) audits, (3) accessing hard-to-get private documents, (4) document examiners, and (5) searches of public sources.

ASPECTS OF DOCUMENTARY EVIDENCE

A fraud examiner should never underestimate the value of documents in a fraud investigation. When faced with a choice between an eyewitness and a good document as evidence, most fraud experts would opt for the document. Unlike witnesses, documents don't forget, they can't be cross-examined or confused by attorneys, they can't commit perjury, and they never tell inconsistent stories on two different occasions. Documents contain extremely valuable information for conducting fraud examinations. For example, as shown in Figure 11–1, the front and back of a canceled check (which is a document) contains the information listed , in addition to possible fingerprints.

This information can be valuable in a fraud investigation. Suppose, for example, you are investigating a kickback or a forgery scheme. The check will direct you to the teller who processed the transaction, who may remember valuable information about the suspect. In addition, a check allows an investigator to complete a paper trail of the entire transaction. Other documents contain similar information.

FIGURE 11–1   *Information on a Check*

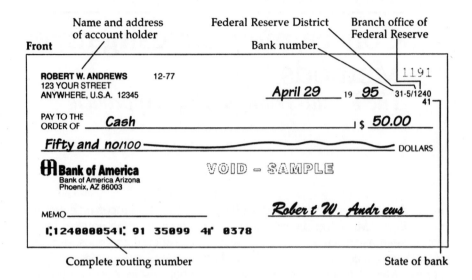

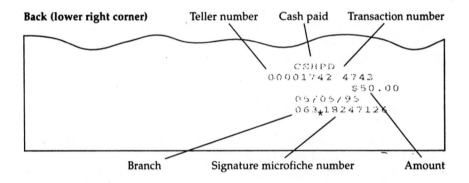

Information about the Maker and the Maker's Bank

1. Name and address of the account holder
2. Bank number of the maker's bank, including:
   a. City and state of bank
   b. Bank name
3. Bank routing number of the maker's bank, including:
   a. Federal Reserve District
   b. Branch office of Federal Reserve
   c. State of the maker's bank
4. Maker's account number

Information about the Bank that Processes the Check

1. Branch number where processed
2. Teller who processed the transaction
3. Sequence number of the transaction
4. Information about the nature of the transaction, including:
   a. Whether the check was cashed
   b. Whether the check was deposited
   c. Whether the check represented a payment
5. Account number of the person who presented the check
6. Date of transaction
7. Amount of transaction

Since documents make up a great deal of evidence in most fraud cases, it is extremely important that investigators understand the legal and administrative aspects of handling them. Specifically, investigators must understand the following aspects of documentary evidence:

Chain of custody of documents

Marking of evidence

Organization of documentary evidence

Rules concerning original versus copies of documents

Chain of Custody

From the time documentary evidence is received, its chain of custody must be maintained in order for it to be accepted by the courts. Basically, the chain of custody means that a record must be kept of when a document is received and what has happened to it since its receipt. Careful records must be maintained anytime the document leaves the care, custody, or control of the examiner. Contesting attorneys will make every attempt to introduce the possibility that the document has been altered or tampered with since it came into the hands of the examiner. A memorandum should be written that describes when the document came into the hands of the examiner, and subsequent memoranda should be written whenever there is a change in the status of the document.

Marking the Evidence

We recommend that when documentary evidence is received, it be uniquely marked so it can be later identified. We suggest that a transparent envelope be used to store it, with the date received and the initials of the examiner written on the outside. A copy of the document should be made, and the original document should be stored in a secure place in the envelope. Copies of the document should be used during the investigation and should be kept in the same file where the original is kept. During the trial, the original can be removed from safekeeping and used.

The Organization of the Evidence

Fraud cases can create tremendous amounts of documentary evidence. For example, in one fraud case in which one of the authors was an expert witness, 100 people worked full-time for over a year to input into the computer key words for documents so that the documents could be called up on demand during the trial. In this case, there were literally millions of documents. In an Arizona case, Lincoln Savings and Loan

Association, the judge created a document depository containing millions of documents, from which attorneys, FBI agents, and others were able to access evidence while preparing for trial.

Because of the possibility of a large volume of documents, it is important that a consistent organization scheme be used. Fraud experts disagree about what the organization scheme should be. Some say that documents should be organized by witness, some argue for a chronological organization, and others argue for organization by transaction. Whichever method is used, a database should be maintained that includes (1) dates of documents, (2) sources of documents, (3) the dates on which documents were obtained, (4) brief descriptions of document contents, (5) subjects of documents, and (6) an identifying or bates number. ("Bates" numbers are used by attorneys involved in litigation to track all documents.)

Original Documents versus Photocopies

Original documents are always preferable to photocopies as evidence. In fact, depending upon the jurisdiction, there are usually only four situations that permit the introduction of photocopies, which are considered secondary evidence, in a court of law. The four situations are:

1. When the original document has been lost or destroyed without the intent or fault of the party seeking to introduce the secondary evidence.
2. When the original document is in the possession of an adverse party who fails to produce it after a written notice to do so, or when the party in possession is outside the jurisdiction of the subpoena power of the court.
3. When the document or record is in the custody of a public office.
4. When the original documents are too voluminous to permit careful examination, and a summary of their contents is acceptable.

In such a situation, it must be shown that an original document existed and that the secondary evidence copy is a genuine copy of the original.

Many frauds have been allowed to be perpetrated and to go undetected because auditors and others were satisfied with photocopies rather than original documents. In the ZZZZ Best case, one of the principals was said to be a master of the copy machine. According to one source, "He could play the copy machine as well as Horowitz could play the piano." Anytime photocopies are used, investigators must be suspicious.

OBTAINING DOCUMENTARY EVIDENCE

Most concealment investigative procedures involve accessing and accumulating documentary evidence. In the remainder of this chapter, we identify several ways to obtain such evidence. Examiners who have computer, statistics, and/or accounting backgrounds usually have an advantage in investigating documentary evidence.

There are five ways to obtain documentary evidence. The first is by chance or accident or through tips. Once in a while, auditors and others are lucky and come across documents that provide evidence of fraudulent activities. Sometimes these documents are recognized by blatant alterations or forgeries. At other times they are brought to an organization's attention by informants. In either case, such instances should be considered luck. We don't know how to instruct you to be lucky, although we do know that awareness training increases a person's ability to detect problems. Rather, we recommend that you follow one of the other ways described here to gather documentary evidence.

Audits

Auditors conduct seven types of tests, each of which yields a form of evidence. The tests are: (1) tests of mechanical accuracy (recalculations), (2) analytical tests (tests of reasonableness), (3) documentation, (4) confirmations, (5) observations, (6) physical examinations, and (7) inquiries. Because gathering documentation is a normal part of their work, quite often auditors can gather documentary evidence as part of an investigation without arousing suspicion.

Auditors can use manual or computer procedures to gather documentary evidence. To illustrate audit procedures, consider the following actual fraud, which has already been discussed in Chapter 6:

> Elgin Aircraft had an insurance claims processing and claims payment department to administer its health care plans. The company was self-insured for claims under $50,000, and claims above this amount were forwarded to an independent insurance company. The claims processing department's responsibility was to verify the necessary documentation for payment and then to forward it to the claims payment department. The payment department approved and signed the payment.
>
> The employees had a choice between two types of insurance plans. The first was a health maintenance organization (HMO) plan in which they went to an approved doctor. Elgin had a contract with a group of medical doctors who treated the employees for a set fee. The second plan allowed employees to choose not to go to the HMO but to have only 80 percent of their bills paid by Elgin.

Management believed the company had an excellent internal control system. In addition, they continually had various auditors on their premises—government contract auditors, defense auditors, bank auditors, CPAs, and internal auditors. These auditors felt, as management did, that controls over health claims were adequate. Each health claim was processed on the basis of an extensive form filled out by the attending physician and a statement from the doctor's office verifying the dollar amount of the treatment. This form was given to the claims processing department, which verified the following:

- That the patient was an employee of Elgin Aircraft.
- That the treatment was covered in the plan.
- That the amount charged was within approved guidelines.
- That the total amount claimed for the year was not over $50,000. (If it was, a claim was submitted to the insurance company.)
- Which plan the employee was on, and that the calculation for payment was correct.

After verification, the claim was forwarded to the claims payment department, which would pay the doctor directly. No payment ever went directly to employees.

In January, a defense auditor observed the manager of the claims department taking the department to lunch in a limousine. The auditor was curious about how the manager could afford such expensive occasions. In speaking with the vice president of finance, he learned that the manager was "one of the company's best employees." He also learned that she had never missed a day of work in the last 10 years. She was indeed a very conscientious employee, and her department had one of the best efficiency ratings in the entire company.

The defense auditor recognized several symptoms in this case, including: (1) the limousine (a lifestyle symptom), (2) never missing a day's work (a behavioral symptom), and (3) not verifying claims with employees (a control weakness). He decided to investigate. His suspicion was that the manager of the claims department was committing some kind of fraud. Reasoning that the easiest way for her to be committing fraud was by setting up phony doctors and billing the company for fictitious claims, he decided to gather documentary evidence in the form of checks paid to various doctors to ascertain whether the doctors and claims were legitimate. The auditor knew it would be impossible to determine conclusively whether or not fraud was being perpetrated without looking at every check. He also realized that, since there was no proof of fraud, his suspicions did not justify personally examining the total population of all 6,000 checks, which were numbered 2000 through 8000.

Faced with the desire to examine the checks but with limited time, he realized he had three audit alternatives. He could audit the checks by selecting a few of them to look at, he could draw a random sample and use statistical sampling techniques to examine the checks, or he could use a computer and examine certain attributes of all checks.

FIGURE 11–2
Statistical Sampling

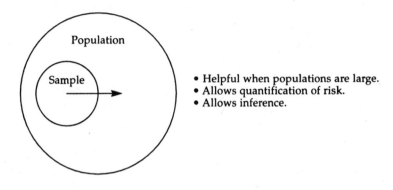

If the auditor took the first alternative and chose, say, 40 of the checks for detailed analysis, he could conclude that the manager was committing fraud if one or more of the selected checks had been made out to a fictitious doctor or doctors. However, if his sample of 40 checks did not include payments to fictitious doctors, the only conclusion he could draw was that there was no fraud in his sample of 40. Without drawing a random sample and using proper sampling procedures, no conclusions could be made about the total population. If he happened to find fraud, he would be lucky. If he didn't, it might be because he was unlucky or because there was no fraud.

Discovery sampling. A better approach to auditing documentary evidence in some situations is to use a form of statistical sampling called *discovery sampling*. Using discovery (statistical) sampling allows an auditor to generalize and make inferences from the sample to the population (Figure 11–2).

Discovery sampling is the easiest of all statistical sampling variations to understand. Basically, if an auditor can read a table, he or she can conduct discovery sampling. Discovery sampling deals with the probability of discovering at least one error in a given sample size if the population error rate is a certain percentage. A type of attribute sampling which is based on normal probability theory, discovery sampling is sometimes referred to as *stop-and-go sampling*. Its use involves two steps: (1) drawing a random sample and (2) using a table to draw inferences about the population from the sample. To illustrate, assume that the defense auditor wanted to use discovery sampling to examine checks payable to doctors. First, he would use a random number generator or a random number table to select the checks to be examined. Figure 11–3 shows a sample list of random numbers.

FIGURE 11–3
Random Number Table

				Column				
Item	(1)	(2)	(3)	(4)	(5)	(6)	(7)	(8)
1000	37039	97547	64673	31546	99314	66854	97855	99965
1001	25145	84834	23009	51584	66754	77785	52357	25532
1002	98433	54725	18864	65866	76918	78825	58210	76835
1003	97965	68548	81545	82933	93545	85959	63282	61454
1004	78049	67830	14624	17563	25697	07734	48243	94318
1005	50203	25658	91478	08509	23308	48130	65047	77873
1006	40059	67825	18934	64998	49807	71126	77818	56893
1007	84350	67241	54031	34535	04093	35062	58163	14205
1008	30954	51637	91500	48722	60988	60029	60873	37423
1009	86723	36464	98305	08009	00666	29255	18514	49158
1010	50188	22554	86160	92250	14021	65859	16237	72296
1011	50014	00463	13906	35936	71761	95755	87002	71667
1012	66023	21428	14742	94874	23308	58533	26507	11208
1013	04458	61862	63119	09541	01715	87901	91260	03079
1014	57510	36314	30452	09712	37714	95482	30507	68475
1015	43373	58939	95848	28288	60341	52174	11879	18115
1016	61500	12763	64433	02268	57905	72347	49498	21871
1017	78938	71312	99705	71546	42274	23915	38405	18779
1018	64257	93218	35793	43671	64055	88729	11168	60260
1019	56864	21554	70445	24841	04779	56774	96129	73594
1020	35314	29631	06937	54545	04470	75463	77112	77126
1021	40704	48823	65963	39659	12717	56201	22811	24863
1022	07318	44623	02843	33299	59872	86774	06926	12672
1023	94550	23299	45557	07923	75126	00808	01312	46689
1024	34348	81191	21027	77087	10909	03676	97723	34469
1025	92277	57115	50789	68111	75305	53289	39751	45760
1026	56093	58302	52236	64756	50273	61566	61962	93280
1027	16623	17849	96701	94971	94758	08845	32260	59823
1028	50848	93982	66451	32143	05441	10399	17775	74169
1029	48006	58200	58367	66577	68583	21108	41361	20732
1030	56640	27890	28825	96509	21363	53657	60119	75385

In using a random number table to select the checks to examine, an auditor must make four decisions:

1. Where to start in the table when selecting check numbers.
2. The direction in which to move through the table.
3. What to do with numbers that are outside the range, in this case, that do not fall between 2000 and 8000.
4. Which four of the five digits to use, since the checks are all four-digit numbers.

Assume, for example, that the auditor decided to start with the top-left number (37039), to move through the table from left to right and from top to bottom, to skip numbers that fell outside the relevant range, and to use the first four digits of each number. The checks selected for examination would be checks 3703, 6467, 3154, 6685, 2514, 2300, and so forth. (How many to select is discussed below.) Randomly choosing the checks to be examined allows the auditor to make inferences about the population, not just about the sample.

Once the checks were selected, the next step would be to use a discovery sampling table such as the one in Figure 11–4 to draw conclusions about the checks.

When examining the checks in the sample, if the auditor found a check to a fictitious doctor, he would be 100 percent certain that fraud existed. If he did not find such a check, he would still have to examine all 6,000 checks to be absolutely certain there was no fraud. If he sampled anything less than 100 percent of the checks and didn't find fraud, discovery sampling would allow him to decide how much risk he was willing to assume. In other words, discovery sampling would allow the auditor to quantify risk. From Figure 11–4, you can see that if the auditor sampled 300 checks and found none made out to fictitious doctors, he would be 95 percent confident that the true population fraud rate did not exceed 1 percent, 78 percent confident that no more than 0.5 percent of the checks were fraudulent, and so forth. The entire table is based on the assumption that no fictitious checks are found. (Again, if the auditor found even one fictitious doctor, he would be 100 percent certain that fraud existed.) The more confident the auditor wanted to be and the less risk of not identifying fraudulent checks the auditor wanted to assume, the larger the sample size that must be examined. Population size seems to make little difference in sample size unless the sample becomes a significant part of the population (usually greater than 10 percent), and then the confidence level is higher and the risk lower than indicated in the table.

Even with discovery sampling, auditors can never be certain that fraud does not exist in a population of checks. While discovery sampling

FIGURE 11–4
Discovery Sampling Table

Probability (percentage) of including at least one error in the sample

Rate of Occurrence in the Population (Percent)

Sample Size	0.01	0.05	0.1	0.2	0.3	0.5	1	2
50		2	5	9	14	22	39	64
60	1	3	6	11	16	26	45	70
70	1	3	7	13	19	30	51	76
80	1	4	8	15	21	33	55	80
90	1	4	9	16	24	36	60	84
100	1	5	10	18	26	39	63	87
120	1	6	11	21	30	45	70	91
140	1	7	13	24	34	50	76	94
160	2	8	15	27	38	55	80	96
200	2	10	18	33	45	63	87	98
240	2	11	21	38	51	70	91	99
300	3	14	26	45	59	78	95	99+
340	3	16	29	49	64	82	97	99+
400	4	18	33	55	70	87	98	99+
460	5	21	37	60	75	90	99	99+
500	5	22	39	63	78	92	99	99+
800	8	33	55	80	91	98	99+	99+
1,000	10	39	63	86	95	99	99+	99+
1,500	14	53	78	95	99	99+	99+	99+
2,500	22	71	92	99	99+	99+	99+	99+

does allow inferences to be made about the problem, there is still the possibility that the sample will not be representative of the population (sampling risk), and the possibility that the auditor will examine a fraudulent check and not recognize it (nonsampling risk). Using discovery sampling, auditors can quantify both risk and samples until they conclude that they have sufficient evidence that fraud does not exist.

Using computers. An alternative to discovery sampling, which allows all checks to be examined, is to use a computer. Using this approach, the auditor selects an attribute of interest, such as addresses of payees, checks mailed to PO boxes, or payments made to certain doctors. If the auditor identifies attributes that signal fraud, this approach can be very effective in determining whether or not fraud exists.

In this actual fraud case that we have been discussing, the claims payment manager embezzled more than $12 million over a five-year period by making payments to 22 fictitious doctors. The payments were sent to two common addresses: The address of a business in a nearby city that was owned by the manager's husband and a PO box that the manager rented. Either discovery sampling or a computer search could have detected the fraud. Using discovery sampling, the auditor would have selected checks and then confirmed whether or not the doctors being paid were legitimate. Legitimacy could have been determined by examining the doctor's listings in telephone books, confirming their medical licenses with the state licensing board, or making inquiries through medical associations. As soon as he found even one fictitious doctor, sampling would have stopped and the entire population would have been examined to determine the extent of the fraud.

Using the computer approach, the auditor would have matched addresses of doctors and found that payments to 22 doctors were being sent to two common addresses. Checking out the addresses, he would have found that one was the business owned by the manager's husband and the other was her PO box.

With discovery sampling, the risk of not catching the fraud is choosing a sample that is not representative of the population (sampling risk) and examining fraudulent checks but not recognizing them as being fraudulent (nonsampling risk). With the computer method, the risk is not selecting the right attribute to query.

Computer searches are valuable audit tools in fraud investigations. For example, a fraud examiner who suspected procurement fraud might make computer searches for and/or comparisons of the following items:

- Timing of bids.
- Pattern of bids.
- Dates of disposal with reorders of goods.
- Amount of work by a given vendor.
- Pattern of hiring new vendors.
- Vendors with PO boxes as addresses.
- Number of sole-source contracts.
- Price changes in purchased items.
- Company employees with vendor officers.
- Vendors with Dun & Bradstreet.
- Vendor addresses with company use.
- Number of rush orders.

Similar computer searches can be made to gather documentary evidence relating to any kind of fraud. The authors believe that using the computer to investigate fraud is the most promising of all investigative procedures for the future.

Hard-To-Get Documentary Evidence

Some documentary evidence, while valuable, is extremely difficult to obtain. The three most common examples are private bank records, tax returns, and brokerage records. Usually there are only three ways to obtain such documentary evidence: (1) by subpoena, (2) by search warrant, and (3) by voluntary consent. *Subpoenas duces tecum* are orders issued by a court or a grand jury to produce documents. Failure to honor such a subpoena is punishable by law. Because only agents of the grand jury or the court (usually law enforcement officers) can obtain documents by subpoena, a need to obtain a subpoena is one reason to coordinate fraud investigations with law enforcement officials.

A second way to obtain hard-to-get documentary evidence is to use a search warrant. A search warrant is issued by a judge when there is probable cause to believe that documents have been used in committing a crime. Search warrants are executed only by law enforcement officials and are generally used only in criminal cases.

The third and most common way to obtain private documents is by voluntary consent, which can be either oral or written. Often an initial interview with a fraud suspect is for the purpose of obtaining permission to access bank or brokerage records rather than to obtain a confession. Figure 11–5 shows an example of a consent signed by a suspect, which allows a fraud examiner to access private bank records.

Document Examiners

Sometimes it is necessary to determine whether a document is authentic. Documents can be genuine, counterfeit, fraudulent, forged, or questioned. A specialized form of investigation that applies forensic chemistry, microscopy, and photography in making determinations about documents is known as *document examination*. Document examiners can make such determinations as whether a document was written by the person whose signature it bears; whether a document has been forged; whether a document has been altered by additives, deletions, obliterations, erasures, or photocopying; whether the handwriting is genuine; whether the entire document was printed on the same machine; whether a document was printed on the date it bears or before or after; whether two or more documents are significantly different or substantially the same; and whether pages have been substituted in a document.[1]

---

[1]Note that document examiners should not be confused with graphologists. The authors strongly recommend that only certified forensic document examiners be used in the investigation of potential fraud.

FIGURE 11–5
Consent Form

XYZ CORPORATION

CUSTOMER CONSENT AND AUTHORIZATION
FOR ACCESS TO FINANCIAL RECORDS

I, _____*Arnold Fox McCune*_____ , having read the
(Name of Customer)

explanation of my rights which is attached to this form, hereby

authorize the _____*XYZ Corporation Credit Union*_____
(Name and Address of Financial Institution)

to disclose these financial records: _____

_____*All bank account records, including checking accounts,*_____

_____*savings accounts, and loans from 1/1/89 to present*_____

to _____*Michael R. Blair and*_____
(Name of Person(s))

_____*Robert W. Jacobs*_____ , for the following purpose(s):

_____*administrative purposes*_____

_____ .

I understand that this authorization may be revoked by me in
writing at any time before my records, as described above, are
disclosed, and that this authorization is valid for no more than
three months from the date of my signature.

_____*1/20/93*_____   _____*Arnold F. McCune*_____
(Date)   (Signature of Customer)

                              _____*318 E. Birch St.*_____

                              _____*Ann Arbor, MI 48159*_____
                              (Address of Customer)

                              _____*Michael R. Blair*_____
                              (Witness)

Figure 11–6 lists the most commonly encountered questions relating to disputed documents or documents of unknown origin. Trained document examiners can usually answer all these questions. For example, in answering questions about handwriting, they might examine the 20 characteristics listed on pages 167–68.

FIGURE 11–6
Questions about Disputed Documents

Handwriting:
1. Is the signature genuine?
2. Is the continued writing genuine?
3. Was the writing disguised?
4. Who did any unknown writing?
5. Can any hand printing that exists, if any, be identified?
6. Can any handwritten numerals, if any, be identified?
7. Which was written first, the signature or the writing above it?
8. Can the forger be identified?
9. Is the handwriting or signature consistent with the date of the document?

Printing:
1. What make and model of printer was used? During what years was the particular make and model used?
2. Can the individual printer that was used be identified?
3. Was the printing done before or after any handwriting and/or signatures?
4. Was the printing done on the date of the document or later?
5. Who did the actual printing?
6. Was the printing on the document all done at one time, or was some of it added at a later time? How much was added later?
7. Were copies made using the original document?
8. Are the copies genuine?
9. Can the printer or the document be identified from a carbon tape?

Alterations and additions:
1. Was the document altered in any way or added to at a later time? Were pages added, parts torn or cut off, purposely wrinkled or stained, etc.?
2. What original date or matter was altered or added to?
3. When was the alteration or addition made?
4. Who made the alteration or addition?
5. Has the photograph on an ID card or other ID document been removed and replaced with another?

FIGURE 11–6 *(concluded)*

Age:

1. Is the age of the document in accordance with its date?
2. How old are the paper, the printing, the ink, the seal, etc.?
3. Is there evidence of the manner or location in which the document was kept?

Copies:

1. Are the photocopies or photostatic reproductions copies of other documents?
2. What type of copy machine was used? What brand?
3. Can the individual copier be identified?
4. In what year was the particular make and model used? Produced?
5. Was any portion of the copy not on the original document? Was it pasted up?
6. Is there any indication that pages are missing on the copies that were part of the original?
7. Can the copy be traced to and identified as the particular original document that was its source?

Other:

1. Can machine-printed matter be identified?
2. Can the check-writer, the adding machine, the addressograph machine, or other machine be identified?
3. Was the envelope resealed?
4. Can the stapler, glue, pin, clip, or other fastener be identified?
5. Is the printed document genuine or counterfeit? If counterfeit, can the original document used as a reproduction source be determined?
6. What processes were used to print the counterfeit document?
7. Could the printing source or counterfeiter be identified if located?

Characteristics of Handwriting:

1. The basic movements of the handwriting—clockwise, counterclockwise, and straight-line,—indicating direction, curvature, shapes, and slopes of the writing motions.
2. Slant—forward, backward, or in between.
3. The manner in which letters with loops are curved, and the size, shape, and proportion of the loops.
4. Peculiarities in the approach strokes and the upward strokes in the first letter of a word and in capital letters.
5. Characteristic initial and terminal strokes; their length and their angle in relation to letters and words.

6. Gaps between letters in specific letter combinations.

7. The manner in which the capital letters are formed, and the additional hooks or flourishes some writers place at the start or end of these letters.

8. Relative smoothness, tremor, or hesitation in the writing. Some writing flows smoothly and is free of hesitation. Other writing shows hesitation in the formation of some letters or defective line quality in the writing as a whole.

9. The manner in which the writer varies pressure in certain pen strokes, and variations in the weight and width of stroke lines.

10. The proportion and alignment of letters; the length or height and size of capital letters compared with lower case letters.

11. The manner in which the letter t is crossed, and the height and slant of the crossing—near the top of the t or lower down, straight or at an angle, with a flourish or plain; whether words ending in t are crossed.

12. The location of the dot over the letter i and its relationship to the location of the letter itself.

13. Types of ending strokes in words ending in the letters y, g, and s.

14. Open or closed letter style, as seen in such letters as a and o, and in letters that combine upward or downward strokes with loops, such as b, d, o, and g. Are the circles in these letters open or closed, broad or narrow?

15. Separation of letters within a word (for example, separating a t from the remainder of the word, or separating a whole syllable from the rest of the word).

16. Characteristics of the portions that appear above and/or below the line in such letters as f, g, and y.

17. Relative alignment of all letters; the uniformity and spacing of letters, words, and lines.

18. Alignment of lines.

19. Use and positioning of punctuation.

20. Indications that the writing instrument was lifted off the writing material between words and sentences.

To become a skilled examiner of "questioned" documents, one must acquire extensive and specialized training. Though most fraud investigators are not trained document examiners, it is important that they understand two important elements relating to questioned document examination: (1) when to have a document examined by an expert and (2) the responsibility of the investigator with respect to questioned documents. As to when to have a document examined, the warning signs listed in Figure 11–7 indicate a need to submit a document for examination.

FIGURE 11–7
When to Have a Document Examined

The following signs indicate that a document should be submitted for examination:

1. Abrasions or chemical pen or pencil erasures.
2. Alterations or substitutions.
3. Disguised or unnatural writings.
4. Use of two or more different colors of ink.
5. Charred, mutilated, or torn pages.
6. Pencil or carbon marks along the writing lines.
7. Existence of lines made during photocopying.
8. Signs of inconsistency or disruption in the continuity of the content.
9. Any suspicious appearance or unusual form.

In dealing with questioned documents, the fraud investigator is responsible for taking the following steps:

- Collecting, protecting, identifying, and preserving the questioned document in as good a condition as possible.

- Collecting and being able to prove to the document examiner the origins of adequate comparison specimens.

- Submitting both the questioned and the comparison documents to the examiner.

There are two well-known organizations of document examiners in the United States. The first is the FBI Laboratory Division, Document Section.

The Document Section, FBI Laboratory Division, provides expert forensic assistance and examinations of physical evidence. These services are available to all Federal agencies, U.S. Attorneys, and the U.S. Military in connection with both criminal and civil matters. These services are available to all duly constituted state, county, municipal, and other non-federal law enforcement agencies in the United States in connection with criminal matters. All expenses for these services, including provision of expert witnesses to testify to the results of their examinations in judicial proceedings and the travel expenses of these experts, are borne by the FBI.

Examinations of questioned documents include the full range of traditional examinations and comparisons, including, but not limited to, the following: handwriting and signatures, hand printing, typewriting, altered and obliterated documents, charred or burned paper, writing materials, photocopies, and many others.

The second is a private group, the American Board of Forensic Document Examiners, Inc. (ABFDE).[3] A description of the ABFDE's background, functions, and purpose follows:

> The need to identify forensic scientists qualified to provide essential professional services for the nation's judicial and executive branches of government as well as the community in general has been long recognized. In response to this professional mandate, the American Board of Forensic Document Examiners, Inc., was organized in 1977 to provide, in the interest of the public and the advancement of the science, a program of certification in forensic document examination. In purpose, function, and organization, the ABFDE is thus analogous to the certifying board[s] in various other scientific fields.
>
> The objective of the Board is to establish, enhance, and maintain as necessary, standards of qualification for those who practice forensic document examination and to certify as qualified specialists those voluntary applicants who comply with the requirements of the Board. In this way, the Board aims to make available to the judicial system, and other public, a practical and equitable system for readily identifying those persons professing to be specialists in forensic document examination who posseses the requisite qualifications and competence.
>
> Certification is based upon the candidate's personal and professional record of education and training, experience, and achievement, as well as on the results of a formal examination.
>
> The Board is a non-profit organization in the District of Columbia. Its initial sponsors are the American Academy of Forensic Sciences and the American Society of Questioned Document Examiners. The Board is composed of officers and other directors who serve staggered terms and are elected from among nominees of designated nominating organizations or serve at-large.

Both of these organizations can suggest experts and offer help in fraud investigation.

---

[3]The authors wish to point out the difference between forensic document examiners and graphologists, as commonly practiced in North America. Forensic document examiners are typically required to actually practice in a laboratory setting, applying such techniques as examining documents for fingerprints, indented writing, handwriting or typewriting similarities, etc. They generally possess accredited degrees in areas of applied science. Graphology (a term used in conjunction with some forensic document examiners in Europe) is practiced in North America by individuals (graphologists) who generally undertake home study courses in handwriting and its application to personalities. We strongly urge caution in differentiating between forensic document examiners and graphologists when seeking the truth in any investigation involving the need for expert review of questioned documents.

CONCLUDING COMMENTS

Concealment investigative techniques usually focus on obtaining documentary evidence. Documents usually make up a significant and reliable amount of the evidence in fraud cases. It is very important to understand both the legal and the administrative aspects of documentary evidence and the various ways in which such evidence may be accumulated and examined. In this chapter, we have identified the legal and administrative issues and have described various ways in which documentary evidence can be accumulated and examined.

Chapter Twelve

Conversion Investigative Methods
The Fraud-Triangle-Plus Approach

Recently one of this book's authors testified in a civil case relating to fraud by a perpetrator who confessed to embezzling $3.2 million. In the deposition, the perpetrator was asked the following question:

> With respect to your lifestyle during the period when the fraud was being perpetrated, how would you describe that lifestyle?

Her response was:

> Extravagant. I drove expensive, very nice cars. We had an Audi 5000 Quattro, a Maserati Spider convertible, a Jeep Cherokee, and a Rolls Royce. We bought expensive paintings, art, and glasswork. We held expensive parties, serving steak and lobster. We bought a condominium for my parents; we took cruises and other expensive vacations. And I wore expensive clothes, fur coats, and diamond and gold jewelry.

While the lifestyle described by this embezzler is extreme, rarely do perpetrators save what they steal. While most begin their thefts because of a perceived critical need (this perpetrator began stealing in order to repay a debt consolidation loan), perpetrators continue to embezzle after the need has been met. They use the money to improve their lifestyles.

One of the most common investigative procedures involves determining how perpetrators converted or spent their stolen funds. Conversion is the third element of the fraud triangle. Some frauds can most easily be detected and investigated by focusing on lifestyle changes and other conversion attempts.

Most conversion investigative techniques involve searching public records and other sources to trace purchases of assets, payments of liabilities, and changes in lifestyle and net worth. These searches are usually performed for two reasons: first, to determine the extent of the embezzlement and, second, to gather evidence which can be used in interrogations to obtain a confession. An effective interviewer, without tipping his or her hand, can get a suspect to admit that his or her only income was earned income. By introducing evidence of lifestyle and expenditures that cannot be supported by the earned income, the interviewer makes it difficult for the suspect to explain the source of the unknown income. Caught in an unexplainable situation, the suspect sometimes breaks down and confesses.

To become proficient at conversion investigative techniques, fraud examiners should understand that: (1) federal, and state, and local agencies and other organizations maintain information that can be accessed in searches; (2) several types of information are available from each of those sources; and (3) the net worth method of analyzing accessed information can help to determine the probable amount of embezzled funds.

OBTAINING PUBLICLY AVAILABLE INFORMATION

Many federal, state, and local agencies maintain public records in accordance with various laws. Much of this information can be accessed by anyone who requests it; some of it is protected under privacy laws which prevent disclosure to the public. While federal records are generally not as useful as state and local records in fraud investigations, they can be helpful. Because of the bureaucracies involved, accessing federal records can be time-consuming and costly. In addition, several private organizations, such as credit reporting agencies and companies that maintain computer databases, can provide valuable information about a person's lifestyle and spending habits.

In this chapter, we discuss sources of information in the following sequence: (1) federal sources, (2) state sources, (3) county and local records, (4) private sources, and (5) publicly available databases.

Federal Sources

Most federal agencies maintain information that can be helpful in investigations of fraud. Some of these agencies and the information they possess are described below.

US Department of Defense. The Department of Defense maintains records on all military personnel, both active and inactive. Military information is maintained by branch of service. The department also contains information on individuals who may be a threat to national security. The department regularly shares information with other federal agencies, such as the FBI and Central Intelligence Agency (CIA).

Military records are not confidential and can provide valuable information relating to the addresses of individuals. Military records can also be helpful in searching for hidden assets, because individuals often buy property and other assets in areas where they previously lived.

US Department of Justice.   The Department of Justice is the federal agency charged with enforcing federal criminal and civil laws. It contains records related to the detection, prosecution and rehabilitation of offenders. The Department of Justice is in charge of US Attorneys, US Marshalls, and the FBI. The Drug Enforcement Administration (DEA) is an agency of the FBI that is charged with enforcing narcotics trafficking.

The FBI is the principle investigative agency of the Department of Justice. Any criminal matter not assigned to another US agency is assigned to the FBI. The FBI is in charge of investigating bank fraud, organized crime, and trade in illegal drugs. The FBI is also responsible for national security within US borders.

The FBI maintains several databases and other records that can be accessed by state and local law enforcement agencies. The major database maintained by the FBI is the National Crime Information Center (NCIC). The NCIC contains information on stolen vehicles, license plates, securities, boats, and planes; stolen and missing firearms; missing persons; and individuals who are currently wanted on outstanding warrants. The FBI also contains the Interstate Identification Index (III), which is an outgrowth of the NCIC and is maintained for the benefit of state and local law enforcement agencies. The III contains arrest and criminal records on a nationwide basis.

Some states maintain databases for their states similar to one maintained by the NCIC. To gain access to all such databases, you must present identifying information, such as birth date or Social Security number; these databases are not generally available to private investigators. A need to obtain access to these databases is a good reason to involve local law enforcement in a fraud investigation.

US Bureau of Prisons.   This agency operates the nationwide system of federal prisons, correctional institutions, and community treatment facilities. It maintains detailed records on persons who have been incarcerated in the various federal facilities.

Internal Revenue Service.   The IRS enforces all internal revenue laws, except the ones dealing with alcohol, firearms, tobacco, and explosives, which are handled by the Bureau of Alcohol, Tobacco, and Firearms. IRS records are not available to the public.

US Secret Service.   The Secret Service is responsible for protecting the President of the United States and other federal dignitaries. It also has responsibility for dealing with counterfeiting, theft of government checks, interstate credit card violations, and some computer crimes.

US Postal Service.   The Postal Service is a quasi-governmental organization that has responsibility for the US mail and for protecting citizens from loss through theft involving the use of the mail system. Postal inspectors are generally recognized as some of the best and most helpful federal investigators. They handle major fraud cases involving the use of mails, and they work for the prosecution of offenders who violate US postal laws. Postal inspectors share jurisdiction with other federal, state, and local agencies.

US postal inspectors can be extremely helpful in investigations of employee fraud, investment scams, or management frauds. It is difficult to perpetrate a fraud in the United States without using the mail system. Bribes and kickbacks are often made through the mail, false advertisements are commonly sent through the mail, and stolen checks and funds are often deposited in banks by sending them through the mail. Because the use of mails is so common in frauds, the federal mail statutes are the workhorse statutes in federal crimes. Every fraud investigator should become familiar with mail fraud statutes and should get to know the local postal inspectors. They can be extremely useful in all kinds of fraud investigations.

Central Intelligence Agency.   The CIA is an executive office of the President of the United States. It investigates security matters outside the United States, whereas the FBI has jurisdiction for security within the US.

Social Security Administration.   The Social Security Administration (SSA) has information about individuals' Social Security numbers. This agency can be helpful in identifying the area where a perpetrator was residing when a Social Security number was issued. Because every Social Security number contains information about the area (first three digits), the group (middle two digits), and the person's serial number (last four digits), Social Security information can be extremely helpful in fraud investigations. Once an individual's unique Social Security number is known, numerous federal, state, local, and private records can be accessed.

State Sources

State Attorney General.   The attorney general for each state enforces all state civil and criminal laws, in cooperation with local law enforcement agencies. Most state attorneys general have investigative arms (similar to the FBI for the Department of Justice), such as the State Bureau of Investigation. This agency contains records relating to individuals who have been convicted of breach of state civil and criminal laws.

Bureau of Prisons. The Bureau of Prisons for each state maintains the network of state prisons and administers state corrections departments. It maintains records on all individuals who have been incarcerated in state prison systems, as well as on individuals who are on probation or parole.

Secretary of State. The secretary of state maintains all types of records relating to businesses and Uniform Commercial Code filings.

Every corporation must file documents in the state in which the organization was chartered. These documents, which are usually maintained by the secretary of state's office, reveal incorporators, bylaws, articles of incorporation, registered agent, and the initial board of directors and officers. These records are public information and can be extremely helpful in gathering information about organizations that are participating in fraudulent schemes. They can confirm whether or not an organization is legally conducting business and whether or not its taxes have been paid, and can also give an investigator the names of partners, principal shareholders, board members, and business affiliations. This information is extremely valuable in tracing assets, establishing conflicts of interest, identifying dummy companies, and determining changes in financial status.

Secretary of state offices also usually maintain UCC filings. Such records contain information about chattel mortgages (non-real estate transactions) and about loans to individuals or businesses on equipment, furniture, automobiles, and other personal property. UCC records can identify collateral on purchased and leased assets, the nature of the lending company, where a person banks, and whether the person has a need for money.

UCC records are sometimes available in a county clerk's office (depending on the state). Much of the information maintained by a secretary of state's office concerning businesses and UCC filings is on-line with such services as Information America, Dun & Bradstreet, and Prentice Hall's Legal and Financial Services database.

Department of Motor Vehicles. Driver's license records are maintained by the Department of Motor Vehicles and are publicly available in most states. These records can be helpful in accessing a person's driving history, address, convictions for traffic violations, name, date of birth, address of birth, and photograph.

Department of Vital Statistics. Maintains birth records. These records, though they are quite difficult to obtain, contain information about a person's date and place of birth and parents.

Department of Business Regulation. Most states have a department of business regulation or a similar agency that maintains licensing information about various professionals. Licensing information is generally maintained about accountants, attorneys, bankers, doctors, electricians, plumbers, contractors, engineers, nurses, police officers, firefighters, insurance agents, bail bondsmen, real estate agents, security guards, stock brokers, investment bankers, teachers, waitresses (food handler's permit), and travel agents.

Information about professionals can be extremely helpful in accessing industry guidelines as well as giving an individual's memberships; specializations; current business addresses; history of business complaints, grievances, and charges; investigations; and professional credentials.

As an example of how this information can be helpful, assume a fraud was being perpetrated by setting up dummy doctors, as in the Elgin Aircraft example in chapter 11. A quick check with the department of business regulation in the relevant state would disclose whether or not the doctors being paid were legitimate.

County and Local Records

Counties and other local agencies contain records that are among the most useful in fraud investigations. The nature of these records varies from state to state and from county to county. Some of the most common and useful sources are described below.

County Clerk. Maintains many records of local citizens, including voter registration records and marriage licenses. Marriage and voting records are extremely useful. Voter registration records, for example, contain information about a person's name; current address; past addresses; age; date of birth; Social Security number; signature; and telephone number, whether listed or unlisted. Even if a person has not voted, his or her family members (such as son, daughter, and spouse) may have voted, and thus voter registrations can still provide valuable information. Marriage records are maintained in the county clerk's office in the county of residence at the time of marriage. They may contain the full legal names of the couple, their dates of birth, their Social Security numbers, their addresses at the time of marriage (and usually their parents' addresses as well) driver's license numbers (if they are US citizens), their passport numbers (if they are nationals), their prior marriages, and the witnesses to the marriage (who may be the couple's best friends). Once this information has been obtained, numerous databases and other sources of information can be accessed.

County Land Office and Tax Assessor's Office.   These offices contain real estate records for land located in the county. There are two common ways to trace real estate records. Land ownership is normally found in the county land office or in the office of the recorder of deeds. Property tax records, maintained by the county assessor's office, also contain property records. Property records are usually indexed by address or legal description; or by the owner's name, or they may be indexed by the name of the seller or the buyer. County land office records identify owned assets, indebtedness, mortgage holders, trustees or straw buyers, and people who knew a suspect before and after a sale. Property tax records contain information about a property's legal description and current assessed value, and about the taxpayer's current status. These records are helpful in identifying assets purchased and liens removed by a perpetrator.

County Sheriff and Other Officers.   Offices such as that of the city police, the county constable, probation officers, bail bondsmen, etc., contain information about criminal charges, indictment statements, pretrial information reports, conviction statements, incarceration information, and probation information.

Local Courts.   Various local courts contain pretrial information, including personal history, employment history, physical identifying information, prior charges, divorces and property settlement agreements, personal injury lawsuits, financial claims and litigation, fraud claims and coconspirators, bankruptcies, wills, and probates.

Bankruptcy information, which is also contained on-line in Information America and by Prentice Hall's Legal and Financial Services database, includes the current status of bankruptcy cases, creditor lists, debts, assets, and information on individuals' characters. These records are helpful in determining how assets are hidden. Information about wills and probates can be helpful in identifying sources of assets of perpetrators. Many perpetrators explain their extravagant lifestyles by claiming to have inherited money. Claims about inheritances can be validated or dismissed by using will and probate information.

Permit Departments.   Permit departments can supply information about fire permits (hazardous chemicals), health permits (pollutants), elevator permits, and building permits. Permit-issuing departments can be helpful in identifying the nature and location of businesses, new leases, and recent construction.

Private Sources

There are hundreds of sources of private information available to those who understand where to find them. Utility records (gas, electric, water, garbage, and sewer), for example, can supply the names of persons billed, can show whether or not a person lives or owns property in the service area, and can identify the kinds of utilities a business uses.

Private credit records are maintained for both individuals and organizations by various credit reporting companies. Essentially, there are two types of reporting agencies: (1) file-based credit reporting agencies, which develop information from their credit files, and (2) public records and investigative credit reporting agencies, which gather most of their information through interviews. Credit bureaus are used primarily by retail organizations. They typically maintain the following information:

- Consumer information, such as addresses, ages, family members, and incomes.
- Account information, such as payment schedules, items purchased, and buying habits.
- Marketing information, such as customer breakdowns by age, sex, and income levels.
- Information on current and former employees.

Information maintained by credit reporting agencies is governed by the Fair Credit Reporting Act of 1971. The purpose of this act is to regulate activities of credit, insurance, and employment investigations. Under the law, a consumer reporting agency must, on request, furnish information to an individual that is also furnished to a third party. If adverse action is to be taken against an employee as a result of third-party information, the employee must be given advance notice of the act.

Publicly Available Databases

An increasing number of publicly available databases provide information that is helpful in investigations. Dialog, for example, contains 500 databases that provide information about individuals' and companies' backgrounds, employment histories, professional papers, and technical information. CompuServ contains the same information as Dialog except it is geared more to personal than to business information. The Prentice-Hall Legal and Financial Services database contains court records and information about bankruptcy, real estate, tax liens, UCC filings, and organization. Redi-Data Services contains information from tax assessors. Vultext, Datatimes, Newsearch, Magazine Index, NEXIS, and Newsnet contain information about individuals that has been published in magazines and newspapers. If, for example, an organization was planning on conducting business with an individual, a quick NEXIS search could determine whether newspaper articles, either positive or negative had ever been written about the individual.

A recent article in *Forensic Accounting Review* contained an extensive list of various types of available datatbases, as follows:[1]

The names and locations of a few selected investigative databases include:

- CBI/Equifax, Brea, CA
- Transunion, Fullerton, CA
- TRW, Orange, CA
- Dun & Bradstreet, Van Nuys, CA
- Metronet, Lombard, IL
- CDB Infotek, Orange, CA
- IRC, Fullerton, CA
- Super Bureau, Monterey, CA
- Prentice-Hall, Monterey, CA
- Damar Corp., Los Angeles, CA
- Data Quick, San Diego, CA
- Redloc, Anaheim, CA
- Redi Real Estate, Miami, FL
- Mead Data Central, Dayton, OH
- NCI Network, Jackson, MI
- CompuServ, Columbus, OH
- Dialog, Louisville, KY
- Dow Jones, Princeton, NJ
- Vultext, Philadelphia, PA
- Western Union, Upper Saddle River, NJ
- Westlaw, St. Paul, MN

Contract database researchers include:

- Information on Demand, McLean, VA
- Research on Demand, Berkely, CA
- Savage Information Service, Torrance, CA

---

[1]Jack Bologna, *Forensic Accounting Review* (Plymouth, Michigan), April 1993, p. 2.

Database directories include:

- *Directory of On-Line Data Bases*, Cuadra-Elsevier Publishing, CA
- *National Directory of Bulletin Board*, Westport, CT

Database wholesalers include:

- US Datalink, Baytown, TX—represents 250 information brokers. One-call access to public documents in all 50 states.
- NCI (Jeff Kirkpatrick), Jackson, MI (skip tracing and credit data).

THE NET WORTH METHOD

Once information about spending and lifestyle has been abstracted from public records and other sources, the investigator must determine the extent of stolen funds. The most common method of making such determinations is by use of *net worth* calculations. Essentially, the net worth method is a calculation (formula) based on a person's assets (things owned), liabilities (debts), living expenses, and income (see Figure 12–1).

From public records and other sources, such as property and UCC records, an individual's purchases of real estate, automobiles, and other assets can be determined. Such records also provide information about whether liens have been removed, thus identifying whether loans have been paid. Information from public sources can be combined with information from interviews of landscapers, furniture and automobile dealers, and other relevant parties, and information can be gathered through subpoena to make a reasonably accurate accounting of assets and liabilities.

When a person has income, he or she either purchases additional assets, pays off liabilities, or increases lifestyle, thus increasing living expenses. When known income is subtracted from unknown income, a reasonable estimate of unknown funds can be determined. When other sources of funds (such as inheritances, gambling winnings, and gifts) are eliminated through interviews and other sources, a good estimate of the amount of stolen funds can be made.

The net worth method has gained prominence among fraud investigators in recent years. The FBI regularly uses it. The DEA uses it to establish whether a suspected narcotics trafficker has income from illegal drug sales. The IRS uses the net worth method to estimate unreported income in tax fraud cases.

Because only assets and reductions in liabilities that can be discovered from public sources enter into the calculation, the net worth method tends to be a very conservative estimate of stolen funds. Indeed, embezzlers usually spend increasing amounts on food, jewelry, vacations, and

FIGURE 12–1
The Net Worth Calculation

Assets	
Less	Liabilities
Equals	Net worth
Less	Prior year's net worth
Equals	Net worth increase
Plus	Living expenses
Equals	Income
Less	Funds from known sources
Equals	Funds from unknown sources

other luxuries that are difficult to assess and cannot be factored into net worth calculations. Because net worth calculations are conservative, amounts determined to be stolen using this method are usually readily accepted as evidence by courts. Even in cases in which net worth calculations are considered only secondary or circumstantial evidence, they can be very useful in helping to obtain confessions from suspects. There is no better way to conduct an interrogation of suspects that to present accurate information regarding their expenditures and lifestyle which they cannot explain.

As an example of how the net worth method can be used, consider the following fraud example:[2]

Helen Weeks worked for Bonne Consulting Group (BCG) as the executive secretary in the administrative department for nearly 10 years. Her apparent integrity and dedication to her work quickly earned her a reputation as an outstanding employee and resulted in increased responsibilities. Her responsibilities included making arrangements for outside feasibility studies, maintaining client files, working with outside marketing consultants, initiating the payment process, and notifying the accounting department of all openings or closings of vendor accounts. During Helen's first five years of employment, BCG subcontracted all its feasibility and marketing studies through Jackson & Co. This relationship was subsequently terminated because Jackson & Co. merged with a larger, more expensive consulting group. At the time of the termination, Helen and her supervisor were forced to select a new firm to conduct BCG's market research. However, Helen never informed the accounting department that the Jackson & Co. account had been closed. Her supervisor completely trusted her and allowed her to sign for all voucher payments less than $10,000. Helen was able to continue to process checks made payable

---

[2]The names of the perpetrator and the company have been changed.

FIGURE 12–2
Financial Data for Helen Weeks

	Year 1	Year 2	Year 3
Assets			
Residence	$100,000	$100,000	$100,000
Stocks and bonds	30,000	30,000	42,000
Automobiles	20,000	20,000	40,000
CD	50,000	50,000	50,000
Cash	6,000	12,000	14,000
Liabilities			
Mortgage balance	90,000	50,000	—0—
Auto loan	10,000	—0—	—0—
Income			
Salary		34,000	36,000
Other		6,000	6,000
Expenses			
Mortgage payments		6,000	6,000
Auto loan payments		4,800	4,800
Other living expenses		20,000	22,000

to Jackson's account. The accounting department continued to process the payments, and Helen would take responsibility for distributing the payments. She opened a bank account under the name Jackson & Co. and deposited the checks in the account. She paid all her personal expenses out of this account.

Assume that you are investigating Helen's fraud. As part of the investigation, you have searched public records and other sources and have accumulated financial information for Helen Weeks (see Figure 12–2).

With this information, you can use the net worth method to make an estimate of how much Helen may have embezzled. Your net worth calculations are shown in Figure 12–3.

Based on this calculation, you determine that Helen had at least $46,800 of unknown income in year 2 and $74,800 of unknown income in year 3. While this information could probably be used in court to obtain a restitution judgment against Helen, it could also be used to obtain a confession. A good investigator, armed with these data, could probably get a confession from Helen. Helen could be asked, without knowing that the investigator had the information, to make statements regarding her income and other sources of funds. After she had explained all her

FIGURE 12–3
Comparative Net Worth–Asset Method

	End Year 1	End Year 2	End Year 3
Assets:			
Residence	$100,000	$100,000	$100,000
Stocks and bonds	30,000	30,000	42,000
Auto	20,000	20,000	40,000
CD	50,000	50,000	50,000
Cash	6,000	12,000	14,000
Total assets	$206,000	$212,000	$246,000
Liabilities:			
Mortgage balance	$90,000	50,000	$—0—
Auto loan	10,000	—0—	—0—
Total liabilities	$100,000	$50,000	$—0—
Net worth	$106,000	$162,000	$246,000
Change in net worth		56,000	84,000
Plus total expenses		30,800	32,800
Total		$86,800	$116,800
Less known income		40,000	42,000
Equals income from unknown sources		$46,800	$74,800

sources, the investigator could provide information to show that she could not have sustained her lifestyle and paid her debts without additional income. Seeing that her story and explanations weren't realistic and not wanting to perjure herself, Helen would probably confess.

CONCLUDING COMMENTS

Conversion investigative techniques focus on how a suspect spends, or converts, stolen funds. A large number of public and private sources reveal information about how a person is spending money, buying assets, paying debts, and improving his or her lifestyle. Federal, state, and local government agencies, private companies such as credit bureaus, and publicly available databases all maintain information that can be extremely valuable in investigations. Investigators can choose to search these records on their own, which can be time-consuming and expensive, or they can hire experts to perform searches. Many companies have accumulated large amounts of publicly-available information and created their own databases. By using these databases and also being proficient at other types of searches, these companies can put together financial profiles quickly and inexpensively. Combined with evidence gained by using other investigative techniques, information obtained from public sources can be helpful in obtaining confessions, convictions, and restitutions.

Chapter Thirteen

Inquiry Investigative Methods
The Fraud-Triangle-Plus Approach

In this chapter, we conclude our discussion of fraud investigation techniques by discussing investigation methods that involve querying people (witnesses or suspects), either through interviewing or through various types of honesty testing. We will first discuss honesty testing, then cover interviewing and interrogation, and conclude with a consideration of lying and deception.

HONESTY TESTING

The most common inquiry investigative methods (and the most common of all investigation techniques) are interviewing and interrogation. However, there are at least four other methods of soliciting information about a person's honesty or whether or not he or she was involved in a fraud: (1) pencil-and-paper tests, (2) graphology, (3) voice stress analysis, and (4) polygraph examinations.[1]

Pencil-and-Paper Tests

Pencil-and-paper honesty tests are objective tests that elicit information about a person's honesty and personal code of ethics. They are used more frequently as employee screening devices than as tools to determine whether someone has committed a crime. Pencil-and-paper tests are alleged to be between 50 and 90 percent accurate. Some of the

---

[1]Again, the authors want to stress that we do not advocate all these types of testing. In particular, we have yet to see convincing evidence that either graphology or voice stress analysis has scientific validity.

more common ones are the Reid Report, the Personnel Selection Inventory, and the Stanton Survey. These honesty tests use questions such as:

True   False   1. It is natural for most people to be a little dishonest.

True   False   2. People who are dishonest should be sent to prison.

Answers to these and similar questions combine to create a profile of an individual's personal code of conduct, on which his or her riskiness to a business can be assessed. According to the developers of these tests, one of their advantages is that the results can be tabulated by a computer in a matter of minutes, making them ideal for applicant screening or initial identification of possible suspects. These tests are now being used by 42 percent of retailers in the United States.

Graphology

Graphology is the study of handwriting for the purpose of character analysis. Its use has increased substantially in the past five years. Graphology is being used in fields in which employee integrity is important, such as banking, manufacturing, and insurance. About 350 graphologists are currently working as consultants to US businesses.

The three primary uses of graphology are in (1) preemployment screening, (2) personality evaluation, and (3) career path evaluations. In addition, fraud investigators sometimes use graphologists to help gather evidence and evaluate suspects.

Voice Stress Analysis

Voice stress analysis is a method of determining whether a person is lying or telling the truth by using a mechanical device to detect variations of a microtremor in the voice. Three of the most common voice stress instruments are the Mark II, the PSE, and the Hagoth. Research has found that voice stress analysis is accurate only 50 to 60 percent of the time, because the instruments frighten users and make them appear dishonest. Recent legislation that makes it more difficult to use polygraph tests also governs the use of voice stress analysis.

Polygraph Examination

A *polygraph instrument* is a mechanical device that is hooked up to a suspect to determine whether he or she is telling the truth. Polygraphs are more complicated than voice stress analyzers in that they attempt to assess stress, and hence lying, by measuring several physical responses.

The theory is that people feel guilty when they lie or are dishonest. The guilt feelings produce stress, which is coped with by changes in behavior. Polygraphs measure pulse rate, blood pressure, galvanic skin response, and respiration. Like voice stress analyzers, polygraphs often lead to incorrect decisions because they frighten innocent people. In addition, they rarely detect psychopathic liars, who feel no stress because they have no consciences.

The Employee Polygraph Protection Act passed by Congress has made polygraphs difficult to use. While the devices are still legal, an investigator must meet 11 specific conditions in order to use a polygraph, one of which is that the investigator must inform the suspects that they don't have to take the test if they don't want to.

Polygraphs and voice stress analyzers are only as good as the experts who administer them. In the hands of an inexperienced administrator, they can be dangerous. Most experts agree that an individual who passes a polygraph examination is probably innocent, but that failure does not necessarily imply certain guilt. One of the most famous examples of a polygraph examination that failed was the one administered to confessed killer Mark Hoffman (described in Chapter 9).

INTERVIEWS

Interviewing, by far the most common technique used in investigating and resolving fraud, is the systematic questioning of persons who have knowledge of events, people, and evidence involved in a case under investigation. A good interviewer can quickly zero in on suspects and can usually get admissions from guilty parties. Interviews can help with the following: (1) obtaining information which establishes the essential elements of the crime, (2) obtaining leads for developing cases and gathering other evidence, (3) obtaining the cooperation of victims and witnesses, and (4) obtaining information concerning the personal backgrounds and motives of witnesses, in addition to the subject of the investigation.

Interviews can be conducted with victims, complainants, contacts, informants, clients or customers, suspects, expert witnesses, police officers, clerks, janitors, co-workers, supervisors, disgruntled spouses or friends, vendors and former vendors, and anyone else who might be helpful in an investigation. There are three types of interviews: (1) friendly, (2) neutral, and (3) hostile. Each type should be handled differently. The friendly interviewee goes above and beyond what is normally expected in order to be, or to appear, helpful. While friendly witnesses can be helpful, the investigator must be careful to determine their motives. In some cases, the motive will be a sincere desire to help. In other cases, the motive may be as complicated as a desire to get even with the suspect or a ploy to direct attention away from the interviewee as a suspect.

Neutral interviewees have nothing to gain or lose from the interview. They have no hidden motives or agendas, and they are usually the most objective and helpful of all interviewees. Hostile interviewees are the most difficult to interview. They are often associated in some way with the suspect or the crime. While friendly and neutral interviewees can be questioned at any time, and appointments can be made in advance, hostile interviewees should generally be questioned without prior notice. Surprise interviews provide hostile interviewees with less time to prepare defenses.

Understanding the Reactions of Interviewees

Fraud, like death or serious injury, is a crisis. People who are involved in or knowledgeable about a crisis generally have a predictable sequence of reactions to the crisis. Interviewers who understand these reactions are much more effective than interviewers who do not. The sequence of reactions is as follows:

1. Denial
2. Anger
3. Bargaining or rationalization
4. Depression
5. Acceptance

Denial functions as a buffer after a person receives unexpected shocking news. It allows people who are affected by or connected with the fraud to collect themselves and to mobilize other, less radical defenses. Denial involves screening out the reality of the situation.

Some studies have shown that carefully balanced psychological and physiological systems must be maintained in order for an individual to function normally. To avoid any sudden and severe disruption of the psychological equilibrium, which may destroy or incapacitate the system, the most immediate recourse is for the individual to maintain the status quo by denial. Since the individual is refusing to acknowledge the stress at either the cognitive or the emotional level, he or she is not motivated to initiate behavioral changes necessary to adjust to the new reality.

Denial may take many behavioral forms: appearing temporarily stunned or dazed; refusing to accept the information given; insisting that there is some mistake; or not comprehending what has been said. The denial reactions act as "shock absorbers" to reduce the impact of sudden trauma. Denial of fraud gives perpetrators time to alter, destroy, or conceal valuable documents and records. It also causes loss of time, which can mean that witnesses disappear or become confused, and can also mean that valuable documentary evidence, for example, gets lost.

When the first stage of denial cannot be maintained any longer, it is replaced by feelings of anger, rage, and resentment. The *anger* stage is difficult to cope with, because anger is usually displaced in all directions and projected onto the environment—at times, almost randomly. Anger usually arises because attempts to return to the old psychological status quo fail and are met with frustration. The anger is sometimes directed not only at the suspect but at others, including friends, relatives, and co-workers. Sometimes the anger is directed inward, resulting in feelings of guilt. Feelings of anger often lead managers and others to become hostile to auditors and investigators—to perceive them as cruel or unfeeling, a reaction not unlike that of the ancient Greeks who murdered messengers bearing evil tidings.

The anger stage is a dangerous time to resolve frauds. While angry, managers or others may insult, harm, slander, or libel employees or others, and may terminate employees, without due cause. The result of these actions is often lawsuits for slander, libel, assault, battery, or wrongful termination. An angry manager of a fast-food restaurant who felt that an employee was stealing had the police handcuff the employee and drag him out of the store in front of customers. The employee, who was later found to be innocent, sued and won a $250,000 lawsuit. In other circumstances, victims' angry reactions have allowed criminals to get legal settlements larger than the amounts they had stolen.

The *rationalization* stage is an attempt to justify the dishonest act and/or to minimize the crime. During this stage, managers see themselves as understanding why the crime was committed and often feel that the perpetrator's motivation may not have been all that bad. Managers often feel during this period that the perpetrator is not really a bad person, that a mistake was made, and that perhaps the suspect should be given one more chance. Interviews during the rationalization stage are often not objective and can even prove detrimental to attempts to determine the truth, or harmful to potential prosecution efforts. The rationalization stage leads to nonprosecution, easy penalties, and weak testimonies. Rationalization is the last attempt to return to the formerly established, psychologically steady state.

As attempts to resolve the problem repeatedly fail, hope diminishes. Managers are faced with the emotional burden of trauma. As trauma occurs, symptoms of *depression* appear: the person appears to be sad, and may become withdrawn or lose interest in the environment. Like the stages of denial, anger, and rationalization, depression is a normal part of the coping sequence necessary for eventual psychological readjustment. In this stage, managers can no longer deny or rationalize the dishonest act. Their anger is replaced by a sense of loss and disappointment—or sometimes embarrassment that a fraud could happen in their environments. During the depression stage, managers and others may become withdrawn and uncooperative. They may be unwilling to volunteer information or assist with investigations. Interviews conducted during this stage may be less useful than those held later, during the acceptance stage. The state of mind of potential witnesses should always be taken into consideration by fraud investigators.

Normal people cannot function in a continued stage of depression. Soon, managers try other behaviors in an attempt to adjust to the new situation. After a small fraud with minimal impact, readjustment to a steady psychological state requires only a small amount of psychological change. After a larger fraud with significant ramifications (such as embarrassment, loss of client, public exposure, or job jeopardy), individuals may repeat the entire coping sequence a number of times, or may fluctuate between two phases, as they try to reach a new psychological equilibrium.

Eventually, they will reach a state in which they no longer experience depression or anger; rather, they just have a realistic understanding of what happened. *Acceptance* is not a happy state; it is an acknowledgement of what happened and a desire to resolve the issue and move on. This phase is often precipitated by a knowledge of the facts surrounding the fraud, including a knowledge of the motivations of the perpetrator. It is during this phase that interviews are most useful and witnesses most cooperative.

To illustrate how these reactions occur when a fraud is committed, consider the following fraud, which was first described in Chapter 7.[2]

This case involves a fraud of over $5,000 by a supervisor in the shipping department of a wholesale–retail distribution center warehouse facility. The supervisor was responsible for the overall general operations of the warehouse and had individual accountability for a cash fund that was used for collecting money (usually amounts between $25 and $500) from customers who came to the warehouse to pick up COD orders. The established procedures called for the supervisor to issue the customer a cash receipt, which was recorded in a will call–delivery log book. The file containing details on the customer order would eventually be matched with cash receipts by accounting personnel, and the transaction would be closed.

Over a period of approximately one year, the supervisor defrauded the company by stealing small amounts of money. He attempted to conceal the fraud by submitting credit memos (with statements such as "billed to the wrong account," "to correct billing adjustment," and "miscellaneous") to

[2]W. Steve Albrecht, and Timothy L. Williams, "Understanding Reactions to Fraud," *Internal Auditor*, August 1990, pp. 45–50.

clear the accounts receivable file. The accounts would be matched with the credit memo, and the transactions would be closed. A second signature was not needed on the credit memos, and accounting personnel asked no questions about the credit memos originated by the supervisor of the warehouse. At first the supervisor submitted only two or three fraudulent credit memos a week, totaling approximately $100. After a few months, however, he increased the amount of his theft to about $300 per week. To give the appearance of randomness, so as to keep the accounting personnel from becoming suspicious, the supervisor intermixed comparatively large credit memo amounts and smaller ones.

The fraud surfaced when the supervisor accidentally credited the wrong customer's account for a cash transaction. By coincidence, the supervisor was on vacation when the error surfaced and was not available to cover his tracks when accounting personnel queried the transaction. Because of his absence, the accounts receivable clerk questioned the manager of the warehouse, who investigated the problem. The manager scrutinized cash receipts and determined that the potential for fraud existed.

Stage 1. Denial. Because of the possibility of fraud, the general manager and the warehouse manager started their own investigation of the warehouse cash fund. Sensing a serious problem, they decided to wait until the supervisor returned from vacation before taking further action.

Both managers became anxious and somewhat irritable during the week before the supervisor returned. Each manager, independently, later said that his ability to perform had been adversely affected by the shock and his preoccupation with the matter. Even though they realized the potential for fraud, both managers rationalized that the error could probably be explained by the supervisor, who had been with the firm for approximately three years and was an individual whom they considered to be a model employee.

After the fact, both managers admitted that they had tried to deny that the falsified credit memos could represent intentional fraud on behalf of the supervisor. Because of their denial, they didn't take advantage of evidence that was readily available during the suspect employee's absence.

Company procedure required managers to contact either corporate security or the internal audit department if a fraud occurred or was suspected. However, both managers had convinced themselves that fraud was not even a possibility, because of their knowledge and trust of the supervisor. When the supervisor returned from vacation, the managers asked him to come into a private office and discuss the situation. Still in the denial stage, the managers simply requested an explanation from the supervisor regarding the handling of the cash fund. The supervisor, now thrown into his own initial stage of crisis, also took a position of denial and advised both managers that he did not know what they were talking about. Had he offered an alternative explanation for the credit memos and accounting error, the managers, who were still denying fraud, probably would have been satisfied and terminated their suspicions and investigation.

Because the supervisor denied the existence of the credit memos, which was an obvious misrepresentation, the managers decided that further investigation would be needed and sent the supervisor back to his job. From an investigative standpoint, sending the supervisor back to his desk was a risky action. He was placed back in control of the original credit memos and cash transaction logs and could have easily destroyed a great deal of evidence. Simply "losing" the records could have concealed the fraud and jeopardized the investigation. At this point, the warehouse managers requested the assistance of internal audit to review the matter further. A full week passed before investigative assistance was made available.

Stage 2. Anger.   During the one-week waiting period, both managers became very angry with the suspect and decided, in their own minds, that fraud had indeed been committed. They discussed their feelings and decided to confront the employee again. This time they vowed that they would get answers. Clearly, both managers were evolving from the denial stage to the anger stage.

Without the additional information that could have been provided through a full investigation, the managers again confronted the supervisor and demanded an explanation. The supervisor simply said nothing. Irate, the managers fired the employee on the spot, without additional information or explanations.

This emotional firing could have jeopardized the investigation and the company in several ways. First, if fraud had not been committed, the company could have been subjected to litigation and sued for wrongful dismissal, slander, or libel. Second, the harsh treatment could have jeopardized further cooperation by the perpetrator in the investigation. The basis for the termination was that several falsified credit memorandums (totaling between $300 and $400) had been located by the managers.

The subsequent audit revealed that there were over 100 falsified credit memos and that the losses were actually more than $5,000. The managers were surprised at the extent of the fraud. In addition, the managers placed the corporation in a position of liability because they had directly accused the supervisor of fraud well before a case was developed that clearly demonstrated his guilt.

Stage 3. Bargaining and Rationalization.   After the termination took place, the general manager rationalized that both he and the warehouse manager might have acted too quickly in terminating the supervisor. Regardless of whether or not the supervisor was guilty, they felt that perhaps they should give him one more chance. They also realized that they had acted too quickly and in anger when they fired the employee; they had begun to worry about the company liability in the matter. Although rehiring the supervisor would have been contrary to company policy, the general manager felt he could "save" this "valued" employee.

Through rationalization, the general manager was trying to come to grips with the fact that a trusted friend and employee had committed a fraud against the firm. He was "bargaining," or trying to change the facts in some way to provide an alternative—a more acceptable explanation, although none existed.

Stage 4. Depression. During the bargaining stage of the crisis, both the general manager and the warehouse manager became less irritated and much more withdrawn. Feelings of depression began to envelop both individuals as the reality of what had happened started to hit home.

The feelings of depression were reinforced by comments and reactions from other warehouse employees, who were beginning to learn what had occurred. The fact that the internal auditors were in the supervisor's office for over a week added to the employees uncomfortableness and concern. It was highly unusual for auditors to be around for more than one or two days, and rumors that the supervisor had been terminated added to misunderstandings. Interestingly enough, during this period neither manager discussed his feelings with the other. Rather, they kept their feelings to themselves, apparently because they felt that the employee had suffered enough and that the case should be closed.

Stage 5. Acceptance. The investigation conducted by corporate security and internal audit revealed the following facts:

- The supervisor had a substance abuse problem involving cocaine and alcohol. As a result of his confrontation with management, he was considering rehabilitation.

- The supervisor had rationalized the theft by believing that he was simply borrowing the money. In his mind, he had every intention of repaying the loan; he had become caught up in the machinations of the fraud and was surprised that in less than one year he had defrauded the company of over $5,000.

- The supervisor informed security personnel that he had spent almost his entire life savings on cocaine and had lost his family in the process. Losing his job was the last straw.

- In discussions with local management, it was learned that several managers and employees had noticed a change in the behavior of the supervisor over the past two to three months. The behavior changes, which no one had acted upon, had included frequent mood changes (he was bright and cheerful in the morning but extremely depressed later in the day); frequent tardiness and absenteeism; and a preoccupation with impressing other employees by taking them out to lunch during which the supervisor talked relentlessly.

Once these facts were known, both managers accepted the fraud as a reality and felt that they were back in control of the situation. Their desire now was to resolve the fraud and move on to normal operations.

Planning an Interview

Whenever you conduct an interview, you should follow specific guidelines to make sure that your objectives will be met. Proper planning will allow you to get the most from the interview and to minimize the time spent on it. Such planning involves ascertaining in advance as many facts as possible about the offense and the interviewee, and establishing a location and time for the interview that are conducive to success.

In obtaining facts about the offense and the interviewee, interviewers should review relevant documents to gather as much other information as possible about the following factors:

The offense

- The legal nature of the offense.
- The date, time, and place of occurrence.
- The way in which the crime appears to have been committed.
- Possible motives.
- All evidence that is available.

The interviewee

- Personal background information—age, education, marital status, etc.
- Attitude toward investigation.
- Any physical or mental conditions, such as the use of alcohol or drugs.

It is usually best (except with hostile interviewees) to conduct an interview at the interviewee's office or workplace, (so that the interviewee will have access to any necessary papers, books, and other evidence). In addition, such a location is generally more convenient for the interviewee. The interview room should be one where distractions from colleagues and telephones can be eliminated or minimized.

Investigators should usually set up an appointment with a friendly interviewee and should allow sufficient (perhaps even excess) time for the interview. When setting up the appointment, the interviewer should identify information that will be needed in the interview. Wherever possible, only one person should be interviewed at a time.

The Interviewer's Demeanor

An interviewer should always be efficient, courteous, polite, and careful with language during an interview. Here are some specific suggestions for interviews:

- Sit fairly close to the interviewee with no desk or furniture between you. Don't walk around the room; stay seated.

- Avoid talking down to the person. (Don't assume the person is less intelligent that you).
- Be sensitive to the personal concerns of the witness, especially in regard to such matters as sex, race, religion, and ethnic background.
- Be businesslike. Conduct the interview in a professional manner. Be friendly but not familiar or social. Remember that you are seeking the truth, not trying to get a confession or a conviction.
- Avoid being authoritarian or attempting to dominate the interview.
- Always be sympathetic and respectful. (If appropriate, tell the subject that anyone else under similar conditions or circumstances might have done the same as he or she did.)
- Give careful thought to your language. Don't use technical jargon.
- Be complimentary to the witness for taking the time and trouble to cooperate.
- Keep pencil and paper out of sight during the interview.
- End every cooperative interview by expressing your sincere appreciation.

The Specific Language of Interviews

Language is very important in an interview. Successful interviewers usually follow specific language guidelines, such as the following:

- Use short questions, confined to one topic, which can be clearly and easily understood.
- Ask questions that require narrative answers; whenever possible, avoid eliciting yes and no answers.
- Avoid questions that suggest part of the answer. (These are called *leading questions.*)
- Require witnesses to give the factual basis for any conclusions they state.
- Prevent witnesses from aimlessly wandering. Require direct responses.
- Don't let witnesses lead you away from the topic. Don't let them confuse the issue or leave basic questions unanswered.
- At any given point, concentrate more on the answer you are hearing than on the next question you plan to ask.
- Clearly understand each answer before you continue.
- Maintain full control of the interview.
- Point out some, but not all, of the circumstantial evidence.

Structuring an Interview

Every interview has three parts: the introduction, the body, and the close. During the introduction, background information about the interviewee should be obtained and the purpose of the interview should be clearly stated. The introduction is the time to get a commitment of cooperation from the interviewee.

It is during the body of the interview that information is obtained. This is when open-ended questions should be asked and facts should be examined in detail. There are several ways to organize questions during this part of the interview. One method is to cover the fraud in chronological sequence. Another is to proceed from the general to the specific. A third is to use documents to control the sequence of questions. The interview should not be terminated until the interviewer has exhausted every possibility of discovering as much information as possible about the who, why, how, what, when, and where of the fraud.

During the closing part of the interview, the investigator thanks the interviewee for his or her cooperation. Every close should include questions such as:

> Is there anything else you would like to tell me?
>
> Have I forgotten anything that I should ask you?
>
> Can you suggest anyone else I should talk to?

Be sure to end every interview by being polite as possible. You may want to interview the person again.

The two most common mistakes investigators make in conducting interviews are poor planning before approaching the interviewee and pushing the interviewee too hard.

INTERROGATIONS

In a confrontational interview or interrogation, suspects or uncooperative witnesses are questioned to obtain evidence not available by other means. The goal may be to give the subject of the investigation an opportunity to volunteer facts and/or to obtain a legally binding confession of guilt. Confrontational interviews can also be helpful in accumulating evidence that neutralizes defenses and that can perjure or impeach the suspect.

Confrontational interviews should not normally be conducted until all other investigative procedures have been completed or until there is evidence that can be obtained only from the suspect. Indeed, investigations should begin as tangentially as possible and should work inward toward

FIGURE 13–1
Investigating a Kickback Scheme

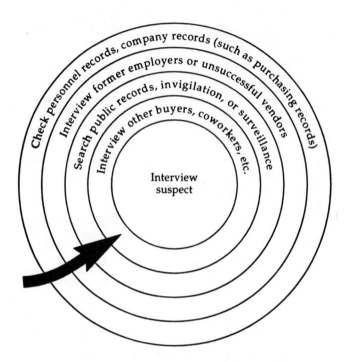

the suspect until, finally, the suspect is interviewed. Figure 13–1 shows how an investigation should proceed for a suspected kickback scheme.

In order to be legally binding, confessions must be given voluntarily. This means that the suspect must be able to terminate the interview at will, and must be free to leave at any time. Interrogations should be carefully controlled by the investigator. They should normally be conducted by surprise, and should be held either in a neutral location or at the interviewer's workplace. The location should be one where privacy can be ensured, where no locks or other barriers prevent the suspect from exiting, and where distractions are minimized.

Strategy

The strategy used in a confrontational interview is quite different from that used in interviewing friendly and neutral witnesses. While the introduction is similar, including the obtaining of background information, the body of the confrontational interview is different. In most cases, interviewers are likely to be successful in obtaining a confession when they confront the suspect directly, rather than trying to elicit information. The interviewer should state the allegations clearly and should identify the interviewee as the primary suspect. Denials and refutations by suspects should be immediately cut off, and partial admissions of guilt should be obtained whenever possible. Partial confessions can be gradually expanded during the interrogation, until a full confession is obtained.

Good confrontational interviewers will realize that there is an artificial wall between them and their suspects. This wall is composed of guilt feelings, fear of consequences, and fear of embarrassment. The wall can be removed and a confession obtained by reducing the crime in the eyes of the perpetrator and maximizing sympathy for the suspect. Statements such as "I can understand why someone would do this" and "Under the same pressure anyone would do the same thing" reduce the crime in the mind of the suspect. Statements such as "I want to help you" and "I will do everything I can to minimize consequences" maximize sympathy.

The Signed Confession

Whenever a hostile witness or a suspect is interviewed, a confession which can be signed during the interview should be prepared in advance. Signed confessions should be witnessed by at least two people and should include a statement to the effect that the confession was made of the suspect's own free will, without threat or promise of any kind.

Figure 13–2 is a sample confession statement.

DECEPTION AND LYING

One of the biggest problems an interrogator has is determining whether a suspect or witness is lying or being truthful. Most people lie to avoid punishment or to receive awards. People defend themselves by lying until the pain of their own conscience becomes unbearable or until outside influences prompt them to reveal their guilt. When people lie, they become fearful and develop nervous symptoms, such as a pulsation of the carotid artery, dry lips, excessive activity of the Adam's apple, and/or swearing to the truthfulness of their assertions.

There are several types of liars. Most common are the following six types:

1. *Panic liar.* Lies because of intense fear of the consequences of confessing. This person feels that his or her embarrassment in front of friends and loved ones would be too great to bear. Confessing would be a blow to his or her ego. This sort of liar believes that confessing would make a bad situation worse.

FIGURE 13–2
Confession Statement

I, Jane Smith, furnish the following free and voluntary statement to Keith Curtis and Julie McElvy, who have identified themselves to me as corporate security investigators/internal auditors for Madison Meats. No threats or promises of any kind have been used to induce this statement.

I have been advised that an internal inquiry is being conducted to determine whether or not I have accepted any unlawful gratuities in my position as manager for Madison Meats. I have also been advised that I am the target of this internal inquiry; that the allegations could constitute a criminal act; and that I have a right to an attorney, should I choose.

I have been employed by Madison Meats since February 2, 1973, and since January 1988, I have been employed as the manager of Madison Meats.

I freely admit that I have accepted gratuities from Mark Thompson, sales representative of Mercury Meats, Denver, Colorado. The total amount of money I have received is approximately __*$10,000*__, which has been paid to me by Mr. Thompson since January 1993. Mark Thompson paid me this money to ensure that I would increase purchases from his company. I was aware at the time I began taking money from Thompson that such conduct was illegal and violated Madison Meats policy. I am truly sorry for my conduct, and I would like to do anything I can to repay damages I have caused Madison Meats. No one else at Madison Meats was involved, or had knowledge of my activities.

I have read the above statement. I have initialed the page and filled in the amount of money received, and I now sign my name because this statement is true and correct to the best of my knowledge.

_____*Jane Smith*_____

Jane Smith   Date
Witnesses:

_____*Keith Curtis*_____

_____*Julie McElvy*_____

---

2. *Occupational liar.* Has lied for years, maybe in sales work, on expense accounts, and so forth. This person is a practical liar.
3. *Tournament liar.* Loves to lie. Lying is a personal challenge. Each person becomes a new conquest. This liar began by deceiving mother and father, and has lied ever since.
4. *Sadistic liar.* Lying is the only weapon available. The sadistic liar realizes that he or she may be convicted but will not give

investigators the satisfaction of confessing. This person is the martyr type, who enjoys seeing his or her family suffer because the law is punishing an "innocent" person.

5. *Ethnological liar.* Was taught by parents that "no one likes a squealer." The creed of the Mafia represents this type of thinking. This person loves to be interrogated.

6. *Psychopathic liar.* Seems to be without conscience, and shows no regret about acts of wrongdoing. This person shows no manifestation of guilt. This is the hardest type of liar to understand—a great actor who can fool most investigators.

Lying is hard work. Telling a significant lie in an interview or an interrogation is tough. Good interviewers can recognize a suspect's struggling, halting, and laboring. Experts have identified several verbal and nonverbal cues to lying (Figure 13–3).

Exhibition of one or more of the cues listed in Figure 13–3 does not in itself mean that a suspect is lying. Good interrogators use a process known as *calibration* to determine whether cues represent evidence of lying or are simply nervous reactions. In this process, the interrogator calibrates or assesses the suspect's behavior and speech when questions are asked about subjects with which the suspect is comfortable. This behavior and speech is then compared to the suspect's reactions to questions about specifics of the crime. In order to properly calibrate the suspect's reactions, it may be necessary to repeat each type of questioning several times. If the types are repeated often enough, differences in both verbal and nonverbal reactions can usually be assessed.

Defense Mechanisms Used to Hide Guilt

Suspects who are lying often use one or more of the following four defense mechanisms to hide their guilt: (1) disassociation, (2) projection, (3) rationalization, and (4) identification. A person who is using the *disassociation* defense will normally be present in body but not in mind. Such individuals appear preoccupied, lack animation, seem vague and evasive, and talk about everything but the crime. When asked about the incident, these persons will describe nonrelated activities in detail. They will say they haven't thought about the crime, do not suspect anyone, and have no idea how the crime could have been committed. They will not take the initiative and will use expressions such as "Not that I can recall" and "To the best of my knowledge." They will often become sullen and stare into space, and will sometimes appear to be physically exhausted.

Suspects who are hiding behind the defense mechanism of *projection* will demonstrate hostility toward everyone. They will project their guilt onto others and will displace outwardly all that becomes troublesome from within. They will blame everyone else for their problems and will appear to be highly indignant while they are being questioned about the crime. They will often attempt to take the offensive and will become incensed when you suggest or even insinuate that they might be guilty. Once a confession has been obtained, such a person becomes docile.

Rationalizing is a defense mechanism that involves substituting good reasons for the real reasons behind the perpetrator's actions. Suspects will probably state that the stolen property was lost, not stolen, or that there must be some kind of mistake. They will also say that the loss is insignificant, and that the company or victim made it easy for the crime to occur or even tempted the perpetrator. They may state that the poor person who stole the money was probably underpaid and was therefore not really stealing. They will take all actions possible to minimize the crime and will state that they believe no one would deliberately steal. These persons will try to justify the intentions of the perpetrator rather than the actions that were taken.

FIGURE 13–3   *Verbal and Nonverbal Cues to Lying*

Verbal Cues

Response to a Question.
Truthful people tend to respond directly to a question; untruthful people tend to be circumspect in their answers.

Length of time before giving response.
People who are telling lies generally take longer to give a response to a question, in order to gain additional time in which to think what to say.

Repetition of question.
Repeating the questions is a specific technique used to gain additional time to think of a response.

Fragmented sentences.
Many untruthful people speak in fragmented or incomplete sentences.

Oaths.
Oaths (such as "I swear to God") are frequently used by deceptive persons, in an attempt to add credibility to their lies. Truthful people have no need to give oaths.

Clarity of response.
Liars frequently mumble their responses to questions, or hedge on their answers.

Use of words.
Untruthful persons tend to answer with "soft" words—for example, "I did not *take* the money."

Assertiveness.
Truthful people tend to be assertive about their innocence, while untruthful people are usually passive.

Inconsistencies.
Inconsistencies in statements are among the best indicators of deception.

Indirect speech.
Truthful people tend to be direct in their answers; liars try to answer difficult questions indirectly.

FIGURE 13–3 (*concluded*)

Nonverbal Cues

Emblems.
Emblems are signals made with the body, the meanings of which are clearly understood. An example is a nod of the head. In some cases involving deception, the emblem is not completed, but is halted abruptly.

Ilustrators.
Illustrators are motions, primarily made with the hands, that are used for expression. Untruthful people sometimes use illustrators that seem out of place or deliberate.

Manipulators.
Manipulators are mostly habitual behaviors in which the person repeatedly touches himself or herself. Examples include grooming the hair and wringing the hands. Use of manipulators tends to increase during periods of stress.

Breathing.
Stress generally produces an increase in breathing rate, which can sometimes be an indicator of deception.

Frequent swallowing.
Frequent swallowing or throat clearing, which is common in stressful situations, may indicate deception.

Microexpressions.
Microexpressions are hidden expressions that are "leaked" for a short period of time—usually for less than a quarter of a second. The expression being leaked always indicates concealed emotion. Through proper training, interviewers can learn to detect these expressions.

Precaution

The evaluation of deception is an art, not a science. It cannot be used for any purpose other than to pursue a line of inquiry. No one cue has any particular meaning; all cues must be evaluated together.

Source: These cues were taken from the video, "How to Tell if Someone *Is* Lying," produced by the Association of Certified Fraud Examiners (ACFE), 1989, 716 West Avenue, Austin, Texas 78701.

Identification is a defense mechanism in which suspects portray themselves as "holier than thou." They would like you to believe that they have never had an off-color or dishonest thought. They repeatedly tell you how honest they are, how often they go to church, and that they are always helping other people. They carry the good-person image to an extreme.

Example

To understand how a perpetrator might start to develop defense mechanisms, consider the case of Harry Brown. Harry, who had been honest until he embezzles a deposit, will be a different person after he becomes dishonest.

You have met Harry Brown a hundred times. He is a typical accounts payable clerk in a major corporation. He is between 35 and 45 years of age, and he is married and has two children. He has been employed by the company for seven years. He has a good record. Not a single complaint has ever been made against him which would necessitate an inquiry by an investigator.

In the last year, however, the routine life of Harry Brown has undergone a severe change. Because of illness in his family, he has become financially encumbered to the desperation point. To Harry, the anguish of his personal problems is unbearable. This change in his life has a direct bearing on his relationship with his company. For the first time, he has become a definite security risk.

One morning Harry arrives at work and notices a deposit bag lying on a desk. He realizes immediately that the night clerk has forgotten to deposit the bag in the night vault. He knows from previous experience that there must be at least $2,000 to $3,000 in this bag. In these few moments, an impulsive idea enters his mind. The money in the bag seems to be a solution to his personal financial problems. Varying thoughts race through his mind.

Unfortunately for Harry Brown, he is placed in a position which is the common denominator to all crime; he has both the *opportunity* to steal and the belief that his crime will go undetected. At this moment, Harry is consumed by *pressure*. The ready-made solution which lies before him is so enticing that it overcomes any personal fears he might have about social and legal reprisals for the act he is contemplating. Harry is *rationalizing* his action.

His conscience or the built-in braking system which has kept him honest all his life, now slips. He reaches out to steal the bag. He secretes the bag in a place where it will not be found, so that he can recover it later. From these moments on, Harry Brown is no longer the same human being. His entire behavior pattern will change, to manifest his guilt.

After the commission of the crime, Harry Brown becomes enveloped by emotions of fear and guilt. The counterpart to the mental experience of an emotion is a physiological feeling. Fear and guilt express themselves in extremely unpleasant sensations. Technically, these unpleasant sensations or feelings are called *stress*. Prolonged stress can take a toll on human beings.

Harry Brown, now possessed of fear and guilt, becomes a victim of terrible stress; but, like all human beings, he possesses a psychological method of coping with stress—development of defense mechanisms.

The defense mechanisms covered in this chapter are the most common ways to handle stress. As an investigator, you must recognize and understand these defense mechanisms when you encounter them in the course of your work.

CONCLUDING COMMENTS

Interviewing is the most common of all investigative techniques. Among the numerous books that have been written on the subject of interviewing, one of the best is *Criminal Interrogation and Confessions*, by Fred E. Inbau and John E. Reid.[4] The authors of this book sponsor the John E. Reid & Associates School of Interviewing which is located in Chicago. In addition, the ACFE, which has its central headquarters in Austin, Texas, sponsors numerous seminars on interviewing techniques. In this chapter, we have only touched the surface of this complex topic. If you are serious about the investigation of fraud, you should work hard to become an excellent interviewer. You should read one or more books on the subject, and you should take advantage of some of the excellent training that is available. Many frauds are solved, and many confessions and restitutions are obtained, because of good interviewing skills. Many other fraud investigations are blown because of interviewing mistakes. Taking counseling courses can be another excellent means of developing the listening and observation skills needed to interview people in fraud inquiries.

---

[4]Fred E Imbau and John E Reid, *Criminal Interrogation and Confessions*, Baltimore, MD: The Williams and Willins Co., 1967.

Chapter Fourteen

Concluding the Investigation
The Fraud Report

Wherever possible, fraud investigations should conclude with the obtaining of a signed confession of guilt from the perpetrator or perpetrators, and with an accurate calculation of the extent of theft and losses. The confession and the loss calculation, as well as the fraud investigative techniques discussed in the last four chapters, must be carefully documented so that civil, criminal, or other actions can be supported. The American Institute of Certified Public Accountants (AICPA), the Institute of Internal Auditors (IIA), the American Society of Industrial Security (ASIS), and the National Association of Certified Fraud Examiners (NACFE) all have reporting guidelines. The following excerpts from the IIA's reporting standards on fraud provide an example[1]:

> A preliminary or a final report may be desirable at the conclusion of the detection phase. This report should include the internal auditor's [or corporate security's] conclusions as to whether sufficient information exists to conduct an investigation. It should also summarize the findings that serve as the basis for such decisions.
>
> A formal [written] report should be issued at the end of the investigation phase. This report should include all findings, conclusions, recommendations, and corrective action taken.
>
> The internal audit report should indicate all pertinent facts uncovered relative to the who, what, where, when, how, and why of the fraud. It should also include recommendations for control improvements to minimize the exposure to similar occurrences in the future. It should not contain recommendations for disciplinary or legal action against anyone suspected of fraudulent or illegal activity, even when the internal audit investigation provides tenable evidence

---

[1]*Deterrence, Detection, Investigation, and Reporting of Fraud*, Statement on Internal Auditing Standards No. 3 (Maitland, Fla.: Institute of Internal Auditors, 1985), p. 9.

of probable culpability and/or complicity. However, the director of corporate security or the internal auditor—usually the director of internal auditing—should participate with management in decision making discussions.

Particular care should be exercised to ensure that the general tone of the internal audit report is neither accusatory nor conclusive as to guilt. Even when a confession of culpability or complicity is obtained from a suspect or suspects during a fraud investigation, such confession may not be considered valid or consequential evidence of guilt of fraud until a court of law so decides. This is so even when management has already taken disciplinary action on the basis of the confession. A security or internal audit report that includes reference to a confession obtained in the course of a fraud investigation should state merely that admission of the alleged or suspected events was obtained—not that guilt was acknowledged.

Attention to language is important to assure absence of subjective, inflammatory, libelous, or other prejudicial connotations. To be objectively factual, unbiased, and free from distortion, the internal audit report should refer to "alleged" irregularities, activity, conduct, etc. Accordingly, the activities investigated and reported should be described as "purported" or "alleged" to have occurred. When audit findings support the allegations, the internal audit report should be couched in language such as the following:

a. "The corporate security investigation disclosed the existence of reasonably credible evidence to support the allegation."

b. "The internal audit investigation concludes with a rebuttable presumption that the allegations or suspicions are tenable."

c. "The internal audit investigation concludes with plausible evidence in support of the allegation."

EXAMPLE OF A FRAUD REPORT

To illustrate the investigation of an employee fraud and the kind of report that should be prepared to document investigative procedures, we present a completed fraud report of the investigation of "Ivan Ben Steelin", a real estate purchasing representative who worked for "Table Deals Inc." Ivan was involved in accepting kickbacks from a company we'll call "Red Hot Real Estate" and in allowing inflation of real estate prices.

The fraud investigation documented by the report involves all four types of investigative procedures. The investigation is predicated on an anonymous tip received in a letter addressed to the company president. The investigation begins with a review of the suspect's personnel records. It includes one theft act investigative procedure—surveillance of the suspects at a local restaurant. It includes several concealment-based investigative procedures, including computer searches of company databases; calculations of total purchase transactions by each real estate buyer; and determinations of the number of real estate agencies used, the average price per acre paid, and the number of purchase transactions made with each vendor. The report documents public records searches and net worth conversion investigative procedures. Searches were made of voter registration and marriage records, the secretary of state's records, and real estate and contracting office records at the county level. Query investigation procedures involved neutral interviews with the company's personnel manager, a home builder, and a company secretary, as well as a friendly interview with another real estate buyer and a hostile interview with the real estate agent who was suspected of making illegal payments to Ivan Ben Steelin. An interrogation of Ivan Ben Steelin in order to gain access to his bank records leads to a signed confession. The investigation concludes with the obtaining of a signed confession statement and the calculation of real estate overpayments (losses) by the company.[2]

While the report is not perfect, it does provide an excellent example of the kinds of investigative procedures and documentation that should be included in fraud investigations. We encourage you to read it carefully.

---

[2]This report was prepared by Scott R. Bulloch, a masters of accounting student in Steve Albrecht's fraud auditing course (winter semester 1993) at Brigham Young University, Provo, UT, and is included here with his permission. The report was written in partial fulfillment of the requirements for the course, and each student prepared a similar report. The fraud, the individuals involved, and the investigative procedures are ficticious but realistic.

INVESTIGATIVE REPORT
ON IVAN BEN STEELIN

Table
Deals
Inc.

Internal Audit (or Corporate Security)
Special Cases File
030369

sb
1-1-93

Table
⌐ Deals ⌐
Inc.

Internal Audit Special Cases File
(IASCF) 030369

Regarding
Ivan Ben Steelin

FILE INDEX

Table
Deals
Inc.

To: IASCF 030369
From: Scott R Bulloch
Date: January 1, 1993
Re: Ivan Ben Steelin
Subject: Unsigned letter regarding Ivan Ben Steelin

On December 28, 1992, an unsigned letter was received by Vic Tumms, president and CEO of Table Deals Inc. The letter, dated December 27, 1992, referred to Ivan Ben Steelin; the letter is self-explanatory.

On December 30, 1992 the letter and its contents were discussed in a meeting at which Scott R Bulloch (Table Deals' internal auditor), Vic Tumms, and Sue U Buttz (Table Deals' legal counsel) were present.

Predicated on the contents of the letter, an investigation was commissioned by Sue U Buttz, and was set to commence on January 1, 1993.

The original letter was initialed by Scott R Bulloch, and is maintained as evidence in IASCF 030369.

1

Table
Deals
Inc.

December 27, 1992

Mr. Vic Tumms
President
Table Deals Inc.
5511 Vero Beach Road
Orem, UT 84057

Dear Mr. Tumms:

I believe you should investigate the relationship between Ivan Ben Steelin, the real estate acquisition manager, and Red Hot Real Estate. I believe we paid significantly more than fair market value for the 200 acres we purchased in the river bottom, as well as for several other properties.

Sincerely,

A Concerned Associate

2
1-1-93

Table
⌐ Deals ⌐
Inc.

To: IASCF 030369
From: Scott R Bulloch
Date: January 2, 1993
Re: Ivan Ben Steelin
Subject: Interview with Rebecca Monson

Synopsis

Rebecca Monson, personnel manager of Table Deals, advised on January 2, 1993, that Ivan Ben Steelin had been employed at Table Deals since January 7, 1985. Steelin's salary in 1992 was $45,000, and his supervisor was RaNae Workman, vice president of external affairs.

Details

Rebecca Monson, personnel manager of Table Deals, was interviewed at her office, 5511 Vero Beach Road, Orem, Utah, telephone (999) 555-3463, on January 2, 1993. Rebecca was advised of the identity of the interviewers, Scott R Bulloch and Sue U Buttz, and provided the following information. Rebecca was advised that the nature of the inquiry was an "internal investigation of misconduct," as per the company's code of conduct.

The personnel records reflect that Ivan Ben Steelin, white male, date of birth August 5, 1956, Social Security 999-06-2828, residing at 1156 North Ocean Boulevard, Orem, Utah, telephone (999) 225-1161, had been employed at Table Deals since January 7, 1985. According to the records, Steelin was married and had four children.

Steelin's initial salary was $38,000 per year, and he was an investment analyst in the external affairs department. Steelin was enlisted into the management training program on his hire date. His supervisor after he became an investment analyst was Mickey Sheraton, vice president of external affairs.

On January 1, 1987, Steelin was promoted to a purchasing representative position, still in the external affairs department. Steelin's salary was $45,000 per year, as reflected by the 1992 salary file.   3

RaNae Workman became vice president of external affairs in August of 1988, and was Ivan's immediate supervisor.

According to the records, prior to his employment with Table Deals, Ivan Ben Steelin was employed by Rockwell Laboratories in St. Louis, Missouri. His reason for leaving Rockwell laboratories as stated on the personnel information card, was that he wanted to be closer to his family in Utah.

No background investigation was conducted by the company prior to hiring Steelin at Table Deals.

First National, Second National, Third National, and Fourth National Banks called in February 1988 to confirm Steelin's employment with Tabl Deals. The personnel department enters the nature of the inquiry in the personnel database each time an outside party asks about Table Deal's employees. No other parties have requested information about Steelin since February 1988.

The original personnel information card and a copy of outside party inquiries, (consisting of 2 pages) were obtained from Rebecca Monson and initialed and dated by Scott R Bulloch. They are maintained in IASCF 030369. Copies were left with Rebecca Monson.

Rebecca Monson was advised to keep the interview and its issues confidential.

4

Personnel Information Card

Hire date: January 7, 1985   Social Security number: 999-06-2828
Name: Steelin, Ivan Ben   Birth date: August 5, 1956

Address at time of hire:
  1156 North Ocean Boulevard
  Orem, UT 84057

Emergency Contact:
  James Clintock   Relation: Father-in-law
  1145 North 8000 West   (999) 555-7974
  Orem, UT 84057

Previous Employers
_____

Rockwell Laboratories   Position: Sales agent
66 Market Street   Supervisor: Jeff Cole,
St. Louis, MO 63101   Sales Manager
                                               Dates: 1980–1984

Reason for leaving: Would like to be closer to family in Utah.

Ethics University   Position: Mail courier
Provo, UT 85926   Supervisor: Joseph Starks,
                                                 Mail Manager
                                               Dates: 1977–1980

Reason for leaving: Graduated from Ethics University and accepted a position in St. Louis.

Reason for leaving:

Other pertinent information

Ivan Ben Steelin   1-7-85
_____
Signature   Date
_____

Administrative Use Only
Background Check: No
Other: None

sb
5
1-2-93

Outside Party Inquiries
Print date: January 2, 1993
Employee: Ivan Ben Steelin
File: 528062828

Date	Party	Contact	Purpose
2/2/88	First National Bank	Loan department	Confirm employment
2/4/88	Second National Bank	None given	Confirm employment
2/12/88	Third National Bank	Loan department	Confirm employment
2/16/88	Fourth National Bank	Credit department	Confirm employment

Table
⌐Deals⌐
Inc.

To: IASCF 030369
From: Scott R Bulloch
Date: January 4, 1993
Re: Ivan Ben Steelin
Subject: Search of voter registration and marriage license records

Voter Registration

Voter registration records were examined on January 4, 1993, to confirm the information about Ivan Ben Steelin maintained by Table Deals personnel department. The registration records substantiated that Steelin's address was 1156 North Ocean Boulevard, Orem, Utah, 84057. Social Security number, phone number, and date of birth were the same as maintained by the personnel department at Table Deals.

Marriage License

The marriage license of Mr. Steelin was inspected on January 4, 1993, at the Moore County Clerk's office. Ivan Ben Steelin was married to Clara Clintock on July 1, 1977. The records indicated that no previous marriages existed for either Mr. or Mrs. Steelin. The marriage license of Steelin revealed that his wife's parents, James and Jennifer Clintock, live at 1145 North 8000 West, Orem, Utah, 84057—the address of Ivan Steelin at the time he was hired by Table Deals.

7

Table
⌐ Deals ⌐
Inc.

To: I   ASCF 030369
From: Scott R Bulloch
Date: January 5, 1993
Re: Ivan Ben Steelin
Subject: Search of records at the Utah secretary of state's office

The office of the secretary of state was visited on January 5, 1993, to survey:

- Business license records
- The UC Code Records

Business License Records

It could not be determined whether Steelin has ever sought a business license in the state of Utah. A computer search on Prentice Hall's national database did not provide information that would substantiate that Steelin has held a business license in any other state in the United States.

Uniform Commercial Code Records

The UCC records for Ivan Ben Steelin, 999-06-2828, 1156 North Ocean Boulevard, Orem, Utah, reported the following information:

- Steelin made an acquisition of a boat at Ron's Boats, 25000 North State Street, Orem, Utah, on November 12, 1988. The record reflected that a loan was not secured against the acquisition, though the cost of the boat was $23,000.
- On May 1, 1989, a purchase was made at Lund Furniture, 1400 West 1200 North, Orem, Utah. The record reflects that the purchase, secured on store credit, cost a total of $9,425, with the acquisition items being the collateral for the credit. The purchase items consisted of:

  One (1) 44-inch Mitsubishi television set.

  One (1) Samsung home entertainment center.

  One (1) Broyhill bedroom set.

8

- On July 1, 1990, two automobiles were leased from Quickie Auto Imports, 1400 South State Street, Salt Lake City, Utah, 84067.

  Auto 1: Audi 100, four-wheel-drive, VIN AUDI1234567891014.

  Auto 2: Subaru Legacy wagon, VIN SUBA1234567892024.

  The bargain purchase price, pending the end of the lease, was $45,000 less the cumulative lease payments of $1,150 per month.

- Cellular Three Telephone, 2200 Martin Parkway, Provo, Utah, sold merchandise to Ivan Steelin on July 13, 1990. The record does not reflect that the acquisition was collateralized, though the cost was $2,000.

- Roger Tones Motors, 1275 South University Avenue, Provo, Utah, sold one automobile to Ivan Ben Steelin on December 19, 1991. The automobile was partially paid for through a dealer loan, with the automobile being the collateral. The auto was a 1991 Volkswagen Passat Turbo touring sedan, VIN VW987654321123459. The purchase price was $26,497, and the amount of the loan was $10,000.

- On June 28, 1992, Bullard Jewelers Company, 1100 North University Avenue, sold merchandise on credit, to Ivan Ben Steelin. The collateral to the purchase was the acquired merchandise, with the credit being extended by US Jewelers Credit Corporation of Denver, Colorado. The total cost of the acquisition was $8,200, with $4,000 being the credit amount. The description of the items identified:

  One (1) ring with 1.24 carat diamonds.

  Two (2) earrings, each with a 1.5 carat diamond.

9

Table

⌐ Deals ⌐
Inc.

To: IASCF 030369
From: Scott R Bulloch
Date: January 7, 1993
Re: Ivan Ben Steelin
Subject: Search of real estate records

On January 7, 1993, the Moore County Land Office and the Moore County
Tax Assessor's Office were visited to determine Ivan Ben Steelin's real estate holdings and their respective values.

County Land Office

The property records of Moore County, Utah, indicate that Ivan Ben Steelin's real estate holdings consist of:

- 1.1 acres of improved property located at 1156 North Ocean Boulevard,
  Orem, Utah, 84057.

As cited by the County Land Office records, Steelin acquired the property
on April 4, 1988, from Red Hot Real Estate. The records maintain that the
property, consisting of 1.1 acres of land and one single-family dwelling, is
indebted to Fourth National Bank. The amount of the indebtedness was
not available from these records.

County Tax Assessor's Office

The Moore County Tax Assessor's office records show a total tax base on
the improved property, 1156 North Ocean Boulevard, Orem, Utah, held by
Ivan Ben Steelin, to be $275,000. The legal description of the property is as
follows:

- 1.1 acres of property, with sewer and water.
- 4,100-square-foot single-family dwelling, built from building permit
  19883000, issued on May 1, 1988.

The status of the tax payments, as reflected in the records, is that Steelin is
current for his annual assessment.

10

Table
⌐ Deals ¬
Inc.

To: IASCF 030369
From: Scott R Bulloch
Date: January 8, 1993
Re: Ivan Ben Steelin
Subject: Search of records at the Moore County Contracting Office

On January 8, 1993, building permit 19883000 was examined at the Moore County Contracting Office.

The permit revealed the following information:

- The permit was issued to Ivan Ben Steelin on May 1, 1988.
- The designated licensed contractor on the building permit was Well's Custom Homes.
- The permit was for a single-family dwelling to be constructed at 1156 North Ocean Boulevard, Orem, Utah 84057.

The records accompanying the permit revealed that the dwelling passed code requirements and was available to be occupied on October 28, 1988.

11

Table
⌐ Deals ⌐
Inc.

To: IASCF 030369
From: Scott R Bulloch
Date: January 8, 1993
Re: Ivan Ben Steelin
Subject: Interview with Jack Wells, owner of Wells Custom Homes

Synopsis

Jack Wells, owner of Wells' Custom Homes, telephone (999) 222-1212, was interviewed over the phone on January 8, 1993. Wells revealed that the charge for building Ivan Ben Steelin's home at 1156 North Ocean Boulevard, Orem, Utah, was $240,000.

Details

Jack Wells, owner of Wells Custom Homes, was interviewed over the phone on January 8, 1993. Wells was advised of the identity of the caller, Scott R Bulloch, but not of the nature of the inquiry or of Scott R Bulloch's position.

Wells stated that custom home construction is charged to clients on a square-foot basis. He stated that the average charge is $60 to $75 per square foot.

Wells remembered building a home for Ivan Ben Steelin. He stated that Steelin's home had been one of the first built by Wells Custom Homes. He revealed that the charge to Ivan Ben Steelin was $240,000.

Wells stated that payment had been received through a construction loan at Fourth National Bank, and that full payment had been received upon the house's passing the code requirements.

12

Table

⌐ Deals ⌐
Inc.

To: IASCF 030369
From: Scott R Bulloch
Date: January 9, 1993
Re: Ivan Ben Steelin
Subject: Net worth analysis of Ivan Ben Steelin

Synopsis

On January 9, 1993, Scott R Bulloch and Sue U Buttz performed a net worth analysis of Ivan Ben Steelin. The analysis revealed, conservatively, that Mr. Steelin may have had estimated income from unknown sources of $17,000, $22,000, $34,000, and $23,000 in the years 1989, 1990, 1991, and 1992, respectively.

Details

On January 9, 1993, Scott R Bulloch and Sue U Buttz performed a net worth analysis of Ivan Ben Steelin. Conservative estimates and interpolations were made with regard to Mr. Steelin's assets and liabilities. The estimates and interpolations were derived from information acquired through public records, interviews, and personnel records maintained by Table Deals Inc.

The net worth analysis indicated that Mr. Steelin may have had unknown sources of income in the amounts of $17,000, $22,000, $34,000, and $23,000 in the years 1989, 1990, 1991, and 1992, respectively.

Attached is the worksheet that details the process of determining the above-stated figures. The worksheet consists of one page; it was initialed by Scott R Bulloch and is maintained in IASCF 030369.

13

Net Worth Analysis

	1989	1990	1991	1992
Assets:				
Home	$275,000	$275,000	$275,000	$275,000
Cars	$5,000	$45,000	$70,000	$70,000
Boats	$23,000	$23,000	$23,000	$23,000
Furniture and other	$10,000	$20,000	$20,000	$28,000
Total assets	$313,000	$363,000	$388,000	$396,000
Liabilities				
Home	$240,000	$240,000	$240,000	$240,000
Cars	$0	$45,000	$55,000	$55,000
Boats	$0	$0	$0	$0
Furniture and other	$10,000	$10,000*	$10,000	$14,000
Total liabilities	$250,000	$295,000	$305,000	$309,000
Net Worth	$63,000	$68,000	$83,000	$87,000
Net worth increase	$10,000*	$5,000	$15,000	$4,000
Living expenses:				
Mortgage	$24,000	$24,000	$24,000	$24,000
Food, etc.	$15,000	$15,000	$15,000	$15,000
Cars	$0	$12,000	$15,000	$15,000
Total living expenses	$39,000	$51,000	$54,000	$54,000
Income	$49,000	$56,000	$69,000	$58,000
Known sources of income(net of taxes)				
	$32,000	$34,000	$35,000	$35,000
Funds from unknown sources				
	$17,000	$22,000	$34,000	$23,000

*Determined from 1988 figures, which are not provided.

sb
1-9-93

Table

Deals
Inc.

To: IASCF 030369
From: Scott R Bulloch
Date: January 11, 1993
Re: Ivan Ben Steelin
Subject: Average prices per acre paid by Table Deals Inc.

Synopsis

The records of the external affairs department were analyzed to track the average prices that each of the purchasing representatives has negotiated per acre of real estate purchased. Ivan Ben Steelin's average price is 23 to 42 percent higher than the average prices of the other three purchasing representatives.

Details

Four real estate purchasing representatives are employed by Table Deals Inc. Each of the representatives is assigned purchasing tasks by the vice president of external affairs. The purchasing representative then initiates contacts and proceeds to fulfill their respective purchasing assignments.

The assignments are distributed equally among the four representatives. The records show that each representatives executed the same number of real estate transactions as his or her counterpart representatives in the years 1989, 1990, 1991, and 1992.

A real estate purchasing project, for example, (project 033189), to acquire 55 acres at 2000 North 8000 West, Jensen, Utah, in 1989, revealed the following information:

- The 55-acre lot was owned by three different parties.
- Each of the three properties was listed by three different agencies, Red Hot Real Estate, Johnson Real Estate, and Monarch Real Estate, respectively.
- Steelin negotiated with Red Hot Real Estate, Peter Principle with Johnson Real Estate, and BJ Integrity with Monarch Real Estate.

14

- Peter Principle's purchase of 21 acres cost $12,000, BJ Integrity's purchase of 20.5 acres cost $10,500, and Steelin's purchase of 13.5 acres cost $10,000.

Data were gathered from purchase agreements, according to the purchasing representative, to determine the average price per acre of the real estate purchased. The data compilations revealed that Steelin's purchases were 23 to 42 percent higher than the purchases of the other purchasing representatives.

Attached (one page) are the data compilations extracted from the records of the external affairs department, as they pertain to the average prices per acre of real estate purchased. Scott R Bulloch initialed and dated the document, and it is maintained in IASCF 030369.

Average Prices Paid per Acre of Real Estate Purchased by Table Deals

Purchasing Representative	1989	1990	1991	1992
Abraham Honest	515	535	543	576
BJ Integrity	507	532	571	561
Peter Principle	555	567	581	592
Ivan Ben Steelin	678	775	898	988

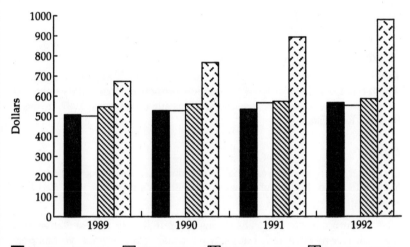

sb
1-11-93

Table
Deals
Inc.

To: IASCF 030369
From: Scott R Bulloch
Date: January 13, 1993
Re: Ivan Ben Steelin
Subject: Computer queries on Steelin's transactions with real estate
           agencies

Synopsis

Table Deals conducts real estate transactions through approved agencies
which have listed the desired acquisition properties. Steelin has executed
over 50 percent of his purchase transactions since January 1, 1989, through
Red Hot Real Estate.

Details

Computer queries on the external affairs database were executed on January 13, 1993, to determine the extent of Steelin's relations with Red Hot
Real Estate.

First, the number of total transactions per purchasing representative was
queried. It was revealed that each purchasing representative has performed 165 purchasing arrangements since January 1, 1989.

Eleven real estate agencies have been utilized since January 1, 1989. The
agencies, all located in Moore County, Utah, are employed based on their
listing of properties which Table Deals seeks to acquire. If a property is not
listed, the purchasing representatives are instructed, as per external affairs
department policy, to rotate their dealings among the eleven agencies. The
policy states "that by rotating among the approved agencies, equity is cultivated, which will encourage the agencies to offer competitive prices."

Since January 1, 1989, each of the four purchasing representatives has dealt
with all the approved agencies. Steelin put 86 transactions through Red
Hot Real Estate during the period in question, January 1, 1989, through
December 31, 1992. Fifty-two percent of Steelin's transactions were made
through Red Hot Real Estate.

The query regarding the distribution of purchasing transactions (one page)
and charts extracted (two pages) were printed, initialed, and dated by
Scott R Bulloch. The three pages are maintained in IASCF 030369.

External Affairs Database

January 13, 1993
User: Scott R Bulloch
Dates searched: January 1, 1989, to December 31, 1992

Real Estate Agency	Abraham Honest	BJ Integrity	Peter Principle	Ivan Ben Steelin
Red Hot	17	10	17	86
Johnson	16	11	12	8
Monarch	19	18	13	9
Rich	10	15	17	7
Martin	7	15	18	8
Labrum	21	19	11	7
Peterson	16	10	20	7
Century 46	22	20	14	9
Littleton	15	13	18	10
Selberg	10	15	16	6
Baker	12	19	9	8
Total	165	165	165	165

sb
1-13-93

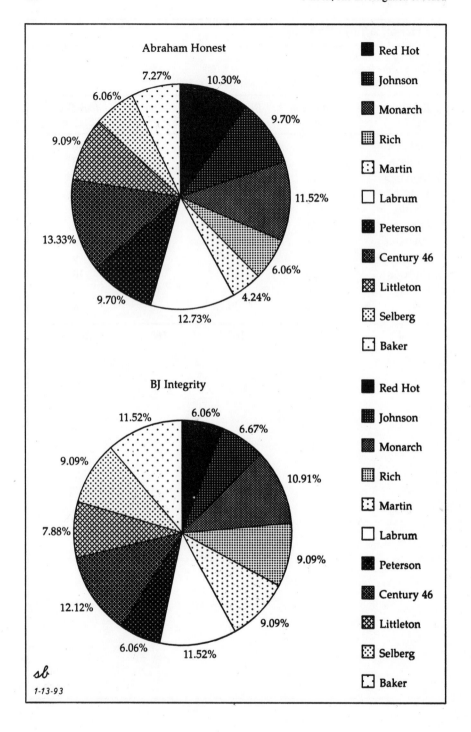

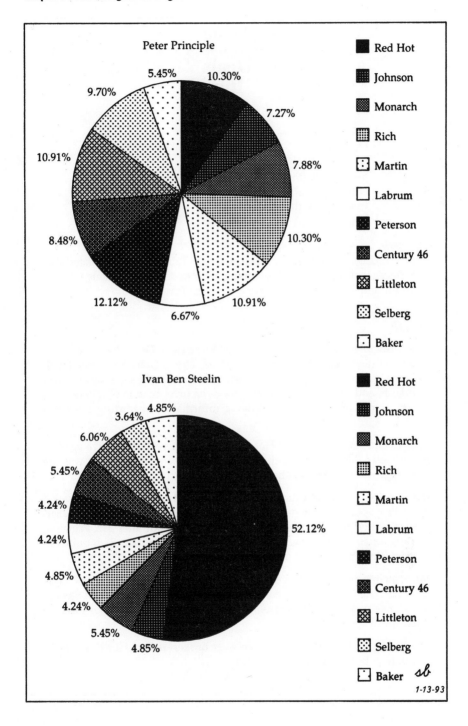

Peter Principle

5.45%   10.30%
9.70%
7.27%
10.91%
7.88%
8.48%
10.30%
12.12%
6.67%   10.91%

Red Hot
Johnson
Monarch
Rich
Martin
Labrum
Peterson
Century 46
Littleton
Selberg
Baker

Ivan Ben Steelin

3.64%   4.85%
6.06%
5.45%
4.24%
52.12%
4.24%
4.85%
4.24%
5.45%
4.85%

Red Hot
Johnson
Monarch
Rich
Martin
Labrum
Peterson
Century 46
Littleton
Selberg
Baker   sb

1-13-93

Table
⌐ Deals ¬
Inc.

To: IASCF 030369
From: Scott R Bulloch
Date: January 20, 1993
Re: Ivan Ben Steelin
Subject: Interview with Peter Principle

Synopsis

Peter Principle, a purchasing representative at Table Deals, Inc., stated that he believes that Ivan Ben Steelin conducts his Red Hot Real Estate transactions through Richey Rich, a broker at Red Hot Real Estate.

Details

Peter Principle, a purchasing representative at Table Deals, Inc., was interviewed in his office, 5511 Vero Beach Road, Orem, Utah, telephone (999)-555-3463, on January 20, 1993. After being advised of the interviewer, Scott R Bulloch, and the nature of the inquiry as an investigation of misconduct, Mr. Principle provided the following information regarding Ivan Ben Steelin:

Mr. Principle stated that Red Hot Real Estate is a very aggressive agency. In particular, Mr. Principle believed that one broker, Richey Rich, was the most aggressive broker that he had dealt with.

Mr. Principle stated that Richey Rich used to call him (Principle) to solicit deals. Principle became a purchasing representative in January of 1985. Mr. Principle cited that Rich became a bother at first, but after Mr. Principle worked for six months as a purchasing representative, Mr. Rich quit calling him (Principle).

Mr. Principle believes that Ivan Ben Steelin works very closely with Richey Rich. He stated that he overheard a conversation between Rich and Steelin, in Steelin's office, in which Steelin conveyed that he'd "send business his [Rich's] way."

Mr. Principle does not know of another broker at Red Hot Real Estate whom Ivan Ben Steelin has dealt with.

18

Table
⌐ Deals ⌐
Inc.

To: IASCF 030369
From: Scott R Bulloch
Date: January 22, 1993
Re: Ivan Ben Steelin
Subject: Interview with Michelle Wang

Synopsis

Michelle Wang, a secretary at Table Deals in the external affairs department, advised that Ivan Ben Steelin had an appointment scheduled for 3:30 PM with Richey Rich on January 22, 1993, at the Burnt Oven Pizza Restaurant.

Details

Michelle Wang, a secretary at Table Deals in the external affairs department, was interviewed at her office, 5511 Vero Beach Road, Orem, Utah, telephone (999)-555-3463, on the morning of January 22, 1993. Ms. Wang was informed of the nature of the inquiry and of the identity of the interviewer, Scott R Bulloch. Ms. Wang provided the following information:

Ms. Wang is responsible for answering all incoming calls at the external affairs department. If the desired party is out or unavailable, Ms. Wang records a message on carbon-copied message slips.

Ms. Wang stated that she answered several calls a week from Richey Rich for Ivan Ben Steelin. On January 21, 1993, Ms. Wang documented a message telling Mr. Steelin to meet Richey Rich at the Burnt Oven Pizza Restaurant at 3:30 PM on January 22, 1993.

The duplicate copy of the message (one page) was obtained from Ms. Wang, was initialed and dated by Scott R Bulloch, and is maintained in IASCF 030369.

19

External Affairs Department

To: Ivan   Date: 1/21/93
                                       Time: 10:15 AM
From: Richey Rich
Of: Red Hot Real Estate

__✓__ Called   _____ Call Back at _____
_____ Stopped by

Message: Meet me at 3:30 PM on January 22—Burnt Oven Pizza Restaurant.

sb
1-22-93

Table
⌐ Deals ¬
Inc.

To: IASCF 030369
From: Scott R Bulloch
Date: January 22, 1993
Re: Ivan Ben Steelin
Subject: Surveillance at Burnt Oven Pizza Restaurant

Synopsis

Ivan Ben Steelin had pizza and drinks with Richey Rich at the Burnt Oven Pizza Restaurant, 2750 East 1800 South, Provo, Utah, on January 22, 1993. Steelin and Rich met from 3:30 PM to 4:45 PM. Steelin picked up the ticket of $14.50 and tipped the waiter a balance of a $20 bill. Rich gave Steelin a piece of paper before they left.

Details

During an interview, Michelle Wang, a secretary at Table Deals, advised of an appointment between Ivan Ben Steelin and Richey Rich. Ms. Wang provided a duplicate of a phone message slip regarding the appointment scheduled for 3:30 PM on January 22, 1993 at the Burnt Oven Pizza Restaurant.

According to the information provided, physical surveillance was established at the Burnt Oven Pizza Restaurant at 3:15 PM on January 22, and was terminated at 4:53 PM on the same date.

During the surveillance, Steelin and a white male, later identified as Richey Rich, had pizza and drinks. Steelin and Rich were observed writing in leather-like ring binders as they carried on a discussion.

After they consumed their provisions, Steelin put a $20 bill on the collection plate. As Steelin and Rich stood to leave, Rich was observed giving a piece of paper to Steelin, which Steelin placed in his left outside coat pocket.

The attached surveillance log furnished additional details. The surveillance log (one page) was initialed and dated by Scott R Bulloch and is maintained in IASCF 030369.

21

January 22, 1993
Surveillance at the Burnt Oven Pizza Restaurant
Surveillance conducted by Scott R Bulloch

3:15 PM   Established surveillance at the Burnt Oven Pizza Restaurant.

3:25 PM   Ivan Ben Steelin arrives at the restaurant.

3:33 PM   White male arrives and sits with Steelin.

3:40 PM   Steelin and white male place orders with waiter.

3:45 PM   Steelin and white male remove zipper ring binders from their
           briefcases, open them, and are observed writing in them as
           discussion takes place.

3:48 PM   Waiter refills glasses with clear fluid.

4:05 PM   Two pizzas are delivered to the table of Steelin and white
           male, and glasses are refilled with clear fluid.

4:30 PM   Waiter takes plates and tableware from table of Steelin and
           white male, refills glasses, and leaves a collection plate.

4:40 PM   Steelin and white male replace their zipper binders in their re-
           spective briefcases.

4:42 PM   Steelin places a form of currency on the collection plate.

4:45 PM   Steelin and white male stand up, white male hands Steelin a
           paper, and Steelin places the paper in his left outside coat
           pocket.

4:45 PM   Steelin and white male shake hands and leave the restaurant.

4:49 PM   Waiter, identified at Martin Lucky, states that the currency
           was a $20 bill and that the charge for the meal was $14.50.
           Lucky intends to keep the change as a tip. He advises that the
           white male is Richey Rich and that Rich is a frequent customer
           of the restaurant.

4:53 PM   Surveillance terminated.

22
1-22-93

Table
⌐ Deals ⌐
Inc.

To: IASCF 030369
From: Scott R Bulloch
Date: January 28, 1993
Re: Ivan Ben Steelin
Subject: Interview with Richey Rich

Synopsis

Richey Rich, a real estate broker with Red Hot Real Estate, advised that he has conducted a few transactions with Ivan Ben Steelin. Rich denied having had any inappropriate relations with Ivan Ben Steelin. Rich denied having ever had meals with Ivan Ben Steelin at the Burnt Oven Pizza Restaurant.

Details

Richey Rich, a real estate broker with Red Hot Real Estate, was interviewed at his office, 3000 South Canyon Road, Provo, Utah, on January 28, 1993. After being advised of the identity of the interviewer (Scott R Bulloch) and the nature of the inquiry as an investigation of misconduct, Rich provided the following information:

"Red Hot Real Estate has done business with Table Deals for more than five years. Rich had conducted real estate transactions through all four of the purchasing representatives at Table Deals: Steelin, Honest, Integrity, and Principle."

Rich stated that he has conducted only a few transactions through Ivan Ben Steelin, because Steelin is "too demanding."

Richey Rich advised that not at any time have he and Steelin met for lunch at the Burnt Oven Pizza Restaurant, nor at any other restaurant.

Rich flatly denied furnishing bribes, kickbacks, or any other form of gratuities to Ivan Ben Steelin, or to any other purchasing representative at Table Deals. Rich stated that he suspects that other, unnamed agencies are furnishing gratuities to the purchasing representatives of Table Deals.

23

Table

┌ Deals ┐
Inc.

To: IASCF 030369
From: Scott R Bulloch
Date: January 28, 1993
Re: Ivan Ben Steelin
Subject: Interview with Ivan Ben Steelin

Ivan Ben Steelin was interviewed at his office, 5511 Vero Beach Road, Orem, Utah, telephone (999)-425-3463, on January 28, 1993. Steelin was advised that the interviewers were Scott R Bulloch and Sue U Buttz, and that an investigation was under way concerning an improper broker relationship.

Steelin was informed that the intent of the inquiry was to obtain a voluntary consent to examine his bank account records. Steelin stated that such a consent agreement was not necessary, and that he wished to meet in private at that time to discuss his predicament.

Ivan Ben Steelin was advised of his rights in regard to self-incrimination, and he executed an advice-of-rights form, a copy of which is attached. Steelin agreed to a videotaping of the interview that followed.

Steelin stated that family pressure to succeed and to measure up to his in-laws' expectations had led to his accepting payments from Richey Rich of Red Hot Real Estate. Steelin provided the attached free and voluntarily signed statement (two pages) regarding his association with Richey Rich, following the interview.

24

Table

┌ Deals ┐
Inc.

ADVICE OF RIGHTS

Place: Table Deals Inc., 5511 Vero Beach Road, Orem, UT
Date: January 28, 1993
Time: 11:30 AM

Before we ask you any questions, you must understand your rights.

You have the right to remain silent.

Anything you say can be used against you in court.

You have the right to talk to a lawyer for advice before we ask you any questions and to have a lawyer with you during questioning.

If you cannot afford a lawyer, one will be appointed for you before any questioning, if you wish.

If you decide to answer questions now without a lawyer present, you will still have the right to stop answering at any time. You also have the right to stop answering at any time until you talk to a lawyer.

WAIVER OF RIGHTS

I have read this statement of my rights and I understand what my rights are. I am willing to make a statement and answer questions. I do not want a lawyer at this time. I understand and know what I am doing. No promises or threats have been made to me and no pressure or coercion of any kind has been used against me.

Signed: _Ivan Ben Steelin_   1-28-93

Witness: _Scott R Bulloch_

Witness: _Sue U Buttz_

Time: 11:30 AM

25

*Private citizens are not required to give Miranda warnings. However, many prosecutors prefer that they be given.

Table

Deals
Inc.

Orem, UT
January 28, 1993

I, Ivan Ben Steelin, furnish the following free and voluntary statement to Scott R Bulloch and Sue U Buttz, who have identified themselves to me as internal auditor and legal counsel, respectively, for Table Deals Inc. No threats or promises of any kind have been used to induce this statement.

I have been advised that an internal inquiry has been and is being conducted to determine whether or not I have accepted any unlawful gratuities and violated the Table Deals code of conduct in my position as a purchasing representative for Table Deals Inc. I have also been advised that I am the sole target of this internal inquiry; that the allegations could constitute a criminal act; and that I have a right to an attorney, should I choose.

I have been employed at Table Deals Inc. since January 7, 1985, and since January 1, 1987, have been a purchasing representative in the external affairs department, in Orem, Utah.

I freely admit that I have accepted gratuities and other considerations form Richey Rich, real estate broker at Red Hot Real Estate, Provo, Utah. The total amount of monies I have received is approximately $115,000 since January 1988. I have also received property, valued at approximately $35,000, from Richey Rich, on which property my personal residence was constructed.

Rich paid me the monies and provided the properties to ensure that I would continue to purchase real estate from Red Hot Real Estate. I was aware at the time I began taking money from Rich that such conduct was illegal and violated the Table Deals code of conduct. I committed these acts because of the financial pressure I felt to live up to others' expectations. I am sorry for my conduct, and I would like to begin to make reparations.

26

No one else at Table Deals was involved, nor did anyone else have knowledge of my activities.

I have read the above statement, consisting of this typewritten page and one other typewritten page. I have initialed the other page and now sign my name because this statement is true and correct to the best of my knowledge and belief.

Ivan Ben Steelin   1-28-93
Ivan Ben Steelin

Scott R Bulloch
Scott R Bulloch   January 28, 1993

Sue U Buttz
Sue U Buttz   January 28, 1993

27

Table
⌐ Deals ⌐
Inc.

To: IASCF 030369
From: Scott R Bulloch
Date: February 13, 1993
Re: Ivan Ben Steelin
Subject: Estimated overpayment to Red Hot Real Estate

Synopsis

Computations indicate that the estimated loss to Table Deals Inc. for the years 1988 through 1992 due to overpayment to Red Hot Real Estate is approximately $436,568.

Details

On February 13, 1993, estimates were prepared concerning possible overpayment to Red Hot Real Estate as a result of activities conducted between Ivan Ben Steelin and Richey Rich.

Data on four of the eleven agencies that Table Deals conducts transactions with were extracted from the external affairs database. The data were extrapolated to determine the average prices paid per acre of real estate purchased through each of the four agencies.

The average cost computation was then applied to the acreage purchased from Red Hot Real Estate to determine an approximate overpayment to that agency over the last five years.

The total of the losses, as reflected on the attached one-page worksheet, is approximately $436,568 for the years 1988 through 1992.

Average Cost Per Acre

	1988	1989	1990	1991	1992
Johnson	$505.00	$525.00	$545.00	$565.00	$576.00
Labrum	508.00	520.00	541.00	560.00	573.00
Century 46	503.00	530.00	548.00	568.00	581.00
Monarch	510.00	524.00	545.00	567.00	575.00
Average cost	$506.50	$524.75	$544.75	$565.00	$576.25

Ivan Ben Steelin's Transactions with Red Hot Real Estate

Cost paid to Red Hot	$130,500.00	$176,280.00	$240,250.00	$332,260.00	$414,960.00
Acreage received	200	260	310	370	420
Average cost	$652.50	$678.00	$775.00	$898.00	$988.00
Expected cost for acreage	$101,200.00	$136,435.00	$168,872.50	$209,050.00	$242,025.00
Estimated overpayment	29,200.00	39,845.00	71,377.50	123,210.00	172,935.00

Total loss = approximately $436,568

sb
2-15-93

IV

THE PREVENTION OF FRAUD

Fraud prevention is the most cost-effective element related to fraud. Once a fraud has been committed, there are no winners. Perpetrators lose because they suffer humiliation and embarrassment as well as legal punishment. They must also make tax and restitution payments, and there are financial penalties and other adverse consequences. Victims lose because of the stolen money, legal fees, lost time, public exposure, and other consequences. The investigation of fraud can be very expensive. Organizations and individuals that have proactive fraud prevention measures usually find that those measures pay big dividends.

There are two major factors involved in preventing fraud. In Chapter 15, we cover the first, creating a culture of honesty, openness, and assistance. Chapter 16 discusses the second, taking away opportunities to commit fraud.

Chapter Fifteen

Fraud Prevention
Creating a Culture of Honesty, Openness, and Assistance

There are no winners when fraud occurs. At best, a scam artist or a fraudulent employee may enjoy a higher lifestyle for a while. In the end, however, the dishonesty usually costs perpetrators much more than they embezzled. As an example of the adverse consequences, consider the following fraud case:[1]

Margaret W. worked for First National Bank. For 34 years she was an "honest and trusted" employee. In the three years prior to her retirement, she embezzled over $600,000. The fraud was discovered after she retired. Once the fraud was known, Margaret suffered tremendous adverse consequences. The bank took possession of her home and her 401 retirement account. Her husband, who supposedly had no knowledge of the fraud, contributed the proceeds of his 401-K from another company to the bank. The bank took possession of virtually every asset the couple owned. In addition, Margaret still owes the bank over $200,000 and has entered into a restitution agreement to make regular payments toward meeting the agreement. Margaret was prosecuted and incarcerated for one year. All of her friends and family members, including her children and grandchildren, now know their grandmother is a crook. When Margaret was released from prison, she was ordered by the judge to seek active employment so she could start making restitution payments. If she fails to make regular payments, she will violate her parole agreement and go back to jail. Margaret and her husband suffered tremendous embarrassment about the fraud. When Margaret's fraud was discovered, it was written up in a local newspaper, and many of her long-time friends called the bank to find out what happened. The bank was required to submit a criminal referral form to the Office of the Controller of the Currency (OCC). By law, the OCC was required to turn over a copy of the referral form to the FBI and the IRS. The FBI investigated Margaret, and the IRS came after her. The IRS levied fines, penalties, interest, and back taxes on Margaret because she had had over $600,000 in income that she had failed to report on her tax returns. Margaret will never be able to get a job, buy life or car insurance, or do many other things without

---

[1]The names of the perpetrator and the bank have been changed.

informing people that she is a convicted felon. In many ways, Margaret's life has been ruined.

Organizations or individuals from whom funds are stolen are also losers. In this case, the bank's name was splashed across the front pages of the local newspaper. Some customers terminated business relationships with the bank for fear that "if the bank can't safeguard funds, then my money is not safe there." The bank also lost the money that Margaret hasn't yet paid, (over $200,000), plus interest on the $600,000 that she embezzled. Margaret will probably never be able to pay back the entire sum she stole, because the kinds of jobs that were available to her upon release from prison don't pay very well. In addition, bank employees spent hundreds of hours investigating, preparing legal defenses, and testifying in the case.

Clearly, fraud prevention is where the big savings occur. When fraud is prevented, there are no detection or investigation costs. There are no bad apples—no examples of fraud in the organization. The organization doesn't have to make tough termination and prosecution decisions. Valuable work time is not lost to unproductive activities and crises.

JUST ABOUT EVERYONE CAN BE DISHONEST

It would be nice to believe that most individuals and most employees are so honest that they would never commit fraud and that, therefore, the kind of culture an organization creates and the fraud opportunities that exist aren't important. Unfortunately, that is not the case. Most people are capable of committing fraud, and many people adapt to their environment. When placed in an environment of low integrity, poor control, loose accountability, and high pressure, people become increasingly dishonest. There are numerous examples of companies in which top management's dishonest practices were adopted by workers. As described in Chapter 3, for example, Equity Funding's management was making up fictitious policyholders and writing insurance policies on them. The fraudulent policies were then sold to other insurance companies or reinsurers. An employee of the company who observed the dishonest behavior thought to himself, "I might as well get in on the action. It doesn't make sense that all these insurance policies are written and no one ever dies." Therefore, he started causing a few of the fictitious people to "die" and collected the death proceeds.

It's possible for an organization to create either a low-fraud or a high-fraud environment. In this chapter and in Chapter 16, we identify two essential factors involved in a low-fraud environment and, thus, preventing fraud. In this chapter, we discuss ways to create a culture of honesty, openness, and assistance—attributes of a low-fraud environment. First, however, to understand the importance of creating the right kind of environment, consider a recent article from *The Wall Street Journal*. This article "Just About Everyone Violates Some Laws, Even Model Citizens," describes the increasing likelihood of dishonest actions in environments where rules don't represent shared values and perceived moral rights. It also states that fraud incidences increase when crimes are perceived as victimless or when examples of appropriate behavior are missing. The article, which includes a self-assessment of honest behavior, points out that everyone is dishonest at times—and, if everyone can be dishonest, it is very important that a corporate culture that discourages rather than encourages honesty be created.[2]

We are a nation of lawbreakers. We exaggerate tax-deductible expenses, lie to customs officials, bet on card games and sports events, disregard jury notices, drive while intoxicated—and hire illegal child-care workers.

The last of these was recently the crime of the moment, and Janet Reno wouldn't have been in the position to be confirmed unanimously as attorney general yesterday if Zoe Baird had obeyed the much flouted immigration and tax laws. But the crime of the moment could have been something else, and next time it probably will.

This is because nearly all people violate some laws, and many people run afoul of dozens without ever being considered, or considering themselves, criminals. The two authors of this article admit, between them, to having committed 16 of the 25 offenses listed in Figure 15–1, carrying maximum jail time of 15 years and fines of as much as $30,000. Most of the dozens of people interviewed for the article have violated eight or more of these laws.

Psychoanalytic approach. Why do we break the law? Is it, as some psychologists suggest, because the law is our symbolic parent, whom we both adore and abhor and whom we enjoy disobeying? Or is it, more prosaically, that many laws seem too foolish, unfair, burdensome, or intrusive for even the most law-abiding to obey slavishly? Or is it simply that we know we can get away with it?

Some people who deal with serious crime scoff at these questions, arguing that routine, nonviolent infractions are too trivial to worry about in a nation threatened by murder, rape, armed robbery, gang warfare, and drug trafficking. But other social scientists take seriously the phenomenon of lawbreaking among the ostensibly law-abiding. They say our willingness to break laws undermines respect for ourselves, for one another, and for the rule of law.

As a practical matter, laws that are often broken with impunity make it difficult for people to predict the consequences of their acts. In the 1970s, Douglas Ginsburg smoked marijuana, as did many of his contemporaries; in 1987 he lost the chance to be a Supreme Court justice as a result. Perhaps a young lawyer who now tosses soda cans into the garbage will be next: In the year 2001, failing to recycle could disqualify someone for the cabinet.

---

[2]Stephen J Alder and Wade Lambert, "Just About Everyone Violates Some Laws, Even Model Citizens," *The Wall Street Journal*, vol. CXXVIII, no. 49, p. A1 (March 12, 1993), Reprinted with permission.

Longtime Practice. Lawbreaking among the mostly law-abiding isn't new, of course. Tax evasion dates back to biblical times. Avoiding jury duty has been common sport at least since the 17th century. Millions drank liquor during Prohibition. People have been driving while intoxicated since the invention of the automobile. Criminologists say they believe that there are more such crimes than used to be, but there are no figures to back up that claim.

Academic studies do show how widespread lawbreaking is today. University of Colorado [Boulder] sociologist Delbert Elliott has tracked a group of young adults since 1976, when they were junior high and high school age. The tally thus far: 905 of the group have broken the law at some time. Other studies yield similar results.

One reason for so much lawbreaking, criminologists say, is that there are so many laws, with new ones being added every year. A state's statutes, including regulations of businesses, can fill 40 volumes or more. State criminal codes average about 1,000 pages each. And on top of the state tomes sit the US laws: Federal criminal provisions fill some 800 pages. Town and city ordinances add to the list.

Pleading ignorance. "There are so many things legally one can get in trouble for breaking, it would be difficult not to be a lawbreaker in our society," says Paul Fromberg, an Episcopal priest at Christ Church Cathedral in Houston, Texas, who admits to having broken 12 of the laws in Figure 15–1. "If you don't know what the rule is, how do you follow it?" wonders Jack Greene, a criminal-law professor at Temple University Philadelphia, Pennsylvania.

Also, in a nation that is increasingly multicultural, many laws don't represent shared values. Laws restricting gambling, drinking, fortunetelling, extramarital sex, sexual behavior, and the use of fireworks, for example, are more acceptable in some communities than in others. In many states, adds James Fyfe, a criminal-justice professor at Temple University, the legislature is still dominated by rural lawmakers whose laws "reflect the values of the farms but not of the urban areas."

Under the circumstances, people who seek to maintain high moral standards often make sharp distinctions between laws they will break and those they won't. Some people who steal, for example, do so only when they believe they have a moral right to what they are taking. "Just because something is against the law doesn't mean it's wrong," says San Francisco author Timothy Ferris. "I've stolen legal pads from every office I've ever been in. But I use those legal pads to write books. That's a good use of the legal pad."

Laws prohibiting crimes that are seen as victimless, or as invasions of privacy, are often broken without much soul-searching. "There is a huge number of people who violate drug laws because they believe use of drugs is their own private business," says Arnold Trebach of the Drug Policy Foundation in Washington, which advocates decriminalization of some drugs. "To a large number of drug users, the law is an ass."

Faceless victims. But people differ as to which crimes are victimless and which victims merit concern. Who is the victim when one cheats on one's taxes or lies to the insurance company or makes illegal home repairs? Whoever the victim is, it is nameless, faceless, and too distant to concern many people. This may be why people so readily cheat the Internal Revenue Service, even though the economy may suffer as a result. "We would have no national debt if people would pay the taxes they owe," says Todd Clear, a criminal-justice professor at Rutgers University in Newark, [New Jersey].

Certainly, the more distant or abstract the victim, the less incentive there seems to be to respect or protect that victim. Kenneth Lenihan, a professor at John Jay College of Criminal Justice in New York, says he witnessed this phenomenon a few years ago when he employed several ex-prisoners. After one apparently stole the professor's checkbook and forged some checks, two of the others indicated that they would cooperate with the bank's investigation. But when they learned the loss would be the bank's and not Mr. Lenihan's, they changed their minds, he says.

Thrilling experience.   Another obstacle to good citizenship is that law-breakers are often admired, both for taking a risk and for profiting from doing so. Says [Professor] Greene of Temple: "There's an under-the-table ideology in this country. People want a good deal."

This attitude seems to be particularly prevalent in the workplace, where competition dictates straddling a fine line between shrewd and shady. "What a lot of people do is, they hang their ethical hat at the door," says Michael Daigneault, whose Falls Church, [Virginia], firm, Ethnics Inc., teaches ethics to business people.

But some law-and-psychology specialists say something far deeper is at work in lawbreaking. "Our emotional stance toward the law isn't one of un-equivocal respect, but one of ambivalence," says Martha Grace Duncan, a professor at Emory University's law school [Atlanta, Georgia].

"From a psychoanalysis perspective, it makes sense that this should be so," she adds, "for the law represents the parent [and] thus serves as a repository of powerful feelings from early childhood—complex feelings of affection and disdain, attraction and repudiation."

If so, the national parent may need a lesson from Dr. [Benjamin] Spock in the virtues of consistent discipline. Civil libertarians warn that when too many rules exist, and only some are enforced, the law becomes capricious and unsettling. The legal system starts to resemble a lottery.

One solution is to repeal or amend laws that don't make sense to a lot of people. Indeed, the Zoe Baird flap seems likely to result in more sensible rules for paying Social Security taxes for domestic employees. But most of the often-disobeyed laws are likely to stay on the books, either because they are sound public policy or because it is easier to pass a new law than to repeal an old one. Particularly when morals are thought to be an issue, many legislators don't want to appear to be on the side of sin. Even some people who admit to occasional lawbreaking say they are happy the laws are there "just so people don't get really out of hand," as Los Angeles teacher Janie Teller puts it.

Inevitably, then, some long-dormant law will awaken periodically and, like a B-movie monster, wreak havoc for a time. But fear of the consequences probably won't increase adherence to the law. Just ask Los Angeles architect Steven Wallock, who says he has violated 22 of the 25 laws [in Figure 15–1].

FIGURE 15–1

Common Offenses: How Many Have You Committed?

Offenses	Penalties If Convicted	Yes
1. Taking office supplies or using office services, such as messengers, for personal purposes	Up to one year in jail and/or up to $1,000 fine	❑
2. Evading taxes (e.g., failing to report tips or other income, including from gambling, or exaggerating deductible expenses)	Up to five years in jail and/or up to $250,000 fine	❑
3. Gambling illegally (e.g., betting on a card game, a sports event, or a political election)	Up to six months in jail and/or up to $1,000 fine	❑
4. Committing computer crimes (e.g., coping software illegally, gaining illegal access to data, altering or destroying data belonging to someone else)	Up to three years in jail and/or up to $10,000 fine	❑
5. Serving alcohol to minors (e.g., allowing a teenager to drink wine with a meal)	Up to one year in jail and/or up to $5,000 fine	❑
6. Drinking in public (e.g., in a park or at a beach, where prohibited)	Up to 30 days in jail and/or up to $100 fine	❑
7. Possessing marijuana in small quantities for personal use	Up to one year in jail and/or up to $5,000 fine	❑
8. Possessing cocaine in small quantities for personal use	Up to four years in jail and/or up to $10,000 fine	❑
9. Committing adultery in states where illegal (also, sex between unmarried partners, in some states)	Up to one year in jail and/or up to $1,000 fine	❑
10. Engaging in prohibited sex acts (e.g., sodomy, in some states)	Up to three months in jail and/or up to $500 fine	❑
11. Patronizing a prostitute	Up to one year in jail and/or up to $5,000 fine	❑

Note: Laws and penalties vary among states.

FIGURE 15–1 *(concluded)*

Offenses	Penalties If Convicted	Yes
12. Appearing nude in public (e.g., nude sunbathing, where prohibited)	Up to one year in jail and/or up to $500 fine	❑
13. Shoplifting	Up to one year in jail and/or up to $1,000 fine	❑
14. Stealing TV signals (e.g., with illegal cable hookup, descrambler, or satellite dish)	Up to one year in jail and/or up to $1,000 fine	❑
15. Speeding or committing other moving-traffic violations	Up to $200 fine	❑
16. Parking illegally	Up to $50 fine	❑
17. Fishing illegally (e.g., without a license, or keeping undersized fish)	Up to $500 fine	❑
18. Smoking in public, where ordinance prohibits it	Up to $50 fine	❑
19. Failing to recycle where required (e.g., failure to separate bottles, cans, and newspapers)	Up to $100 fine for repeat offender; $25 for first offense	❑
20. Lying to a customs agent to avoid duties	Fine not to exceed value of merchandise at issue	❑
21. Importing prohibited products (e.g., Cuban cigars; tortoise-shell jewelry; various foods, plants, and animals)	Up to one year in jail and/or up to $100,000 fine	❑
22. Lying on an application for a government job or benefit, when the form states that false statements are punishable	Up to one year in jail and/or up to $1,000 fine	❑
23. Disregarding a jury summons	Up to six months in jail and/or up to $750 fine	❑
24. Buying stolen goods (e.g., watches, books, stereo equipment, or newspapers from a street vendor, is known to be stolen)	Up to one year in jail and/or up to $1,000 fine	❑
25. Unauthorized sale of tickets to sports or music event, for above the listed price	Up to six months in jail and/or up to $1,000 fine	❑
	Total: _____	

Some of the prohibited acts "are just too much fun" to resist, he explains. And, like most of us, he doesn't expect to get caught. "Why would somebody doubt me?" he asks. "I'm a good guy, and I look honest."

In many ways we have created a high-fraud environment in the United States. In this environment, even individuals who perceive themselves as being moral and ethical commit dishonest acts. Once it is understood that almost anyone can be dishonest, it is easy to understand why proactive fraud prevention measures must be taken. Organizations must create low-fraud environments and must have explicit fraud prevention programs.

TOTAL QUALITY MANAGEMENT AND THE CONTROL ENVIRONMENT

Before discussing the control environment, it is appropriate to consider the implications of recent changes in management practices for the whole area of internal control. Traditional hierarchical organizations with their "military" management are in full retreat, giving way to the concept of *empowerment*, in which power shifts downward and there is an emphasis on informal values such as ethics, competence, shared vision, teamwork, morale, commitment, and communication. These practices and values are included in management concepts popularly referred to as *total quality management (TQM)*. Does this shift toward "softer" management practices have negative implications for internal control? The authors are not sure.

The traditional paradigm of internal control assumes a direct link between the level of internal control and the existence of formal controls, including multitiered management, bureaucracy, detailed procedures manuals, and elaborate approval processes, which have been relied upon for years to provide most of a company's control needs. These formal controls are expensive to maintain, and their effectiveness during recent years has been called into question. In fact, research has shown that the factor that contributes most to employee fraud is *failure to enforce existing internal controls.* Approximately 71 percent of all employee frauds have been committed by perpetrators acting alone, without collusion, and most of these frauds could have been avoided if a good system of internal controls had been in place and complied with.

Traditional formal controls are often not consistent with TQM concepts. At the same time, informal control mechanisms such as organization structure, ethical standards, and leadership (in fact, the very culture of an organization) are very powerful influences on the control environment. We certainly don't support the wholesale elimination of traditional formal controls, but we are suggesting that reliance on a more balanced combination of formal and informal controls may provide a stronger deterrent to fraud in many circumstances. Though methods for assessing the effectiveness of internal controls that can enhance the effectiveness of the control environment have been developed, they are outside the scope of this book.

A CULTURE OF HONESTY, OPENNESS, AND ASSISTANCE

Five major factors in fraud prevention relating to creating a culture of honesty, openness, and assistance are discussed below. These five factors are: (1) hiring honest people and the provision of fraud awareness training; (2) creating a positive work environment, which means having an open-door policy, not operating on a crisis basis, and having a low-fraud atmosphere; (3) having a well understood and respected code of ethics, (4) providing an employee assistance program (EAP) that helps employees to deal with personal pressures, and (5) creating an expectation that dishonesty will be punished.

Hiring Honest People and Providing Fraud Awareness Training

Effectively screening applicants so that only "honest" employees will be hired is very important. As stated earlier in this book, studies have indicated that nearly 31 percent of Americans are dishonest, 30 percent are situationally honest, and only 40 percent are honest all the time. It is also a fact that 25 percent of all frauds are committed by employees of three years or less. Individuals with gambling, financial, drug, or past criminal problems should not be hired, or, at least, if they are hired, the adverse information about their backgrounds and/or character should be known.

With today's stringent privacy laws, it is essential that companies have good employee screening policies. Even in a highly controlled environment, dishonest employees and employees with severe pressures will often commit fraud.

Because of stringent privacy laws and because polygraph examinations often can no longer be used when making hiring decisions, organizations must become creative in their hiring processes. Many banks, for example, are using CHEX systems to determine whether prospective customers have had past credit problems.[3] Banks are also fingerprinting new employees and customers and comparing the fingerprints with law enforcement records. Other organizations are hiring private investigators

---

[3]Alder and Lambert, "Just About Everyone Violates Some Laws, Even Model Citizens," pp. A1, A4.

or using publically-available databases to search out information about people's backgrounds. Honesty testing is increasingly being used as a screening tool. Some companies are having trained interviewers conduct thorough interviews, as well as checking multiple references.

One such company, for example, extensively trained several centralized interviewers. The company trained these interviewers to know which questions were legal to ask and which were illegal; to recognize deception and lying; and to probe, legally, into applicants' backgrounds. It also adopted a policy of calling three previous references instead of the usual one. It developed a rule that if no gratuitously positive information were received in the three background checks, checks would be viewed as negative. (Of course, the interviewers had to call references who personally knew the applicants rather than just personnel officers who didn't know them.) Over a three-year period of hiring, this company found that 851 prospective employees, or 14 percent of applicants, had undisclosed problems, such as previous unsatisfactory employment, false education or military information, criminal records, poor credit ratings, physical or mental illness, alcoholism, or uncontrolled tempers. People with these types of problems generally find it easier to rationalize dishonest acts, and preventing them from being hired can reduce fraud.

As an example of poor screening, consider the following actual fraud:

> A controller defrauded his company of several million dollars. When the fraud was investigated, it was discovered that the controller had been fired from three of his previous five jobs, in the last eight years. He was discovered in the defrauded company when the CEO appeared on the premises one night and found a stranger working in the accounting area. The nocturnal stranger was a phantom controller and was actually doing the normal work of the corporate controller, who wasn't even trained in accounting.

Once employees have been hired, it is important to have them participate in a good employee awareness program that informs them about what is acceptable and unacceptable, how they are hurt when someone is dishonest, and what actions they should take if they see someone being dishonest. A comprehensive awareness program should educate employees about how costly fraud and other types of business abuses are. Employees must know that fraud takes a bite out of their benefits and that no dishonest acts, of any kind, will be tolerated. Companies with successful fraud awareness programs have packaged fraud training with other issues that are important to employees, such as employee safety, discrimination, substance abuse, and the availability of employee assistance programs.

One company, for example, educates all employees about abuses and gives them small cards to carry in their wallets. The cards list four actions employees can take if they suspect that abuses are taking place. They can: (1) talk to management, (2) call corporate security, (3) call internal audit, or (4) call an 800 hot-line number. Employees are told that they can either provide information anonymously or disclose their identities. This company has also made a video about abuses including fraud, which is shown to all new employees. New posters relating to the awareness program are posted conspicuously throughout the organization on a regular basis. Because of these awareness programs, fraud and other abuses have decreased.

A Positive Work Environment

The second factor in a culture of honesty, openness, and assistance is a positive work environment. Such an environment will not grow by itself; it must be cultivated. Employee fraud and other dishonest acts are more prevalent in some organizations than in others. Organizations that are highly vulnerable to employee dishonesty can be distinguished from others that are less vulnerable by comparing their corporate climates. Two elements that contribute to the creation of a positive work environment and, hence, that make the organization less vulnerable to fraud are: (1) open-door policies and (2) positive personnel and operating procedures.

Open-door policies prevent fraud in two ways. First, many people commit fraud because they have no one to talk to. Sometimes, when people keep their problems to themselves, they lose perspective about the appropriateness or inappropriateness of actions and about the consequences of wrongdoing; thus, they make senseless decisions. Second, open-door policies allow managers and others to become aware of employees' pressures, problems, and rationalizations. This awareness enables managers to take additional steps to prevent and/or detect fraudulent behavior. Approximately 71 percent of all frauds are committed without collusion. Having someone to talk to might prevent many of them. One person who had embezzled said, in retrospect, "Talk to someone. Tell someone what you are thinking and what your pressures are. It's definitely not worth it . . . It's not worth the consequences."

As an example of a person who committed a fraud that probably could have been prevented had the organization had a open-door policy, consider Micky R:[4]

> Micky R. was the controller for a small fruit-packing company. In that position he embezzled over $212,000 from the company. When asked why, he said, "Nobody at the company, especially the owners, ever talked to me. They treated me unfairly, they talked down to me. They were rude to me. They deserve everything they got."

---

[4]The name of the perpetrator has been changed.

Research has shown that many personnel and operating policies contribute to high-fraud environment. Uncertainty about job security, for example, has been associated with high-fraud environments. Other personnel and operating conditions and procedures that contribute to a high-fraud environment are:

- Managers who don't care about or pay attention to honesty (who model apathetic or inappropriate behavior).
- Inadequate pay.
- Lack of recognition for job performance.
- Unreasonable budget expectations.
- Employees' expectations of a high lifestyle.
- Perceived inequalities in the organization.
- Inadequate expense accounts.
- Autocratic management.
- Low company loyalty.
- Short-term focus.
- Management by crisis.
- Rigid rules.
- Negative feedback and reinforcement.
- Repression of differences.
- Poor promotion opportunities.
- Hostile environment.
- High turnover and absenteeism.
- Cash flow problems,/or other financial problems.
- Reactive management.
- Managers who model wheeler-dealer, impulsive, insensitive, emotional, or dominant personalities.
- Rivalrous relationships.
- Poor training.
- Lack of clear organizational responsibilities.
- Poor communication practices.

Each of these conditions or procedures helps to create a high-fraud environment. For example, during crises or rush jobs, there are additional opportunities to commit fraud. When a special project is being hurried toward completion, for example, the normal system of internal controls is often pushed aside. Signatures are obtained to authorize uncertain purchases. Reimbursements are made rapidly, with little documentation. Record keeping falls behind and cannot be reconstructed. Materials come and go rapidly, and can easily be manipulated or misplaced. Often, no one is sure who had responsibility for doing what. In a recent interview, the controller of a large Fortune 500 company indicated that his company had experienced three large frauds in the past year. Two of these, both in the millions of dollars, had occurred when the company was rushing to complete crash projects.

Though it would be easy to include many examples of fraud that have been facilitated by each of these factors, we include only two. The first is an example of fraud associated with inadequate pay. The second is an example of fraud associated with unreasonable expectations.

> A long-time employee of a company believed that he had a good record, but he was passed over for a raise he felt he had earned. He was earning $30,000 a year and decided he was entitled to a 10 percent raise. He stole $250 a month, which was exactly 10 percent of his salary. His moral standards permitted him to steal that much because he felt it was due, but he could not embezzle one cent more, since that would have been dishonest.

> A division manager of a large conglomerate was told he would increase his division's segment margin by 20 percent during the coming year. When he realized he was not going to meet budget, he decided to fabricate his reports and overstated assets. He concluded that it was better to be dishonest than to not meet his assigned budget.

A Company Code Of Ethics

The third factor in a culture of honesty, openness, and assistance is a well-defined and respected company code of ethics. Literature on moral development suggests that if you want someone to be honest, you must both label and model honest behavior. The role of modeling in creating a positive environment was covered previously. Companies that are successful in preventing fraud must also have effective labeling programs, which are usually known as *code of ethics.* A clearly defined code of ethics labels for employees exactly what is acceptable and unacceptable. Having employees periodically read and sign the company code of ethics reinforces their understanding of appropriate and inappropriate behavior. A clearly specified code takes away rationalizations, such as "It's really not that serious," "You would understand if you knew how badly I needed it," "I'm really not hurting anyone," "Everybody is a little dishonest," and "I'm only temporarily borrowing it." When the company specifies what is acceptable and what is unacceptable, and requires employees to acknowledge that they understand the code, they realize that fraud hurts the organization, that not everyone is a little dishonest, that the organization won't understand dishonest acts, that dishonest behavior is serious, and that unauthorized borrowing is not acceptable. Codes of ethics eliminate confusion about what is expected.

The Employee Assistance Program (EAP)

The fourth factor in a culture of honesty, openness, and assistance is formal EAPs. One of the three elements contributing to fraud is pressure. Usually the pressures are ones that the perpetrators consider to be unsharable or for which they perceive no solution. Companies that effectively provide employees with an avenue for dealing with personal pressures eliminate many potential frauds. The most common method of assisting employees with pressures is through formal EAPs. EAPs help employees to deal with problems such as substance abuse (alcohol and drugs); gambling; money management and debts; and health, family, and personal problems.

A recent study of Fortune 500 companies found that 67 percent of the companies surveyed had formal EAPs.[5] Most respondents felt that fewer than 10 percent of their company's employees had ever used their EAPs, and 50 percent of respondents felt that the EAPs returned less than $1 for every $1 spent. When asked what type of problems their EAPs dealt with, 67 percent cited alcohol and drug problems, 63 percent emotional problems, 57 percent family and marital problems, 38 percent gambling problems, 37 percent personal financial problems, and 32 percent legal problems. In addition, 11 percent provided investment counseling. Ninety-two percent of all respondents felt that assisting employees with their personal financial pressures would help to prevent employee fraud.

As examples of frauds that might have been prevented with EAPs, consider the following two cases:

An unmarried woman became pregnant. She didn't want her parents or anyone else to know. Needing money desperately, she stole $300 from her company. Then, realizing how easy the theft had been, she stole another $16,000 before being detected.

An employee of a large bank embezzled over $35,000. When she was caught and asked why, she stated that her son was "hooked on herion at a cost of nearly $500 per day." Because she could not stand to see him go through withdrawal pains, she had embezzled to support his habit.

Both of these employees might have been helped by effective EAPs.

The Expectation of Punishment

The fifth factor in a culture of honesty, openness, and assistance is an expectation that dishonesty will be punished. One of the greatest deterrents to dishonesty is fear of punishment. In today's business and social

---

[5]W Steve Albrecht and Jerry Wernz, "The Three Factors of Fraud," *Security Management*, July 1993, pp. 95–97.

environment, merely being terminated is not a meaningful punishment. The real punishment is having to tell family members and friends about the dishonest behavior. Fraud perpetrators are usually first-time offenders who suffer tremendous embarrassment when they are forced to inform their loved ones that they have been fraudulent. When fraud perpetrators are merely terminated, they usually give others a morally acceptable, but false, reason for the termination, such as, "The company laid me off."

A strong prosecution policy that lets employees know that dishonest acts will be harshly punished, that not everyone is dishonest, and that unauthorized borrowing from the company will not be tolerated, is essential in reducing fraud. While prosecution is usually expensive and time consuming, and while it stimulates concerns about unfavorable press coverage, not prosecuting is a cost-effective strategy only in the short run. In the long run, failure to prosecute sends a message to other employees that fraud will be tolerated and that the worst thing that can happen to perpetrators is termination. Because of today's tough privacy laws and high job turnover rates, termination alone is not a strong deterrent. Like a good code of ethics, a strong policy of punishment helps to overcome rationalizations.

CONCLUDING COMMENTS

Fraud prevention involves creating a culture of honesty, openness, and assistance (as discussed in this chapter) and eliminating fraud opportunities (as discussed in Chapter 16). There are five major factors in such a culture, as follows: (1) the hiring of honest people and the provision of fraud awareness training, (2) a positive work environment, (3) a well-understood and respected company code of ethics, (4) an EAP, and (5) an expectation that dishonesty will be punished. To reduce fraud effectively, one or more of the three elements of the fraud triangle that was discussed in detail in Chapters 2 through 5 must be reduced or eliminated. These elements are pressure, opportunity, and rationalization. The first, third, and fifth factors that were discussed in this chapter work to eliminate or reduce rationalization. The second and fourth of these factors work toward assisting employees with or removing pressures. When rationalizations and pressures are eliminated or reduced, fraud becomes less likely. Chapter 16 discusses the elimination of opportunities to commit fraud.

Chapter Sixteen

Fraud Prevention
Eliminating Opportunities for Fraud

In Chapter 2 the fraud triangle—pressure, opportunity, and rationalization—was introduced to explain why fraud occurs. When pressure, opportunity, and rationalization come together, fraud is likely. If one of the three elements is missing, fraud is unlikely. In Chapter 10, for example, invigilation was introduced as a theft act investigation method that involves making fraud impossible by eliminating the opportunity to commit fraud. Chapter 15 discussed the importance of creating a culture of honesty, openness, and assistance, with a focus on two elements of the fraud triangle: pressure and rationalization. This chapter discusses elimination of opportunities to commit dishonest acts as a second element in preventing fraud.

This chapter covers six methods of eliminating fraud opportunities: (1) having a good system of internal controls, (2) discouraging collusion between employees and customers or vendors, (3) clearly informing vendors and other outside contacts of the company's policies against fraud, (4) monitoring employees, (5) providing a hot line for anonymous tips, and (6) conducting proactive auditing. Each of these six methods reduces the opportunity for fraud, and all of them together combine with the prevention factors described in chapter 15 to provide a comprehensive fraud prevention program.

A GOOD SYSTEM OF INTERNAL CONTROLS

The most widely regarded mechanism for the deterrence of fraud is a good system of controls. The Institute of Internal Auditors' standard on fraud, for example, states the following:[1]

Deterrence of fraud

Deterrence consists of those actions taken to discourage the perpetration of fraud and limit the exposure if fraud does occur. The principal mechanism for

---

[1]*Deterrence, Detection, Investigation, and Reporting of Fraud* (Maitland, Fla.: Institute of Internal Auditors), pp. 3–4.

deterring fraud is control. Primary responsibility for establishing and maintaining control rests with management (See SIAS No. 1, *Control: Concepts and Responsibilities*).

Internal auditing's responsibilities

Internal auditing is responsible for assisting in the deterrence of fraud by examining and evaluating the adequacy and the effectiveness of control, commensurate with the extent of the potential exposure/risk in the various segments of the entity's operations. In carrying out this responsibility, internal auditing should, for example, determine whether:

a. The organizational environment fosters control consciousness.

b. Realistic organizational goals and objectives are set.

c. Written corporate policies (e.g., code of conduct) exist that describe prohibited activities and the action required whenever violations are discovered.

d. Appropriate authorization policies for transactions are established and maintained.

e. Policies, practices, procedures, reports and other mechanisms are developed to monitor activities and safeguard assets, particularly in high-risk areas.

f. Communication channels provide management with adequate and reliable information.

g. Recommendations need to be made for the establishment or enhancement of cost-effective controls to help deter fraud.

We have already stated that the *internal control structure* of an organization should provide (1) a good control environment, (2) a good accounting system, and (3) good control procedures (see Chapter 3). The *control environment* is the tone that management establishes by the way it models and labels honest and acceptable behavior. As stated in a report by the Committee of Sponsoring Organizations (COSO), the control environment sets the tone of an organization, influencing the control consciousness of its people.[2] It is the foundation for all other components of internal control, providing discipline and structure. Control environment factors include the integrity, ethical values, and competence of the entity's people; management's philosophy and operating style; the way management assigns authority and responsibility, and organizes and develops its people; and the attention and direction provided by the board of directors. The control environment also includes hiring practices, organization, and a good internal audit department. A good accounting system was described as one designed so that the information provided is valid; complete; timely; and properly valued, classified, authorized, and summa-

---

[2]Committee of Sponsoring Organizations, *Internal Control—Integrated Framework*, Treadway Commission, 1992.

rized. Good control procedures involve policies and practices that provide physical control of assets, proper authorizations, segregation of duties, independent checks, and proper documentation. A control system that meets these requirements provides reasonable assurance that the goals and objectives of the organization will be met.

Obviously, if a person owns his or her own company and is that company's only employee, not many controls are needed. The owner would not be likely to steal from the company or to serve customers poorly. When there is an organization of thousands of individuals or even two or three, controls are needed to ensure that employees behave the same way as a sole proprietor does.

An internal control structure can never be completely effective, regardless of the care followed in its design and implementation. Even if an ideal system is designed, its effectiveness depends on the competency and dependability of the people using it. Take, for example, a company that has a policy requiring the dual counting of all incoming cash receipts. If either of the two employees involved in the task fails to understand the instructions, or if either is careless in opening and counting incoming cash, money can easily be stolen or miscounted. One of the employees might decide to understate the count intentionally to cover up a theft of cash. Dual custody can be maintained only if both employees pay full attention to the task and completely understand how it is to be performed.

Because of the inherent limitations of control, a control system by itself can never provide absolute assurance that fraud will be prevented. Trying to prevent fraud only by having a good control system is like fighting a fire in a skyscraper with a garden hose. In combination with the other methods described below, however, controls are an extremely important part of fraud prevention.

In determining what kind of control procedures an organization should have, it is important to identify the kinds of risks involved and the types of errors that could result from these risks. Based on the assessment of risks, controls that would eliminate or mitigate the risks are identified. Once identified and put into place, the controls need to be tested to ensure that they are effective and are being followed.

In determining what kinds of controls to implement, it is important to assess their costs and benefits. For example, while the most appropriate control from a risk point of view might involve segregation of duties, this control is rather expensive. Particularly in small businesses with only a few employees, segregation may be too expensive or even impossible. In such cases, it is important to identify less expensive or more appropriate compensating controls that can offer some assurance. For example, in a small service business with eight employees, the owner could personally sign all checks and reconcile all bank statements, to control cash.

Often the problem is not a lack of controls, but the overriding of existing controls by management and others. Consider the role of controls in the theft of $3.2 million from a small bank—a case that we have discussed previously.[3]

Marjorie S., head of accounting and bookkeeping in a small bank, was responsible for all proof reconciliations and activities. Over a seven-year period, she embezzled $3.2 million, or approximately 10 percent of the bank's assets. Auditors and management recognized the lack of segregation of duties in her department but believed they had compensating controls in place that would prohibit such a theft—that would provide "reasonable assurance" that no fraud would be possible within the bank. Some of the compensating controls and the ways they were overridden to allow her fraud were as follows:

1. All deposits and transfers of funds were to go through tellers. Yet, proof employees were making transfers for bank officers and for themselves directly through proof. Most people in the bank were aware of this practice, but because it was being done at the president's request, they didn't think it was wrong.

2. All documents were to be accessible to external auditors. Yet Marjorie kept a locked cabinet next to her desk, and only she had a key. A customer whose statement had been altered by Marjorie complained, but he was told that he would have to wait until Marjorie returned from vacation, because the documentation relating to his account was in Marjorie's locked cabinet.

3. Auditors were supposed to have access to all employees, but Marjorie told her employees not to talk to auditors. Thus, all questions were referred to Marjorie.

4. Every employee and every officer of the bank was required to take a two-week consecutive vacation. At Marjorie's request, management allowed this control to be broken. Based on her memos, that "proof would get behind if she took a two-week vacation," Marjorie was allowed to take her vacation one day at a time. In addition, no one was allowed to perform Marjorie's most sensitive duties while she was away.

5. General ledger tickets were supposed to be approved by an individual other than the person who completed the ticket. In order to override this control, Marjorie had her employees presign 10 or 12 general ledger tickets, so she wouldn't have to "bother" them.

6. There were supposed to be opening and closing procedures in place to protect the bank, but many employees had all the keys necessary and could enter the bank at will.

7. An effective internal audit function was supposed to be in place. For a period of two years, however, no internal audit reports were issued. Even when the reports were issued, internal audit did not check employee accounts or perform critical control tests, such as surprise openings of the bank's incoming and outgoing cash letters to and from the Federal Reserve.

---

[3]Throughout this chapter, the names have been changed.

8. Incoming and outgoing cash letters were supposed to be microfilmed immediately. This compensating control was violated in three ways. First, letters were not usually filmed immediately. Second, for a time, letters were not filmed at all. Third, Marjorie regularly removed items from the cash letters before they were filmed.

9. Employees' accounts were not regularly reviewed by internal audit or by management. On the rare occasions when they were reviewed, numerous deposits to and checks drawn on Marjorie's account that exceeded her annual salary were not questioned.

10. Loans were supposed to be made to employees only if the employees met all lending requirements, as if they were normal customers. At one point, a $170,000 mortgage loan was made by the bank to Marjorie, without any explanations as to how the loan would be repaid or how she could afford such a house.

11. Employees in proof and bookkeeping were not supposed to directly handle their own statements. Yet, employees regularly pulled out their own checks and deposit slips before the statements were mailed.

12. Managers were supposed to be reviewing key daily documents such as the daily statement of condition, the significant items and major fluctuation report, and the overdraft report. Either managers didn't review these reports, or they didn't pay close attention to them when they did perform them. There were daily fluctuations in the statement of conditions of over $3 million. The significant items and major fluctuation report revealed huge deposits to and checks drawn on Marjorie's account. In addition, Marjorie appeared on the overdraft report 97 times during the first four years she was employed.

If these compensating controls had been in place and effective, Marjorie's fraud would have been prevented or at least detected in its early stages. Because management and internal auditors were overriding controls, the bank's "reasonable assurance" became no assurance at all.

A good internal control system is the single most effective tool in preventing and detecting fraud. Control procedures such as authorizations, physical safeguards, and segregation of duties help to deter fraud. Control procedures such as document and record verification and independent checks can assist in the detection of fraud. Unfortunately, in practice, control procedures are rarely followed the way they are intended. Sometimes, the lack of compliance occurs because employees emulate management's apathetic attitude toward controls. At other times, managers properly model and label good control procedures, but employees do not comply because of disinterest, lack of reward for following or punishment for not following controls, lack of focus, or other reasons. Because control procedures can provide only reasonable assurance at best, controls are only one element of a comprehensive fraud prevention plan.

DISCOURAGING COLLUSION BETWEEN EMPLOYEES AND OUTSIDE PARTIES

As noted in Chapter 15, approximately 71 percent of all frauds are committed by individuals acting alone. The 29 percent of frauds that involve collusion are usually the most difficult to detect and often involve the largest amounts. Because collusive fraud is usually slower to develop (it takes time to get to know others well enough to collude and to "trust" that they will cooperate rather than blow the whistle), many collusive frauds could be prevented by mandatory vacations, rotations, and job transfers. When an organization leaves an employee in close proximity to the same vendors or customers for a long period of time, there is a risk that the relationships will encourage development of situations in which the individuals will decide to profit personally. In this book a number of frauds in which such relationships developed have been described. An example is the fraudulent situation discussed earlier where an accounts receivable employee "managed" a customer's receivables to benefit both himself and the customer at the expense of the company.

Two recent developments in business may increase the incidence of collusive frauds. The first is the increasingly complex nature of business. In complex environments, trusted employees are more likely to operate in isolated and/or specialized surroundings in which they are separated from other individuals. The second is the move toward total quality management (TQM), in which oral agreements replace paper trails, and in which individuals are trusted with more responsibility and work in more isolated environments than before.

While we stated previously that we believe the increased trust and openness of these relationships can more than compensate for decreased controls, and that TQM may not result in increased fraud, there is significant disagreement among experts about what will happen to the incidence of fraud as TQM becomes more widespread. Certainly there are increased cost savings and increased productivity from using these new management methods. Whether or not fraud will increase remains to be seen. Generally, it is people we "trust" and "have confidence in" who can and do commit frauds. The reaction of one manager to a recent fraud involving a trusted employee was, "I just couldn't believe he would do it. It's like realizing your brother is an ax murderer."

The problem with trusting people too much is that opportunity and temptation increase. An appropriate analogy is that of a man who was looking for someone to drive his wagons over a rugged mountain.

In interviewing drivers, the wagon owner asked the first driver, "How close to the edge of the ledge can you get without going over?"

"Why, I can maneuver within six inches without any problems," was the response.

When asked the same question, the second interviewee responded, "I can drive within three inches of the edge without going off the cliff."

When the third and final applicant was asked, he responded, "I will drive as far away from the edge as I possibly can, because it is foolish to place yourself in a risky position."

Guess which one got the job!

Fraud is similar. If the risk is higher, there will be more problems. Especially in environments where preventive and detective controls are minimal or absent, employees should be regularly reviewed, periodically transferred or rotated, or required to take prolonged periods of vacation. If any of these procedures had been in place, Robert S. probably would not have been able to commit the following fraud:

> Robert S. was the chief teller in a large New York bank. Over a period of three years, he embezzled more than $1.5 million. When the fraud was discovered, it was learned that Robert had a compulsive gambling habit. He had taken money by manipulating dormant accounts. When a customer would complain about his account, Robert S. would always be the one to explain the discrepancy. He usually used the excuse, "It's a computer error." He later said that the bank had placed far too much trust and supervisory authority in him. He stated that if there had been one other supervisor with the same responsibility, or if a one-week mandatory vacation requirement had been combined with periodic rotations, he would not have been able to defraud the bank.

When employees are responsible for large contracts, bribes and kickbacks are likely to occur. In some cases, employees can double or triple their salaries by allowing increases in costs of purchased goods of less than 1 percent. Purchase and sales frauds are the most common types of fraud. When the opportunity is too high, even individuals whose professional lives are guided by professional codes of ethics will sometimes commit fraud, as was illustrated in the ESM fraud, which has already been described.

> In the famous ESM fraud case, for example, the CPA firm partner accepted under-the-table payments from his client, in return for keeping quiet about fraudulent financial statements. The fraud being perpetrated by the client exceeded $300 million. The CPA had been the partner in charge of the engagement for over eight years. For hiding the fraud, he accepted gifts totaling $150,000. If his firm had not allowed him to be managing partner of the job for such a long time, his participation in the fraud and erosion of integrity would probably have been impossible.

ALERTING OUTSIDE CONTRACTORS TO THE COMPANY'S POLICIES

Sometimes otherwise innocent vendors and customers are drawn into fraud by an organization's employees because they fear that if they don't participate, the business relationship will be lost. In most cases, such customers or vendors have only one or two contacts within the firm. They are often intimidated by the person who requests illegal payments or suggests other types of fraudulent behavior. A periodic letter to vendors that explains your organization's policy of not allowing employees to accept gifts or gratuities helps vendors to understand whether or not buyers and sellers are acting in accordance with the organization's rules. Many frauds have been uncovered when, after such a letter, vendors expressed concern about their buying or selling practices.

> A large chicken fast-food restaurant discovered a $200,000 fraud involving kickbacks from suppliers. After investigating the fraud, they decided to write letters, to all vendors, explaining that it was against company policy for buyers to accept any form of gratuities from suppliers. The result of the letters was the discovery of two additional buyer-related frauds.

A related precaution that is often effective in discouraging kickback-type frauds is printing a "right-to-audit" clause on the back of all purchase invoices. Such a clause alerts organizations with which a company does business that the company reserves the right to audit the vendor's books at any time. Vendors who know that their records are subject to audit are generally reluctant to make bribery payments. A right-to-audit clause is also a valuable tool in fraud investigations.

MONITORING EMPLOYEES

Employees who commit fraud and hoard the stolen proceeds are virtually nonexistent. Almost always, they use the money to support expensive habits or to pay for expenses already incurred. If managers and other employees paid close attention to lifestyle symptoms resulting from these expenditures, fraud could often be detected early. Most stolen funds are spent in conspicuous ways. Fraud perpetrators usually buy automobiles; expensive clothes, and new homes; take extravagant vacations; purchase expensive recreational toys, such as boats, condominiums, motor homes, or airplanes; or support extramarital relationships or outside business interests. Consider again the case of Marjorie S.

> Marjorie first started working for the bank in 1980. During her first four years as an employee, she took out a debt consolidation loan of approximately $12,000 and had 97 overdrafts. During the next seven years, while she was committing the fraud, her salary never exceeded $22,000 per year. Yet, fellow employees and officers of the bank knew that she had done the following:
>
> • Taken several cruises.
> • Built a home costing $600,000.
> • Bought the following cars:
>   Rolls Royce.

> Jeep Cherokee.
> Audi.
> Maserati.
- Bought the following personal items:
> Expensive jewelry, including 16 diamonds and sapphires.
> Computers.
> Stereos.
> VCRs.
> Electronic gear.
> Snowmobiles.
> Golf cart.
> Expensive gifts for fellow employees and relatives.
> Fur coat.
> Suntanning machine.
> Expensive clothes.
- Taken limousines everywhere.
- Held extravagant parties for employees and others.
- Bought a condominium for her mother-in-law.
- Purchased an expensive glass art collection.
- Taken many trips to buy glass art, all over the United States.
- Had her home decorated very nicely.
- Gone to Broadway shows.

Anyone who had paid attention would have realized that her lifestyle was unrealistic. When management did finally ask, she explained her lifestyle by saying that her husband had received one-third of an inheritance of $250,000. This story wasn't true, but even if it had been true, the $83,333 that her husband had supposedly inherited wouldn't have paid for the Maserati, let alone all the other luxuries that managers knew she had bought.

Management and employees who pay attention to lifestyles of their co-employees and to the reasonableness of these lifestyles may be able to save an organization from experiencing large frauds of the type committed by Marjorie S.

PROVIDING A HOT LINE FOR ANONYMOUS TIPS

The most common way in which fraud is detected is through employee tips. In one company, for example, 33 percent of all frauds were detected through tips, while only 18 percent were detected by auditors. In a company that experienced over 1,000 frauds in one year, 42 percent were discovered through tips and complaints from employees and customers. Chapter 9 discussed several methods of encouraging tips and complaints. A good whistle-blowing program is one of the most effective fraud prevention tools. When employees know that colleagues have an easy, nonobligatory way to report suspected fraud, they are reluctant to get involved in dishonest acts. As previously stated, the fear of being caught is a tremendous fraud deterrent.

Unfortunately, too few organizations have effective tip programs. In a study of Fortune 500 companies conducted by the authors, only 52 percent of the survey respondents indicated that their companies had formal whistle-blowing systems. Of the companies that did provide a way for employees to report suspicious acts by their co-workers, 16 percent had toll-free hot lines, 17 percent directed employees to discuss the matter with their managers, and 29 percent told them to contact corporate security directly.

CONDUCTING PROACTIVE FRAUD AUDITING

Very few organizations actively audit for fraud. Rather, their auditors are content to conduct financial, operational, and other audits, and to investigate fraud only if they find it. Organizations that proactively audit for fraud create an awareness among employees that their actions are subject to review at any time. By increasing the fear of getting caught, proactive auditing reduces fraudulent behavior.

Good fraud auditing involves four factors: (1) knowing risk exposures, (2) knowing fraud symptoms, (3) building audit programs to look for symptoms and exposures, and (4) following through on symptoms. Fraud auditors make extensive use of discovery sampling and computer auditing. One company, for example, decided to use computer auditing techniques to compare employees' telephone numbers with vendors telephone numbers. The search revealed 1,117 instances in which telephone numbers matched, indicating that the company was purchasing goods and services from employees—a direct conflict of interest.

CONCLUDING COMMENTS

Fraud is prevented by creating a culture of honesty, openness, and assistance and by eliminating fraud opportunities. Chapter 15 discussed ways to create an appropriate culture or atmosphere to deal with employees' pressures and rationalizations. This chapter introduced six factors that help to eliminate fraud opportunities: (1) a good system of internal controls, (2) discouragement of collusion between employees and customers or vendors, (3) clearly informing vendors and other outside parties about the company's policies against fraud, (4) monitoring employees, (5) providing a hot line for anonymous tips, and (6) conducting proactive auditing.

Eliminating opportunities for fraud is also important in dealing with frauds such as investment scams and management fraud. Investors should follow good control procedures before they invest. For example, they should ask questions such as: "Does this investment make business sense?" "Is this company audited?" and "How long has this business been around?" They should also do Dun & Bradstreet checks, and should not rely on verbal representations by friends or other people. Investors who take these precautions usually avoid being victimized. Similarly, auditors and others who are concerned about management fraud should look at the motivations (pressures) and drives (rationalizations) of a client's managers, as well as at the controls that are supposedly in place in the organization, to reduce exposure to management fraud.

The risk of fraud can be reduced to a low level. Money spent on prevention measures is usually far more effective than money spent on investigation. Combinations of the prevention factors discussed in this chapter and in Chapter 15 can significantly reduce the occurrence of fraud.

A COMPREHENSIVE FRAUD PREVENTION PROGRAM

In this book we have discussed most aspects of fraud. Chapters 1 through 5 defined fraud, provided statistics about the extent of fraud, and introduced the fraud triangle, which is comprised of pressure, opportunity, and rationalization. In Chapters 6 through 9, types of symptoms that can signal fraud were covered as a means of detecting fraud. Once fraud is suspected or detected, it must be investigated. Chapters 10 through 14 presented the ways in which fraud is investigated and reported. Chapter 15 and 16 discussed fraud prevention, the area in which real savings can occur. In the final chapter, we will tie all these elements together into a comprehensive fraud prevention, detection, and investigation plan—an organizational program for dealing with fraud. Fraud policies are discussed and illustrated. In addition, a 12-step program for reducing the occurrence of fraud in an organization is outlined.

Chapter Seventeen

Prevention, Detection, and Investigation of Fraud
An Organizational Program

As mentioned in Chapter 16, the authors conducted a fraud study that involved surveying the Fortune 500 companies. Questionnaires were sent to each of the 500 companies, with instructions that the individual in the company who was most responsible for fraud prevention should respond. Of the 500 companies that received questionnaires, 242 sent back responses. Of these 242 responses, 62 percent (150 responses) came from directors of internal audit, 28 percent (67 responses) from directors of corporate security, and 10 percent (25 responses) from personnel or human resource directors. Many respondents wrote that their organization had no one person who was "most responsible for fraud prevention," but that they personally were taking the responsibility for completing the questionnaire.

The diversity in the job titles of respondents, combined with the many comments to the effect that no one in the organization was primarily responsible for preventing fraud, adds up to a sad commentary on the status of fraud prevention in America. Fraud is an extremely costly problem for organizations in the United States and in the world. Yet the control of fraud in an organization is often seen as someone else's responsibility. Independent auditors say they can't detect fraud because it isn't their responsibility and because their materiality levels are too high.[1] Internal auditors stress that their functions are to evaluate controls and to improve operational efficiency. If they happen to find fraud, they'll pursue or report it, but fraud isn't their primary responsibility. Corporate security officers, in most organizations, take the posture that theirs is an investigative role and that they will pursue specific reported frauds. They don't see their role as including prevention. Managers usually perceive running the

---

[1]Independent auditors are examining the consolidated financial statements of an organization. In that role, they are primarily concerned only with amounts significantly large enough to effect the final statements. In some cases, amounts in the $ millions can be insignificant.

business as their responsibility and seldom even acknowledge the possibility that fraud could happen in their organization. Fraud, to them, is something that happens to other people and other organizations. They don't know how to handle fraud situations. Employees, who are usually in the best position to prevent and detect fraud, often don't know what to do when their suspicions are aroused, and they also often feel that it is unethical or unwise to blow the whistle or report fellow employees.

Because of the nonchalant attitude that is prevalent in most businesses, frauds like the one described below will continue to occur.[2]

Jerry Watkins had been working for Ackroyd Airlines for 17 years. During this time, he had held several positions in accounting, finance, and purchasing. Jerry was the father of three children, two boys and one girl. Over the years, Jerry and his family had been active in the community and in their church. Jerry coached both Little League baseball and football. He and his wife, Jill, both had college degrees, both worked full-time, and both had a long-term goal of sending their children to college. Despite their plans for college, each year the Watkins spent most of what they made and saved very little money for college tuition and other expenses.

After Jerry had been working at Ackroyd for 15 years, Steve, Jerry and Jill's oldest son, started school at a well-known Ivy League university. He performed well, and both Jerry and Jill were proud of his and their other children's accomplishments. Approximately a year later, Jerry, who handled all the family finances, realized they could no longer pay Steve's college expenses, let alone pay future college expenses for their other two children. Jerry, a proud man, could not bring himself to admit his financial inadequacy to his wife and children. He already had a large mortgage and several credit card and other debts, and he knew he could not borrow the money needed for college.

Because of this financial predicament, Jerry decided to embezzle money from Ackroyd Airlines. He had heard of several other thefts in the company, and none of the perpetrators had been prosecuted; in fact, the fraud that he knew about had resulted in the company's merely transferring the employee. In addition, Jerry rationalized that he would pay the money back in the future. In his current position as purchasing manager, he found it easy to take kickbacks from a vendor who had previously approached him with favors to get business. At first, Jerry took only small amounts. As the kickbacks proceeded, however, he found that he increasingly relied on the extra money to meet all kinds of financial "needs" in addition to college expenses. He felt guilty about the kickbacks but knew that the company auditors never thought about fraud as a possibility. Anyway, he felt the company would understand if they knew how badly he needed the money. Significant good was coming from his "borrowing": His children were getting an education they could otherwise not have afforded, and Ackroyd didn't really miss the money. Because of his pressure, his opportunity, his rationalization, and Ackroyd's inattention to fraud prevention and detection, the company's honest employee of 17 years became dishonest.

---

[2]Although the case is real, the names have been changed.

What is alarming is that Jerry's case is not unusual. Jerry had never signed a code of ethics. Ackroyd's auditors had never proactively searched for fraud. The company didn't have an EAP to help employees with financial and other needs. Furthermore, as Jerry was well aware, the company had never taken harsher action than terminating previous fraud offenders.

ORGANIZATIONS AND FRAUD

The Current Model

Like Ackroyd Airlines, most organizations do not have a proactive approach to dealing with fraud and reducing fraudulent behavior. Since fraud prevention is not emphasized in most companies, there is significant confusion about who has responsibility for the detection, prevention, and investigation of fraud. Figure 17–1 shows the current model most organizations typically use, often by default, for dealing with fraud.[3]

This model is characterized by four stages. In stage 1, a fraud incident occurs in an organization. This fraud incident is not preceded by formal awareness training or other prevention measures. Once the incident occurs, the firm shifts into a crisis mode, because it (a) needs to identify the perpetrator, (b) wants to avoid publicity, (c) wants to attempt to recover the losses, (d) wants to minimize the overall impact of the occurrence on the organization, and (e) is caught up in the emotion of the crisis.

Stage 2 is investigation. Here security and/or internal audit become involved. Most of the investigative work involves interviewing and document examination. Investigation may or may not lead to resolution, can take extensive time, and may be relatively costly.

In stage 3, after the investigation has been completed, the company must decide what action to take. The choices are: (a) take no action, (b) terminate only, and (c) terminate and seek prosecution.

Stage 4 in the current model of the fraud cycle involves closing the file, tying together loose ends, replacing the employee (obviously incurring additional costs), perhaps implementing a new control, and otherwise resolving the problem. Once these four stages have been played out, no further action is taken—until another fraud occurs. Unfortunately, in this scenario, fraud will never decrease. Instead, it will become a recurring problem.

---

[3]Part of the material that follows has been previously published in "How Companies Can Reduce the Cost of Fraud," W S Albrecht, E A McDermott, and T L Williams, *The Internal Auditor*.

FIGURE 17–1
Dealing with Fraud: The Current Model

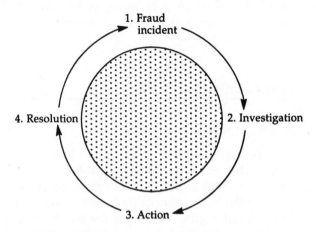

A Proactive Model

A more complete model for dealing with the growing problem of fraud would include the 12 stages shown in Figure 17–2. This suggested fraud process includes eight stages that are currently not included in the fraud programs of most organizations. Stage 1 is implementation of prevention programs (such as those discussed in Chapter 15) designed to educate employees about the seriousness of the problem and to tell them what to do if they suspect fraud. As we have repeatedly said, it is fraud prevention, not detection or investigation, that can result in big savings. Therefore, the greatest attention should be given to instituting proactive fraud prevention initiatives, rather than to dealing with losses that have already occurred.

Companies that have successful fraud prevention programs usually package fraud together with other loss issues such as safety violations, substance abuse, discrimination, environmental programs, and other concerns. This practice helps to ensure that fraud will be detected at an early stage, which limits financial exposure to the corporation and minimizes the negative impact on the work environment.

In the model shown in Figure 17–2, the second stage will be a fraud incident. Unfortunately, no organization can totally eliminate fraud, no matter how good its prevention programs are. However, catching frauds early is the key to minimizing their impact on the organization.

Stage 3 involves fraud reporting. It is extremely important that fraud reporting be facilitated. Fraud is a subtle crime, and thus is very different from other types of crimes. With murder, bank robbery, or assault, there

FIGURE 17–2
Dealing with Fraud: A Proactive Model

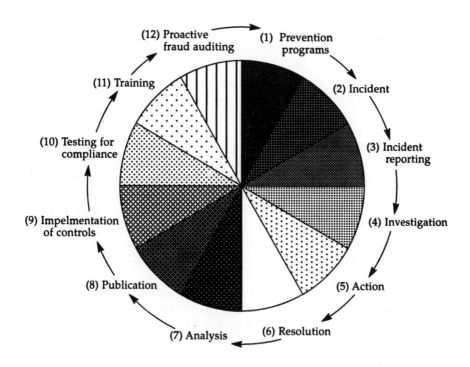

is usually no question about whether or not a crime has been committed. With fraud, however, there are usually no obvious or definitive signs of the crime. All that is usually seen are symptoms or red flags, such as the ones discussed in Chapters 6 through 9. Because hot lines and other reporting systems usually don't exist, employees rarely come forth to present information on possible fraud. The lack of reporting is unfortunate, because employees are in the best position to recognize dishonest behavior or to question red flags that show up in operations with which they are more familiar than anyone else is.

Stage 4, investigation, is different in this proposed model because of the existence of formal fraud policies stating who will carry out all elements of investigation. The procedures are well established, including: (a) who will conduct the investigation; (b) how the matter will be communicated to management; (c) whether and when law enforcement officials will be contacted; (d) who will determine the scope of investigation; (e) who will determine investigation methods; (f) who will follow up on tips of suspected fraud; (g) who will conduct interviews, review documents, and perform other investigation steps; and (h) who will ultimately determine the corporate response to fraud, disciplines, control, etc.

The action phase, stage 5, differs significantly in this proposed program. Taking no action is not even a possibility; rather, whenever possible, fraud perpetrators will be prosecuted to the fullest extent. A strong prosecution policy must have the support of top managers and top managers should also be informed if someone commits fraud and is not prosecuted. Gone are the days when prosecution necessarily resulted in bad publicity. Most people know that fraud exists in every organization. Most people also realize that organizations that take a tough prosecution stance will reduce future frauds significantly and will ultimately be more profitable because of the deterrent effect of prosecution.

As stated previously, the single greatest factor in deterring dishonest acts is the fear of punishment. Companies with successful prosecution policies have developed their own internal investigation experts. They recognize that in order to obtain cooperation from law enforcement officers and the justice system, it is almost always necessary to conduct a thorough and complete investigation (including obtaining a signed confession) before the overworked US law enforcement and criminal justice systems can accommodate the prosecution.

Stage 6, resolution, is no different from the resolution stage in existing fraud policies. Resolution includes replacing the employee, counseling fellow employees, entering into restitution agreements, and closing the case.

The next six stages are new and are not common in business environments today. It is our belief that they are very important in reducing fraud. Stage 7 is the analysis stage. Analysis involves determination by people in management, audit, security, human resources, control, and finance of why and how the fraud occurred. The focus is on the individuals who were involved, the controls that were compromised or absent, the environment that facilitated the fraud, and related factors. This stage is important in understanding the kinds of preventive measures that are needed within the individual culture and environment in which the fraud occurred. It usually does not take long for the appropriate solution to be developed, once all the parties listed above begin to work together to resolve the problems.

Stage 8 is publication of the fraud. Publication does not mean making sure the case and all its accompanying details are in the newspapers. Indeed, until there is a conviction, such publication is ill-advised, because it can lead to slander or libel suits. Rather, what "publication" means in this context is depersonalizing the case (that is, disguising the identities of the perpetrators and other people involved) and publishing it internally in a security newsletter or a memo that is distributed to auditors, security personnel, and appropriate management and employees. Even generic publication of fraud has a tremendous impact, because it makes readers understand that these types of problems happen in their own company and are not only horrible nightmares that happen elsewhere. Publication makes readers much more aware of the kinds of problems that can occur within their own company and more alert to similar schemes or vulnerabilities in their operations.

Stage 9 involves the explicit implementation of the controls and other measures necessary to prevent future occurrences of the fraud problem. Obviously, additional or new controls must meet the cost-effectiveness test and may not be implemented. However, the decision not to implement must based on costs and benefits, not made by default because the proper analysis was not conducted.

Stage 10 includes the testing of controls for compliance. Stage 11 involves the training of appropriate audit, management, security, and other personnel. Unfortunately, fraud training is not very common.

Stage 12 involves proactively auditing for fraud. Using discovery sampling and computer query procedures, auditors identify fraud characteristics and search databases looking for them. Unfortunately, in many organizations, proactive fraud auditing is not even considered.

A FRAUD POLICY

The authors' survey of Fortune 500 companies, which we described earlier, revealed a significant amount of "turf protection" in security, audit, legal, and personnel departments, in terms of dealing with fraud. An organization that seeks to implement a comprehensive fraud prevention, detection, and investigation plan, comprising the stages described above, must determine who will be involved at each stage. Our recommendations are outlined in Figure 17–3.

While the actual organizational structure needed to facilitate interaction between functional disciplines will vary from organization to organization, the structure must allow for and actively facilitate such interaction. *Preventing and resolving* problems, not protecting turf, must be the focus on the interaction. In fact, an overall fraud program such as the one described here usually works best when there is a formal, written *fraud policy* in place. A good fraud policy can raise all parties' awareness of the seriousness of the problem and can establish clear responsibility for the various elements involved in prevention, detection, and investigation. When fraud takes place, emotions run high and investigations are often mishandled. A fraud policy that is well understood can provide order, thus increasing the chances of recovery of stolen assets and successful litigation, and reducing the trauma to the fellow employees.

Figure 17–4 is an example of a fraud policy that encompasses most of the elements described in this chapter.

FIGURE 17–3
The Stages of a Comprehensive Fraud Policy

Recommendations for Involvement of Personnel

Stage	Line Mgt.	Internal Auditing	Security	Human Resources	Legal	Commun-ication
1. Prevention program	Yes	Yes	Yes	Yes	Yes	No
2. Incident	Yes*	Yes	Yes	Yes	Yes	Yes
3. Incident reporting	Yes*	Yes	Yes	No	Yes	No
4. Investigation	Yes	Yes	Yes	Yes	Yes	No
5. Action	Yes	No	Yes	Yes	Yes	No
6. Resolution	Yes	Yes	Yes	Yes	Yes	No
7. Analysis	Yes	Yes	Yes	Yes	No	No
8. Publication	Yes	Yes	Yes	Yes	Yes	Yes*
9. Control implementation	Yes	Yes	Yes	Yes	Yes	No
10. Testing	No	Yes	No	No	Yes	No
11. Training	Yes	Yes	Yes	Yes	Yes	Yes*
12. Proactive fraud auditing	No	Yes	No	No	No	No

*As appropriate.

FIGURE 17–4
MTC Company Fraud Policy

I. Purpose
This fraud policy is designed to minimize MTC Company's exposure to dishonest acts, fraud, gross misconduct, and criminal acts performed by individuals within and outside the company.

This policy focuses on implementing a balanced approach so as to reduce the pressures, opportunities, and rationalizations associated with fraud. The following guidelines will be implemented for handling situations associated with dishonest, fraudulent, and criminal acts.

II. Prevention programs
The following prevention programs will be implemented to educate employees and help reduce the pressures that lead to fraudulent acts:

A. The board of directors and management will be responsible for cultivating an environment in which employees understand the importance of honest behavior and the consequences of dishonest behavior. The board of directors and management will also be responsible for directing and delegating the duty of providing for appropriate controls.

B. Attendance at a mandatory training session designed to educate new employees concerning MTC Company's fraud policy and how to report fraudulent acts will be required of all newly hired employees. The training session will also be used to communicate appropriate and inappropriate behavior. New employees will be informed that perpetrators will be terminated and will be prosecuted to the fullest extent.

FIGURE 17–4 *(continued)*
MTC Company Fraud Policy

New employees will also be required to read and sign a code of conduct defining acceptable and unacceptable behavior. The code of conduct will be renewed yearly during employee evaluations.

C. Notices will be placed on all bulletin boards, informing employees of options available for reporting fraud. Directions will also be available in all company directories. Possible options for reporting fraud are included below, in the section on incident and incident reporting.

D. MTC Company will also implement EAPs to help prevent dishonest and fraudulent acts. Such programs will include the following:

　1. Supervisors will maintain an open-door policy, so that employees can communicate existing pressures and obtain help if needed.

　2. Employee support programs will be implemented to assist employees with problems related to alcohol and drug abuse, gambling, marital problems, and money management.

E. Managers will be responsible for ensuring that work conditions are positive for employees. Items that may make work unbearable include no recognition for job performance, unreasonable expectations, and unfair compensation.

F. Managers and employees will be trained to recognize signals that may indicate dishonest and fraudulent activities. Managers will then be responsible for watching for indicators of dishonest behavior.

III. Incident and incident reporting

Options available to individuals who suspect the occurrence of fraud include the following:

A. Employees can call an 800 hot-line number if they suspect or know that fraud is taking place. The 800 number is the number of a service hired by MTC Company to ensure the anonymity of the caller. The caller can report the suspected fraud to the service, which in turn will contact the internal audit department at MTC Company. The caller reporting the incident can choose either to provide his or her identity or to remain anonymous.

B. Employees can discuss the suspected wrongdoing with their supervisors, who will in turn report the incident to the appropriate department (internal audit or security).

C. Employees can call either internal audit or security directly to report the problem.

D. In any event, neither employees nor managers should confront suspects or investigate the incident in any way. Individuals should contact the appropriate authorities and let them take care of the situation.

IV. Investigation

In situations in which fraudulent acts are reported, the following procedures will be observed:

A. The internal audit department (or corporate security), with the assistance of legal counsel, will coordinate the investigation and will determine what actions will be taken. The internal audit department (or corporate

FIGURE 17–4 *(continued)*
MTC Company Fraud Policy

---

security) will be responsible for determining the scope of the investigation and will determine what investigation methods will be used. The following guidelines will be observed in each investigation:

1. Only individuals who need to have access to the information relating to the investigation will receive such information.
2. Investigations will not include illegal activities. Specialized equipment (recorders, cameras, etc.) that may be regarded as illegal will not be used in the investigation.
3. Information relating to the investigation will be adequately secured by the individuals involved in the investigation. Such measures should include necessary locks, controlled areas, passwords, and other essential security devices.
4. All interviews and interrogations will be conducted so as not to discredit the individual being interviewed or interrogated.
5. Appropriate procedures will be developed and implemented to guard against successful allegations of false imprisonment, defamation, assault, attempted assault, extortion, blackmail, malice, malicious prosecution, invasion of privacy, and violation of expectation of privacy.

B. Information regarding fraudulent incidents and investigations will be communicated from internal audit to top management through reports designed for such situations.

C. The internal audit department or corporate security will be responsible for determining whether, and when, federal, state, or local law enforcement officials should be contacted. The internal audit department will consult with top management to determine when law enforcement officials will be contacted. MTC Company will provide all reasonable assistance to law enforcement officials and regulatory agencies when requested.

V. Action

When sufficient evidence shows that specific federal or state laws have been violated, XYZ Company will seek prosecution of the person or persons involved to the fullest extent of the law.

Individuals who are guilty of fraudulent acts will be terminated immediately. Reasons for termination will not be made publicly available, to avoid allegations of slander or libel.

VI. Resolution

Once the investigation has been completed and actions have been taken, appropriate measures will be taken to return to normal operations. If a person or persons have been terminated, necessary replacements will be found. Good screening policies should be employed to assure t.he hiring of honest employees.

When possible, restitution agreements will be made to recover stolen assets.

VII. Analysis

After an incident has been resolved, a thorough investigation will be performed to determine how and why the fraud took place. The investigation will include all departments and individuals associated with the fraud. The analysis should include the following measures.

FIGURE 17–4 *(continued)*
MTC Company Fraud Policy

A. If possible, interview the individual or individuals involved in the fraud incident. Determine the motives, pressures, and opportunities that allowed the fraud to take place. A report of the findings should be made, and measures to prevent future occurrences of the same act should be implemented.

B. An analysis of the controls that were compromised or absent should be made. If the persons who compromised the controls are still employees of the company, they should be properly reprimanded for their actions.

C. Depending on the severity of the case, the analysis should include people in management, audit, security, human resources, and accounting. Each department will be responsible for determining what actions could have been taken to help reduce the likelihood of the occurrence.

D. The internal audit department will be responsible for identifying alternative ways in which the fraud could have been committed. The internal audit department should then design appropriate controls to protect against frauds committed by the alternative methods.

VIII. Publication

Once the case has been resolved, the incident will be depersonalized and published in the monthly security newsletter. The article will include a generic description of the fraud and the actions taken by MTC Company.

The article may also include information that will make employees more informed as to what kinds of problems can take place, and may reinforce steps that should be taken if someone has information relating to other possible fraud operations.

IX. Implementation of controls

The internal audit department will be responsible for assuring that additional cost-effective controls are put in place to avoid recurrences. Information received from the analysis of the case should be helpful in determining what controls should be implemented.

Audit tests should also be instituted to expose the existence of the same type of fraud if it should occur in the future.

X. Testing for compliance and training

The internal audit department will be responsible for testing controls in place to make sure that current controls are being observed. When controls are not being properly observed, the internal audit department will develop a program to ensure that controls will be complied with in the future.

XI. Training

Management will be responsible for ensuring that internal auditors receive proper training to perform the responsibilities given to the internal audit department. Management will accomplish this objective by appropriating the necessary funds for training, arranging for professionals to carry out the training, and doing all else necessary to adequately train the auditors on their assigned duties and responsibilities.

FIGURE 17–4 *(concluded)*
MTC Company Fraud Policy

XII. Proactive fraud auditing
Finally, the internal audit department will use appropriate techniques to proactively audit for fraud. Such techniques include using discovery sampling and computer query procedures to search for fraudulent transactions. The internal auditors will be responsible for keeping up to date on current developments in techniques that can be used to audit for fraud.

Source: This fraud policy was written by Kevin Brotherson, a student in Steve Albrecht's forensic accounting class (winter semester 1993) at Brigham Young University, Provo, UT, and is included here with his permission. The policy was written in partial fulfillment of the requirements for the course. The policy is generic and may not fit every organization. Some companies may want corporate security to coordinate fraud investigations. Others may want legal counsel or internal audit to be the coordinators. We are not overly concerned about who takes charge of investigations, but it is extremely important that all groups work closely together.

Obviously, this policy is not perfect. It serves, however, as an example of the kind of policy that could be developed to facilitate communication, assign responsibility, and bring order to a company's way of dealing with emotion-laden and unpleasant fraud occurrences. Such policies should be developed in advance and in a calm environment, before "good old Tom" is suspected of fraud and a crisis results.

CONCLUDING COMMENTS

Writing this book has been fun. The principles discussed herein have been tried and have proved successful in various organizations and in numerous consulting engagements. The incidence of fraud in the United States is definitely increasing. Honesty is definitely decreasing. The reasons for this combination of unfortunate circumstances are as follows: (1) The causal factors of fraud—pressure, opportunity, and rationalization—are intensifying; (2) organizations do not have well-designed prevention, detection, and investigation programs; and (3) the labeling and modeling of appropriate behavior are decreasing significantly. In this chapter, we have outlined a suggested fraud program that includes 12 stages. We have explained each of these stages and suggested the individuals who should be involved in each.

Implementing an overall fraud program, including a formal fraud policy, will reduce fraud losses. The thin line between profitability and red ink will continue to perplex management well into the 1990s, along with globalization, cost cutting, shrinking margins, and related problems. Implementing a process to reduce such direct losses as fraud provides another opportunity to protect bottom-line profits. Given the current environment of stretched resources and controls, together with an insecure work force and greater rationalizations to commit fraud at all levels, "surprises" throughout this decade will unfortunately abound. Such surprises can be caught and prevented before they become unmanageable. Only time will tell whether a given organization is smart enough to implement more preventative approaches to fraud, or whether it will continue to react after the losses occur.

We wish you success in your fraud prevention, detection, and investigation efforts. We trust that your job will become easier and more productive after you read this book.

Index

A

Acceptance stage, 191–92, 194
Accounting anomalies, 57–58
Accounting equations, 79
Accounting ledger, definition of, 81
Accounting symptoms, 59
Accounting system, 31
Acid test; *see* Quick ratio
AFCO fraud, 42, 51, 65, 66, 106, 111
Akst, Daniel, 109
Albrecht, Scott, 121
Albrecht, Steve, 88, 89, 121
Alexander's, 123
American Academy of Forensic
  Sciences, 170
American Board of Forensic Document
  Examiners, Inc. (ABFDE), 170
American Continental, 61, 95
American Express, 127
American Institute of Certified Public
  Accountants (AICPA), 67, 206
American Society for Industrial
  Security (ASIS), 206
American Society of Questioned
  Document Examiners, 170
AMI, 111
Analytical anomalies, 59
Analytical fraud, symptoms, 98–104
Anger stage, 190, 193
Anonymous tips, providing a hot line,
  270–71
Antar, Eddie, 125
Apathy, 41–72
Apple Computer, 104
Arthur Andersen & Co., 64, 105
Audi, 219
Auditors' responsibility, 67–72
  engagement characteristics, 68–69

Auditors' responsibility—*Cont.*
  management characteristics, 68
  nature of the symptoms, 69–72
  operating and industry
    characteristics, 68
Audits, 157–63
Audit trail, lack of, 42–43
Automatic teller machines (ATMs), 70,
  71
Awareness training, 255-57

B

Baird, Zoe, 249, 251
Bakker, Jim, 44, 45
Balance sheets, 84
Bargaining, 193–94
Baskin-Robbins, 34
Behavioral symptoms, 59, 126
Biancci, Charles; *see* Ponzzi, Charles
Billy Graham Home, 45
Bloomingdales, 123
BMW, 65
Boeing, 11
Broyhill, 218
Bureau of National Affairs, 8
Bureau of Prisons, 176
Burns, William J., 151

C

Cadillac, 52, 100
Calibration, 201
California Department of Consumer
  Affairs, 37
California Highway Patrol, 37
Cash flow, statements of, 84
Cash inflows, example of, 92